NO TIME TO CLEAN!

NO TIME TO CLEAN!

HOW TO REDUCE & PREVENT CLEANING THE PROFESSIONAL WAY

AMERICA'S #1 CLEANING EXPERT!

DON ASLETT

*Illustrated and Designed by
Craig LaGory*

MARSH CREEK PRESS

NO TIME TO CLEAN!

Published by Marsh Creek Press,
PO Box 700, Pocatello, Idaho 83204
1-888-748-3535.

Distributed by Betterway Books,
an imprint of F&W Publications, Inc.,
1507 Dana Avenue, Cincinnati, OH 45207.
1-800-289-0963.

ISBN 0-937750-22-0
Illustrator/Designer: Craig LaGory
Editor: Carol Cartaino
Production Manager: Tobi Flynn

Quotes from *Make Your House Do the Housework* and *Who Says It's a Woman's Job to Clean*, used by permission of the publisher. Some of the material in this book is a revised and updated version of portions of the books *How Do I Clean the Moosehead?* and *Not for Packrats Only*.

Library of Congress Cataloging-in-Publication Data

Aslett, Don, 1935-
    No time to clean! :how to reduce & prevent cleaning the professional way / Don Aslett ; illustrated and designed by Craig LaGory.
      p.   cm.
    ISBN 0-937750-22-0 (pbk.)
    1. House cleaning. I. Title.

TX324 .A75832 2000
648'.5--dc21
               00-035122

ALSO BY DON ASLETT

Other books on home care:

Is There Life After Housework?

The Cleaning Encyclopedia

Don Aslett's Clean in a Minute

Don Aslett's Stainbuster's Bible

Do I Dust or Vacuum First?

How Do I Clean the Moosehead?

Make Your House Do the Housework

Who Says It's a Woman's Job to Clean?

500 Terrific Ideas for Cleaning Everything

Pet Clean-Up Made Easy

Painting Without Fainting

Books on decluttering and personal organization:

Clutter's Last Stand

Not for Packrats Only

Clutter Free! Finally & Forever

Lose 200 Lbs. This Weekend!

The Office Clutter Cure

How to Have a 48-Hour Day

How to Handle 1,000 Things at Once

Business books:

How to Have a 48-Hour Day

The Office Clutter Cure

Keeping Work Simple

How to be #1 With Your Boss

Everything I Needed to Know About Business
I Learned in the Barnyard

Speak Up!

For professional cleaners:

Cleaning Up for a Living

The Professional Cleaner's Personal Handbook

How to Upgrade & Motivate Your Cleaning Crews

Construction Cleanup

Acknowledgments

Few books reach the finish line without the aid of other people, who are kind enough to contribute their knowledge to the end result. This book was no exception. There was no time to clean (or reach the bottom of today's to-do list), but they found time to help!

My sincere thanks to all of the following, especially:

- My readers and audiences over the years, whose comments and questions keep me in close touch with the home cleaning scene, and keep me learning.

- Mark Browning, Senior Vice President of Varsity Contractors, my longtime partner and sometimes coauthor, who double-checked facts as needed and resolved niggling questions whenever they arose.

- Laura Dellutri of America's Cleaning Connection, the "Duchess of Dirt," who shared her expertise on "quick cleaning" and 21st-century cleaning methods and materials. Laura, a popular presenter at home shows and on television, and a consultant and training resource for the cleaning industry, shares her know-how online at www.lauradellutriduchessofdirt.com.

- Jim Doles, Vice President of Marketing, Varsity Contractors, for his input and assistance, especially on the state of the art of the cleaning industry and the interests of modern home cleaners.

- Laura and Grant Aslett, Rose Galera, and Carey Widder of Solutia, who provided their specialized knowledge for key parts of the book.

- Jenny Behymer, Martha Jacob, John Binkley, Shannon Heaton, and Beth Racine, who helped improve the manuscript in small but important ways.

- My friends at Betterway Books, especially Budge Wallis, David Lewis, and Richard Hunt, among others, who were encouraging and helpful, as ever.

- A big thank-you also to the Soap and Detergent Association, and the many manufacturers of cleaning products, cleaning equipment, and new home materials, from Proctor & Gamble to Pergo flooring, Astroturf to Eureka, who cheerfully and efficiently provided all the information we asked for, and more.

TABLE OF CONTENTS

No Time to Clean!

That's no news to you! I don't need to tell you we are *busy* and only getting busier—all of us, even our kids, have too much to do! Just ask a "retired" couple how much spare time they have these days! We are not only battling too busy, but "too much" as well. We have too many possessions, too many responsibilities, too many opportunities, too much on our minds. We have no time to do many things we want to do and some things we *have* to do, like cleaning. No matter how we feel about cleaning, it does have to be done. If we don't clean up our messes we'll be buried—germed or cluttered to death.

We can't alter the clock or calendar, nor can we quit our jobs or neglect our family, so what do we do?

If it seems you have no time to clean, or it is getting in the way of some of the better things in life, then may I offer a solution: you can *prevent* most of it. And do the rest of it so fast and well it will be fun. The "no time to clean problem" will be solved.

Experts say we spend an average of five years of our lives on household cleaning and maintenance—that's a lot of "life" taken out of our time on earth! What if we cut that five years to only one year and make it an enjoyable year to boot? That's a good deal, and it can be done.

This is the 21st century, and there are new surfaces, new tools, and new approaches to cleaning. Let's put them to work for us. This book will give you seven ways to solve your "no time to clean" worries:

1. prevent cleaning
2. do it faster (use better tools and pro techniques)
3. get help with it
4. dejunk your home and life to reduce the need to clean
5. new approaches to cleaning that work within our hectic, helter-skelter lifestyle
6. design cleaning out
7. and even some help with the "big D" of housework—the desire to do it!

I'll explain all of these in detail in these pages, but I've focused on the #1 way to cut cleaning—**PREVENTION**. I know from the astounding popularity of an earlier book my daughter and I wrote on just one aspect of this subject—*Make Your House Do the Housework*—that today's home managers are smart enough to see the truth. Cutting the problem at its source—**preventing** cleaning—is the truly modern approach to it, and the best solution in the end.

Good cleaning,

Don Aslett

CHAPTER 1

Modern Cleaning's Biggest Mystery:

The Time to Do It

Time to clean and care in the new century

Our goal today more than ever is minimum time and money spent on the "maintenance chores" of life. Cleaning and home care are important, worthwhile parts of our lives, but we don't want to be doing these things all the time or too often. It's hard to be edified or inspired with your hand always on a toilet brush or your head in a cluttered closet. Sometimes we get so endlessly busy with "the chores" that we have no time for the children and the other truly cherishable parts of living.

As I said earlier, the "time scientists" estimate we spend an average of five years of our lives years just in cleaning and home maintenance. This may be true, but it's crazy. We should do the necessary in one year and have those other four years left over to enjoy the mountains and sea coasts and smell the flowers—begonias, instead of ammonia!

How can we manage to do this?

I was doing one of my "how to clean faster" seminars once for a parent/educator organization in Hawaii. Everyone in this large group of typical modern homemakers, fathers and mothers, was really struggling with the modern busy life syndrome, and having a hard time fitting cleaning and maintenance into the schedule. I had my usual wisdom on the subject ready, but ended up gaining a profound insight myself when one of the women present did a preliminary warm-up for the group right before my seminar started.

She drew a circle, called it a clock or a pizza, and had all the attendees do the same. Then she asked them to slice the circle into wedges that showed how and where they were using their twenty-four hours a day right now. Much moaning and groaning followed as the participants attempted to analyze the what and when of their activities. Most had more things to fit in than space in the circle, and suddenly the overall problem became clear. There is so

much we have to do, and so much we feel we *should* do, that there is rarely room in the pie for the wedge of "what we **most** want to do." Because things like jobs and travel to them, cleaning, cooking, repairs, caring for the kids and taking them to soccer, caring for the yard and pets, etc., use up every bit of the space. Everyone there was almost depressed after the warm-up. It was clearer than ever that the battle of modern life is "too much... too busy."

When I was addressing another group a month later, using this woman's idea, I had them do the same exercise. Got the same moaning and groaning and frustrated sighing. Then I had the audience draw another circle and put the leftover wedges in it. I called the first circle the "have-to's" and the second the "want-to's." Was this interesting! The second circle contained life's most valuable uses of time, like "spending time with my spouse and children," "expanding my hobby," "reading more," "learning to play an instrument," "writing some poetry," "working in the garden," "getting more exercise," "helping others," "getting in touch with myself and my Creator." This second circle, which held most of the activities that would truly bless and enhance our lives, was in fact the things we seldom get around to.

As none of us have two clocks and never will, no matter how smart, powerful, or rich we may be, the only choice we have is to combine these circles. We can't throw out all the "have to's" or we would starve and the place would fall to ruin. We can't throw out the second circle, either, or what's the use of living? Pulling wedges out of number two and simply substituting them for those in number one is often impossible. If circle number one is too tight, you and I are the ones who have to do something about it. We, after all, are the ones who determine and control our own slices in the clock of life. No one else, not our bosses, the Lord, the government, the major, or mother. That means we have to shrink the slices in that first circle to fit in the ones we want to wedge in. And we can. This book is going to help you do this with one big one, cleaning. **If you are cleaning more than a couple of hours a week, you are cleaning too much or inefficiently.**

Remember—YOU choose and control the size of those wedges.

For example: Of the cleaning wedge, forty percent of the time, effort, and money here is usually spend on excess stuff—junk and clutter. Cut and control clutter, and your cleaning will drop forty percent. That leaves lots of new room to transfer in some "want-to's."

The secret of cutting down cleaning, doing it faster and better, is just a combination of the following: getting rid of junk, using professional techniques and the right cleaners, and getting some help (yes, from those messer-uppers, family members and guests!). You can also get help from outside, such as from professional cleaners. You can decorate, design, and build things into your home to cut cleaning, too, and make many other sensible if not obvious moves to reduce cleaning by preventing it. Adjusting your approaches to cleaning to fit the new circumstances of our new day will help, too, as will adjusting your attitude toward this often dreaded chore. These simple steps, which I will explain in the chapters that follow, will cut cleaning down to size and give it a much better chance of being fit into our ever busier lifestyle.

Let's get started now!

Adjusting Our Standards

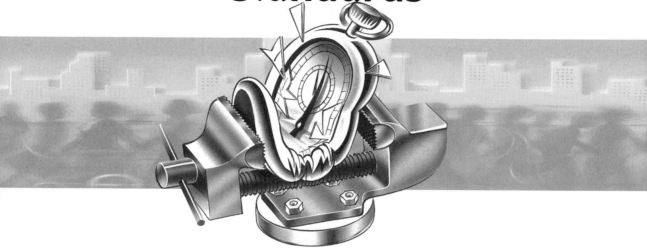

& Schedules

In our quest to cut cleaning, we need a little perspective first—century 2000 is different from the day of our grandparents and great-grandparents, or even our parents.

The bad news, from a cleaning and maintenance standpoint:

1. There are more people now and we live closer to one another than ever before.
2. The average home is larger now (with more to care for, both inside and out). The size of our homes has about doubled, and we also have more and larger garages. Many of us have large yards full of "furnishings," too.
3. We have almost twice as much furniture as earlier.
4. Triple the amount of clothes.
5. And tons more "stuff" (possessions of all kinds) to clean, clean around, and organize.
6. We make several moves in a lifetime, and some of us, many more! This is a big cleaning and organizing job in itself.
7. We all have at least three times as busy a schedule as we did years ago.
8. We have more pets, and they are more likely to share our home than ever before.
9. We have many more disposable things, and more packaging, which creates more trash and litter.
10. Our sanitation standards are also often higher today, which puts more pressure on the cleaning agenda.

THERE'S A LOT OF GOOD NEWS, TOO:

1. Homes today are better lighted and much better insulated, which means better sealed against windblown dust.

2. There is not as much soiling. With all of the paved surfaces we have now, there isn't as much dirt, mud, straw, grass, and gravel being tracked in. And cleaner industrial smokestacks mean less airborne soil.

3. Household surfaces are much easier to clean—not the flaking paint, easily stained wallpaper, and worn linoleum of yesteryear.

4. The majority of our floors are now durable and easy-to-clean nylon carpet.

5. Many modern furnishings have built-in soil, stain, and germ resistance.

6. Machines now quickly do many things that took a lot of time and attention in the past.

7. We have better than ever tools and cleaning chemicals to help us clean, too.

8. We are at home less, and cook at home less. We don't use and dirty up our homes like we used to. There's a lot of difference between mom at home all day with the kids and mom and dad at work while the kids are in day care.

9. We have more health safeguards now, and modern surfaces are easier to sanitize, which means less germ and disease potential.

10. There are more convenient community ways to dispose of trash and garbage.

All of this adds up to the fact that it's easier to clean today, and it has to be done less often. The larger square footage of our homes has more than been offset by the new and better tools available now, and better designed surfaces and structures. Since our furnishings and surfaces resist soil better and show it less, this gives us some leeway to do the housework at our convenience, instead of an exact scheduled time.

If you look at the lists above carefully, you'll see that one of the best ways of gaining additional efficiency here is by reducing the amount of "stuff" we have around. The "too much" we surround ourselves with often undoes all we've gained from technological assistance in the battle of housework. Chapter Five will help here.

Let's look at some other ways to reduce housework now.

Avoid "overkill"

Interesting, how many of our concerns about cleaning are guilt and worry about not doing it enough—falling short of the shine we want or that our neighbors have. When there is on the other side a bigger problem: Cleaning too much, unnecessarily, dusting ahead of the dust.

I call this "overkill"—overdone or excessive cleaning—cleaning things that don't need to be cleaned, or cleaning things too often. When we have no time to clean we sure don't want to be wasting any effort on overkill!

"Overkill"—totally unnecessary cleaning—is almost as common as dirt.

How easily we can see the overkill of others. When I was only six or seven years old, I remember listening in as my mother, aunts, and some neighborhood women were having a sewing session that seemed to be darning more husbands than socks. Then their conversation settled on another neighbor who wasn't there to protect herself.

One of my aunts said, "Do you know that that woman actually irons her husband's socks?" That sure impressed me, thinking about ironed socks, and it was truly what could be referred to as overkill. Now in the new century my wife thinks it is overkill to iron shirts. And you know, she has something there. Buy no-iron or little iron-fabrics, and take them out of the washer and dryer when you should, and the work will be done for you. Or send your shirts out to a laundry that does things in big batches with efficient machines. This is inexpensive, and uses minimum time and resources per shirt. I'm not saying you have to stop ironing shirts or cleaning windows, only that you should consider if what you are doing to get things "clean" is worth the time and money.

I could write a whole chapter on this and include many of the letters I've received reporting and confessing problems from overkill in cleaning. But the following excerpt from Ann Landers' newspaper column does a pretty good job of outlining the problem and the damage it can do.

❝Dear Ann Landers:

I used to do the supper dishes until I watched my wife get up and rinse them again and restack them 'the right way.'

I used to put groceries away. The next time I opened the refrigerator the groceries would all be put back 'where they belong.'

I used to fold towels. I would open the closet and find them all refolded.

Every time I put a cup down my wife washes it. Maybe I'm not finished yet but she never asks. If I make a sandwich she stands next to me. I cut the tomato and she wipes up the juice. I take some mayonnaise out of the fridge and she grabs the jar and puts it back. I set down the knife; she snatches it and washes it.

Finally, I got sick of staying home on Friday night. I go out by myself to the movies and bars and concerts. My wife stays home to dust the ceilings and wash the walls. Her parents let me know what a holy, hardworking woman she is. The preacher tells me a good housewife is better than rubies. I asked her to go with me to a marriage counselor. She says, 'If you have a problem, you go.'

I've thought about divorce, but the lease is in my name. I'm 23 and feel 100. Nobody understands what it is like to live like this, except me and the dog. She puts Clorox in his dish. Sign this letter—TOO Perfect is Hard to Live With.❞

I don't have to give you Ann's answer here, we all already know it. A house this clean isn't worth it.

If you've been caught up in long-established cleaning habits and schedules, stop and think about it a little. Times change, things change, you change, and above all your household has changed. The traffic patterns in your house aren't the same as they were ten years ago. Many of us are still sweeping, dusting, and polishing things THAT ARE NEVER USED AND DON'T NEED IT! Mindlessly disciplined habits may have their place in the army, but in your own home, where you can do things your own way, you should only clean things that really need cleaning.

I'm not saying you should ignore dirt, junk, or filth, I'm just telling you, as a professional cleaner, that many things don't need cleaning for months or weeks or years. And in our disposable society many things aren't even worth cleaning. Some housework that's burning up a lot of hours (and human and kilowatt energy) doesn't really need to be done often—or at all. There are more interesting ways to get exercise, if that's what you're after.

IF IT ISN'T DIRTY DON'T CLEAN IT!

Someone asked me once: "When something is only partly dirty, you don't have to clean it all, do you?" That is one intelligent question. I see people cleaning the whole house or the whole room because one little part is soiled or in need of attention. You clean the cruddy corner, not all the corners if they don't need it.

If you rewash the whole window when it's just been cleaned perfectly and the dog licks the bottom corner, you are a victim of overkill!

HOW CLEAN DOES IT HAVE TO BE?

Not everything has to be perfectly clean to function well and look okay. I have a pair of heavy coveralls, for example, that I haven't washed in three weeks of nonstop assault on outdoor projects now. They look bad, but feel comfortable and don't smell. Why wear out the washer washing them every day or consume electricity in the dryer keeping them spotless—it isn't necessary for what I'm doing and who really cares, anyway? I don't and so far no neighbors have put up any picket signs.

Let's have a few more examples here:

- **Overwashing:** The average family uses two thousand towels in a year—that's a lot of laundry. Used towels aren't dirty, they're wet. They don't have to be tossed right in the hamper. Likewise, many people throw their work/yard clothes or children's play clothes in the wash after a single wearing.

- **Overwaxing:** Here's one thing you can adjust out of your life for sure. Hard floors that have the right finish applied to them (professional grade of wax or sealer) will look good for a long time with only light maintenance. The floors in some of the commercial buildings we clean still have the same wax we put on them five years ago. Overwaxing (especially of corners and edges and other non-traffic areas) only creates unsightly wax buildup that has to be removed by the tiring and time-consuming process known as stripping.

- **Vacuuming:** There must be something seductive about the hum of a vacuum, because some people vacuum twice as much as they need to. High-traffic areas might need daily or every-other-day vacuuming, but bedrooms only need a weekly going over—and some parts of a home need only be done once a month!

- **Windows:** We all have a fetish about windows. Why? Most glass, even when dirty, looks clean enough so you don't have to wash it every week or every month or be-

cause the neighbors do. When windows become visually offensive, clean them. If they don't bother you and the light can still penetrate and people can still find their way around inside, leave the windows un-washed and enjoy life a little.

- **Bathrooms:** Bathrooms, with all their hard surfaces, are basically the cleanest, most sanitary rooms in the house. Bathrooms almost clean themselves, if you think about it. Whenever we use them it generally in-volves soap and water. Toilets may call for frequent cleaning, but that little bit of min-eral (hardwater) buildup on other things isn't dirt.

- **Carpet shampooing:** We've gone eight years in our ranch home without cleaning our carpet and I have a carpet shampooer downstairs (and professional truck-mount units available free at the snap of a finger)! With good door mats and regular vacuum-ing and spot-cleaning, carpet in the aver-age home can go two to three years between shampooings; much upholstery even longer.

- **Polishing and shining metal** (such as sil-ver, brass, and copper) that will only tar-nish again soon—otherwise known as van-ity cleaning. Worrying about a few water spots on interior chrome or stainless steel also qualifies here.

- **Polishing furniture:** some people do it ev-ery time they dust—which makes the fur-niture look good for a little while, but soon creates a sticky, streaky, dust-collecting layer of gunk on the surface.

- **Cleaning anything blackened**—from the barbecue grill to the aluminum pot you cook the artichokes in—that will shortly only be blackened again.

- **The twice-yearly washing** of everything in the upper cupboards and china closet. Yes that stuff does get dusty and grease-filmed, but why not just wait till you need some-thing to serve company?

- **Washing walls:** With today's much cleaner forms of heating and cooking, the walls in most homes don't need to be cleaned nearly as often as they used to. And since ceilings are up and out of the way of many sources of soiling, you don't have to clean them every time you clean the walls—every third or fourth time is enough.

- **Closets:** Need to be dejunked regularly, but except for maybe a quick vacuuming of the floor, they don't need much cleaning.

- **Dusting endlessly:** If your dust conditions are such that the knickknack shelf needs a redo every other day, you might want to consider glassing the shelf in, retiring the knickknack display, or learning to live with a slight white film on everything. At least stop picking things up to dust under them! And see p. 133 for some dust control mea-sures.

- **Drying dishes:** A waste of time, unless you have many sinkfuls that need to be done at once, or you're the washer and you just want company. Otherwise, let the dish drainer do what it was designed for.

- **Sinks:** These too have a built-in sanitation factor, and if you just take the time to rinse and wipe the sink after use, you may be able to postpone "sink cleaning" indefi-nitely.

- **Cleaning non-self-cleaning ovens:** Ever take a close look at a barbecue grill? Well, it's healthy enough to provide safe food. Your oven, even with two years of buildup, is much cleaner than a grill, and the heat will keep things sanitary. It may look like a little cave, but if you have no choice, let it go.

- **Refrigerators:** Those magnets and mes-sages on the outside are always so ugly we don't even notice the inside. Here again, temperature helps keep things sanitary, and as long as you don't have a major spill and chuck leftovers within a reasonable time, the inside can go months and months without cleaning.

- **Removing footprints** from carpet and rump prints from plush or velvet furniture.

- **Playing bodyguard** and handmaiden to fancy and easily stained, dirtied, or damaged decorations and furnishings, from

white cotton rugs to delicate brocades to silk anything, unless you really, truly, enjoy them.

- **Ironing** anything you don't have to. Looking at some of the irons and other pressing equipment from the past two centuries would almost make you want to cry over the time, effort, and labor that went into "doing the ironing." All to have something wrinkle-free for about the first five minutes of wear or use.

- **Overcleaning corners** and other little used or seen places.

- **Washing the car** twice a week.

I can't make your own list of "overkill," or what isn't necessary, for you—you have to do it yourself. Just ask: "What am I doing? When? Why? Does this really need to be done, or am I just in the habit of doing it?"

Remember, you aren't downgrading your standards, just upgrading your values!

DON'T TRY TO CLEAN AWAY DAMAGE

Surfaces do get old, faded, worn, and damaged with age and use—so when something won't come clean, you need to stop and determine: Is it dirt or damage? This doesn't mean you need to run out and replace everything, but understanding it can cut needless cleaning hours and chemicals. It's not necessarily your fault—years go by, and things wear out!

There are many more, but let's look at the six most frequent "this won't come clean" complaints:

1. **No-wax floors.** These are great floors, and with little traffic, stocking feet, and no kids in the house, they will stay bright and shining for years. But if you have a little ruffian or two in residence, and lots of tracked-in soil, before too many months have gone by that no-wax floor may lose its shine. The clear plastic coating on top gets scratched and worn, so it doesn't look as sharp and sparkly as before. Nothing wrong, the floor is still fine and it will probably last another twenty or thirty years. It just needs a little floor finish (or yes, "wax") on it now to touch up that worn top coat.

2. **Showers,** especially the one-piece fiberglass or plastic bath and shower units. These will glisten for a few years, and then a combination of wear from use and cleaning, and buildup of hardwater deposits and soap scum can reduce the sheen. Even after you remove the buildup from an older unit, it often won't shine as brightly anymore. This isn't a matter of life or death, so live with it!

Another problem we often see here is yellowing. I've owned these tub/shower units myself and cleaned them perfectly with gentle professional techniques and products and yet often in four or five years they will turn yellow on the bottom. If you've cleaned it right and it's still yellow, it's damaged. Let it be. Most of us don't show our tub and shower bottoms on home tours anyway. Whatever you do, don't bleach or clean the yellowed area vigorously with powdered cleanser—you'll just damage the surface even more and worsen the yellowing.

3. **Stove tops.** Anywhere there is repeated (or constant) high heat, the best of materials may darken or discolor. Even heat vents have this problem. If a finish reacts to exposure to heat, the resulting discoloration isn't likely to clean off. So forget it or put a pretty teakettle over it and go on living!

4. **Marble.** We think of it as "rock hard," but this is a beautiful but relatively *soft* stone. Marble floors, especially, will wear fast and start looking dull. When this happens you need to use a marble restorer, which fills in the pores and levels the surface and restores its reflective quality. Or if money is no object, you can have a marble floor ground and polished. The best thing to do is avoid having or using marble in any location that gets hard use.

5. **Varnish.** With exposure to sun (ultraviolet rays) it will yellow, even "non yellowing" varnish or finish. Live with it! Stripping it off and revarnishing so it can yellow again is not the wisest way to go!

6. **Water stains**. Almost anything—especially wood—will darken or discolor with prolonged exposure to water. You won't be able to scrub those dark patches away. So you have a choice of ignoring them, or refinishing or replacing the wood AND being sure to find and remove the source of the water leaks or spills.

We can either tolerate and accept some wear, age, and damage in our surroundings, and not feel guilty about it... or spend a lot of our limited time and energy trying to hide or heal it. This is a call only you can make, so let me just remind you of one of my favorite slogans here: "Houses are made to live in, not live for." We should decide early in life, like with our very first home of our own, whether its purpose is to be **shown or shared**... and live accordingly.

How much cleaning needs to be done at your house?

One of the questions I'm asked most often is, "how often should I clean this?" Many factors go into when something needs to be cleaned, or how much cleaning needs to be done in a home, so you can't chart or schedule the chores by any overall standard. Adjusting things to your own highly individual conditions is modern, and smart. Before you overdo, underdo, or feel frustrated about your ability to keep things clean and neat, let the following principles guide or relieve you:

1. Use and activity level

How many people use the item or the area? How much traffic does it get, and what kind of use is it? Rough and tumble and full of spills and crumbs, or quiet and refined?

How a home is used is the #1 determinant of how much cleaning needs to be done. A couple who eat out most of the time and take their shoes off at the door might be able to go weeks without dusting and vacuuming, months without spot cleaning or doing floors, and years without washing the walls. A home that is heavily used by a large family or has a lot of guests, on the other hand, may need cleaning twice a day. *Clean to the need, not the calendar.*

2. The age of the place, or the article

Time and wear take their toll, and older materials or design can mean more cleaning. Old surfaces (such as floors and fixtures) may be of lesser quality, faded, discolored, rough, porous and absorbent, located way up high, etc. If you have an older place it will usually take longer to clean it.

3. Structure/design

What is your home like and what is it made of? The basic design of a home—simple or complex—and the type of wall, floor, and counter coverings in it, the kind of grout that's been used, how high things are, the type and amount of furniture, the number and style of windows, and the like has a great deal to do with how much cleaning needs to be done. If a home has a lot of fancy detail and corners and "gingerbread" this will not only slow us down and discourage us, but hide dust and dirt, and limit sanitation. (See Chapter Six.)

4. How much is in the way of cleaning?

A key word in easy cleaning and carefree living is "unobstructed." This means floors, furniture, counters, and shelves, for instance. The less "stuff" and structures are in the path or way of maintenance, the better things will look and the more quickly and easily we can do what needs to be done. (See Chapter Five.)

5. Location

What is the input from the surroundings and Mother Nature? Do you live in downtown Detroit or on a Dakota north forty? They each bring different soil loads and cleaning problems. Some areas have very little dust in the atmosphere or surroundings, and some are the dust bowl revisited. Some have extra-hard water and some ocean salt spray to contend with. Some homes are bone dry and others humid enough to rust stainless steel. Some homes are surrounded by strongly colored soils or pollution-creating industrial plants, and others are not. Where you live can make a big difference in how much cleaning you have to do.

6. Standards

Some people clean constantly, by habit or to assuage their ego, and the laid-backs let things go till they crawl away by themselves. Somewhere in this range is where you are, and you need to recognize and establish the level of neat and clean YOU need and want in your surroundings.

In the spectrum between "clean freak" and "slob," where do you want to be? What standard or level of cleanliness and neatness do you want or need—fair, average, or gleaming and spotless? This will have a lot to do with how much and often you clean. While dirt and disorder drive some people wild, they are a comfort for others. Only you, and the need for family harmony, can determine your cleaning standards.

Use standards, not charts or schedules, to clean

When the average person knows that something, a chore or maintenance operation, needs to be done, their automatic response is to schedule it. We pros call this "frequency cleaning"—establishing how often something should be done, whether it's every Wednesday, five days a week, once a month, or once a year. The cleaning frequencies in a place add up to something we professionals call "specifications," telling us which areas of a building to clean and how often. For years, when something didn't seem to

be clean enough, we added to the specs and before long some of those lists of specifications were as big as the Manhattan phone book. But often the building still had cleaning problems.

The reason was that, as we just discussed, many different factors are involved in how dirty things get, from atmospheric conditions to how many people use an area. And clean is a value judgment in the end, not a precise scientific determination.

Then we came up with a new concept: why not establish **how clean you want something**—a standard or level of cleanliness—instead of how often it should be cleaned? This will keep us from either neglecting things or cleaning things that don't need cleaning.

This means that instead of saying:
"Clean the windows once a week"
(specification or schedule).

We say:
"The windows shall be free of marks and smudges" (a standard).

I love using cleaning standards. I pioneered this concept for corporations years ago and many other cleaning companies have adopted it. You'll find it works well at home, too.

Here are some samples of what you will find on a professional's set of "building cleaning standards":

▹ DUST CONTROL No accumulation of dust on any exposed surfaces.

▹ RESTROOMS Fixtures will be clean, bright, and sanitized, free of odor, dirt, and foreign matter. Floors will be sanitized and free of dirt and litter.

▹ MIRRORS Shall be free of smudges, spots, and film.

▹ SHOWERS/TUBS Shall be clean and mildew and film free.

▹ DESKS Shall be free of dust and smudges.

▹ TELEPHONES Shall be free of dust and soil.

▹ TV AND CONTROLS Shall be dust and smudge free.

▹ WALLS All wall surfaces shall be dust, spot, and smudge free.

▹ BASEBOARDS Shall have no dust buildup.

▹ CARPETS Will be free of debris, stains, and spots.

▹ DOORS Shall be free of fingerprints, smears, spots, and dust.

▹ STORAGE AREAS/CLOSETS Shall have no unnecessary items, and contents shall be neat and orderly. Floor shall be clean and free of litter.

▹ DOOR MATS Will be free of visible dirt, dust, lint, pebbles, or other foreign matter.

▹ BUILDING EXTERIOR Will be free of trash and debris. Grass and shrubbery will be kept trimmed and neat. Entrances to be clear of snow.

Using this as a guide, get together with your family and set the standards for the living room, the kitchen, the kids' rooms, the garage, and so on. Establish clear standards and then clean to the need and condition, not the hour and calendar.

We should clean by necessity, not schedule, habit, or appointment. Why mop the floor twice a week if it's still clean and shiny, or vacuum daily if there is no dirt? Wall charts and schedules that list what to clean when are great for helping insure that you don't forget anything, but pinpointing exactly when to do things leaves you a slave to a schedule (and possibly doing lots of unnecessary cleaning, while perhaps overlooking some that is truly necessary). Over-scheduling things can lose you in a discouraging quagmire of arbitration between hourly, daily, weekly, semimonthly, monthly, quarterly, annually, seasonally, occasionally, and the heck with it.

HERE'S AN EXCERPT FROM MY OWN HOUSEHOLD'S CLEANING STANDARDS:

- Dishes are always done before you go to bed.
- Empties are put in the trash or recycle bin immediately.
- Sinks and faucets shall always be clean and shiny.
- Projects shall be put away or covered after use.
- Floors shall be free of dust, debris, and black marks.
- Showers and tubs shall be clean and mildew free.
- Kids' rooms must be crossable at all times.
- Lights shall be free of dirt and dead bugs, and bulbs changed as soon as they go out.
- Closets shall be free of unused clothes, excess hangers, and other clutter.
- Dispensers (soap, etc.) in kitchen and bathroom shall be refilled as soon as they run out.

- Dirty clothes shall be taken to the laundry area immediately and sorted immediately.
- Counters shall be cleared and cleaned after every use.
- Beds shall be made directly after use, and sheets changed as necessary.

All of this establishes clean as a life value, not a duty.

When judging when to clean, you can go by your senses: what you see, feel, smell, and yes, even hear (the complaints!).

But how often should *we do it, Don?*

In spite of everything I've said up to here, I know you still want me to tell you "how often," so here goes:

Carpet

In the average home, I would police the carpet daily (remove large debris) and vacuum it once a week. If you live alone and have no pets, twice a month might do it. If there are more people around, two or three times a week should do it, unless the room is directly connected to an exterior area (which will mean more tracking in and more frequent vacuuming).

Shampooing a carpet once every two or three years should be sufficient.

Hard floors

The more you sweep and otherwise keep the dirt and grit off them, the longer they will stay bright and shiny. You can keep a kitchen floor clean and sanitary with a good once-a-week mopping, as long as you clean up spills and dropped food as you go along. Other floors should be mopped a couple of times a month.

Keeping floors waxed, too, will help them last longer and look better. Rewax when wax wears down or off (I've seen some floors go years before they reach this point).

Walls

It's a good idea to spot-clean handprints and smudges off the walls once a week. It only takes a minute or two and will keep things at a nice clean standard that discourages dirtying and abuse. If you live alone, spot cleaning once a month will probably be enough.

I'd wash the walls in the average home every other year or so, except for the kitchen, which should be washed once a year.

Bathrooms

Here again if you wipe the sink, tub, and spills as you go along, then a once-a-week cleaning of the toilet and shower walls (using a light acid cleaner like Showers-n-Stuff) should be enough to keep the bathroom a pleasant and sanitary place to be. Every month or so you need to clean the inside of the toilet with acid bowl cleaner, and remove any hardwater buildup from places like around the faucets and the shower door.

Appliances

Keep them clean daily, as you use them, and you can do the biggies (like cleaning the oven, and cleaning out the refrigerator) twice a year.

Windows

No schedule here! Glass is a non-depreciating material—it won't wear out, rot, or deteriorate, no matter how dirty it gets. So whenever the windows displease or embarrass you, clean them with a squeegee if possible.

Dishes

Do them **right now!**

Neat or clean?

Neat means organized, in place, dejunked, and is the first principle of cleaning. What is neat is one-half cleaned.

Clean means the absence of dirt and soil.

Cleanliness can be undone by disorder, and neat can only get by so long without clean. Which do you go for, when there's too much to do, and little time to clean? The best formula for this I've seen is from a premium building contractor, who is always inundated with materials, equipment, and onlookers, and always managing multiple jobs, many workers, and a demanding schedule.

His motto:
Neat *while doing*
Clean *when leaving*

Bad day cleaning

One last note now about schedules and standards. When you're having a bad day, when three new big headaches (that weren't even on any of your lists) have cropped up and already taken half the morning, and things aren't getting any better, how clean does the house need to be? As long as no one you don't know well is coming, a friend of mine on the Potomac—Sue Lau—offers the perfect philosophy to judge things by at times like this: "The house only has to be clean enough to look good when viewed from a trotting horse (and on a bad day, the horse can be galloping)."

I love it!

CHAPTER 3

Cleaning on the Run

In recent years there are all kinds of "progressive" obstacles to cleaning.

1. Most families are two-career families—no one's full-time job is tending the house and doing the cleaning.

2. All family members now have a world of other interests, activities, and commitments, besides home and work and school.

3. We are home less and less.

4. Home entertainment is competing for every available minute of free time when we are there.

All of this adds up to the fact that cleaning isn't and often won't be the top priority on our list. Cleaning is important, but it still gets squeezed out of our schedule and put off, often until we end up in a "must do or else" situation.

The desire for a clean, neat, and organized home is still there (maybe even stronger than ever), but the actual accomplishing of this seems to have slipped behind these other new realities of our lives today.

What's the answer?

I've been teaching people to clean for more than forty years now. I've taught the why, when, where, and "what with?" of cleaning to millions. There is one big "W," however, it seems impossible to teach.

Yet this particular "W" has more effect on our cleaning efforts than all the others put together—the WANT to clean.

Finding the missing "W"

The first step is adjusting our attitude toward cleaning. If we don't like to do something we'll never make it a priority. There is still plenty of time to clean—IF we really want to do it. The secret is just liking it enough to get around to it.

Unfortunately, cleaning has been and still is clearly branded one of the "have-to's" of life. Parents punish their kids with it, "Behave, or you'll have to clean your room!" and teachers threaten with it, "You students better study or you'll end up like poor Mr. Harris—A JANITOR!" [A cleaner.] Even in the cleaning industry, the image of the profession is the #1 problem, bar none. Because of all the bad associations we have with cleaning, its reputation as "low-class drudgery" won't go away. Not even today, when the majority of cleaning is done by dials, triggers, and buttons, by one finger in five minutes instead of an aching back and five hours. We may admit cleaning is a necessity, but for most it remains a **hard sell**.

After all, the work we do in business, inventing, landscaping, architecture, art, and so on may last 20, 200, or even 2000 years... while the results of our cleaning efforts often last less than twenty-four hours. Our cleaning accomplishments seem so perishable, and we're so quickly faced with the frustration of having to do it all over again. Add to this the fact that cleaning is often taken for granted; it's something people don't even notice unless it isn't done. And last, we are a society ruled by convenience now, not a "take care of it, save it, do it yourself" society. We're too affluent and valuable to spend our time cleaning, that's something peons and lesser people—maids, janitors, and mothers—do.

All of these negatives can and do create a bad attitude toward cleaning. We even flinch saying the word!

On the other hand, our antennae are searching twenty-four hours a day for **anything** that will make us **feel good**. We'll drink, eat, buy, try, travel, even cheat for it. We'll commit all kinds of ethical no-nos for a few hours or minutes of gratification—so much do we love the elation of those sensory "good feelings." How come we overlook the "feelgood" rewards of cleaning?

Why do we get such pleasure from a bath or shower—it's the epitome of clean. We've all savored the sweet sleep of a clean bed, and the solace of clean hands and a pure heart. We've all had the pleasure of shedding soiled clothes and putting on fresh, clean ones. We know how we feel when we use or behold something neat and clean, or when we "come clean" in confessing or amending a dirty deal.

We all like a clean slate or a clean restroom. We've seen the selling-day strength of a clean vehicle or clean house and yard. Clean is right up there when it comes to providing and creating good feelings.

Although important, **cleaning's #1 value is not the removal of the physical dust, dirt, and disorder around us**. It is the revitalization of our soul and spirit. Cleaning is one of the healthiest activities around, physically and mentally, because it improves our quality of life.

I read a list of the benefits of hugging once, composed by a true champion of good feelings. You can substitute the word "cleaning," and I think you'll find the benefits of cleaning a pretty close parallel here.

The Perfect Cure for What Ails You:
Low energy consumption
High energy yield
Inflation proof
Healthy
Relieves tension
Reduces stress
Combats depression
Improves blood circulation
It's invigorating
It elevates self-esteem
It generates goodwill
It has no unpleasant side effects
It is nothing less than a miracle drug
Happy ~~Hugging~~ Cleaning!

The more efficiently you clean, with the aid of pro knowhow and tools and timesaving design, the easier it is to do, and more enjoyable. I'll make you a promise here. Once you learn to clean well and reap its rewards, you'll be eager to drop some of the less beneficial activities once in a while so you can do more of it.

Make cleaning a "feel better" activity and it will fit into any time slot or opportunity. There are always minutes, even hours that are "nothing" spaces in our lives.

When you need exercise, need to meditate or to feel good about something, cleaning is the answer.

Sure relaxing is a wonderful thing and people are always telling us to do it, but sometimes doing something satisfying and worthwhile is more restorative than relaxing. Substitute cleaning for some of the routine, rerun "entertainments" and expeditions. I can tell you what you'll enjoy and benefit from most... the cleaning and dejunking.

"Finding" more time just won't happen. We don't find time, we only use it. And we MAKE time for what we really want to do.

HERE IS A SUMMARY AND REMINDER YOU MIGHT WANT TO POST SOMEWHERE...

Why Clean?

We clean for space. Aren't we all, today, everywhere, feeling emotionally and physically crowded?

Sanitation and health. Clean conditions help assure physical and mental well-being.

Aesthetics. Dirty and cluttered is ugly; neat and clean looks good and makes us feel good.

To prevent wear and damage. Things not cleaned will be damaged, and worn out before their time.

For safety's sake. Clutter and uncleanliness are the unsaid reasons for many accidents and injuries.

For the environment. Taking care of what is ours collectively, the planet, is an individual—not a public—responsibility.

Clean will help us master management. Mastering "clean" will aid and enhance our other management skills.

For the message we give. Admit it or not, like it or not, how we keep things sends a message to others about us.

For how we are treated. How clean we are affects how "the world" treats us, and our family, employees, and workmates, too. Our cleanliness level even determines how we treat ourselves!

For the carryover! As a building follows a blueprint, cleanliness gives a clean pattern for the rest of our lives. The word "clean" ranks second only to the word "faith" as a universal problem preventer and life improver.

Clean creates harmony, peace, safety, and security. Clean speaks with a clear voice that all is well and in control.

Cleaning sooner means cleaning quicker

Once we actually launch into the cleaning, one big way to save time is an easy to understand and apply word called NOW. Shifting from doing things "later" to doing them NOW will, all by itself, reduce your cleaning by up to thirty percent, and improve your attitude at least ninety percent. *Now* is the only magic cleaning word I know!

For example: If we do the dishes, pick up that dropped thing, repair the loose hem, or tighten the loose screw right now when it happens or we discover it, it will only take minutes or seconds to do it. If we let it go, it'll take much longer because the egg will have hardened on the plates, the dropped grape will have been squashed into the carpet, the hem will be all out instead of part out, and the loose screw will have fallen out and rolled away somewhere, and what it held together will fall apart all over the place. A fresh spill can be taken care of in ten seconds. Try to clean it up later—after it's soaked in, seeped down, spread, and had a chance to set—and you'll be at it at least ten or fifteen minutes (plus all the time you'll lose anguishing over the fact that the carpet or whatever now has a permanent spot or stain on it). If you let it go that one piece of cake below the high chair won't be just one piece, after it gets stepped on and then tracked around and ground in and scattered. You now have a five- or ten-minute roundup facing you instead of a one-second pickup.

Likewise, if we wipe the spattered hotcake batter off something right now, when it's still liquid, it only takes seconds. If we wait until later, till it's hardened, it'll take three times as long to remove. You'll use twice as much chemicals and hot water, and the cleaning process will be much harder on the surface (if not damage it), because now we have to rub and scrape and pry.

Don't leave spills or broken things until later. **Later only increases the labor.** The number one reason people hate to clean is not the actual process of cleaning—it's the fact that they let the mess back up until it is a massive job to deal with it. Now it'll take hours of prime time. If a thing is taken care of now, as it happens, it can be done quickly, simply, easily, and won't have to be added to the big list for chores day. Another chance to transfer one of your want-to's from the "wish I could" to the "I will" circle.

Anything done later—picking up, putting away, or balancing your checkbook—always has an added "interest charge" of being harder to do.

Practice "KEEP UP" cleaning

Another great way to cut down cleaning is to not let things around the house ever get to the point of being a cleaning problem. The Navy has a term for this: "Keeping things shipshape." Meaning everything is kept up all the time. You don't leave dishes undone or clothes dropped or drawers ajar or piles anywhere. If you do things as you go along, and do regular policing, THERE IS NO NEED FOR A BIG CLEANING CAMPAIGN. When I come home at night, for example, I hang up my coat as soon as I take it off, and carry my box of papers from the office into the den and put them on my desk, where they belong, and not on the kitchen table or the dresser in the bedroom. When I change to my "home" clothes, I hang up what should be hung back up and put any dirty clothes right in the hamper. Simple little things, but they all add up in the course of a day or week.

We've all been places where someone with one of those little brooms and a long-handled dustpan patrols the area and instantly whisks up any bit of dropped litter. I'm not saying you have to do this, or make the bed when you get up in the middle of the night to hit the bathroom. Just keep things policed up and put back as you progress through the day.

Anytime, anywhere you pass inches from a dropped newspaper, a crooked picture, an open drawer or door, a dead leaf, something spilled or wrinkled, something that needs to be tucked in, thrown out, adjusted, put back, DO IT! It only takes seconds, and when done regularly, eliminates the need for a big cleaning binge.

Lots of smart people **don't ever have cleaning days**, they never schedule "time for cleaning." They do it as they go along: they wipe the sink and shower right after they use them, clean the stovetop while doing the dishes, pick up, fix up, as they go along. They touch up paint, remove scuffs, tighten bolts, oil the hinge, etc., right in the course of daily living. So they rarely if ever have to face a full-scale campaign of restoration.

MAKE THE CLEANING PART OF THE DOING

We have to stop thinking in terms of going in after things are finished and cleaning. Instead, make the cleanup part of the doing. We have cleaning classed as an unpleasant facing of the aftermath of something fun... now comes the pain of the cleanup. Whenever possible, cleaning should be **included with,** not done later.

While my company's new corporate office was being built, many people stopped and said we had the most amazingly clean construction site ever. My contractors cleaned up everything every night as they went, so they didn't have to allow five days at the end of the whole job for a big siege of cleanup (and there were no fines or accidents, either).

In any kind of project, it pays to keep things clean as you go, even if you might re-mess things up a bit in the next step. If done during the project the cleaning will not only go quicker, but reduce the chance of mishaps and accidents, and foul-ups of the next stage,

Some keep-up customs
Pick it up, don't pass it up.

Clean up little messes when they happen.

Close closets, cupboard doors, and drawers before you leave a room.

Clean up as you go when following a recipe.

When you fix something to eat, put away everything you used before you sit down to eat it.

After you've eaten, wash those few little dishes right away.

Take ten minutes to put the main living areas of the house in order before you go to bed at night.

too. So sweep the sawdust up when you're finished making the birdhouse and before you paint it, not at the very end of the job. When things are in hand they're handy, and generally the scraps and trimmings and the like are done for anyway, so you may as well get rid of them. Cleaning as you go makes all the difference, and it makes you feel better, too.

Six "C's" for cutting cleaning

The key things to do as you go along, every day, all the time. The six unfailing principles that will eliminate "the big cleanup."
1. Capture it before it spreads.
2. Clean it or put it away as soon as you're done with it.
3. Clean it if you pass it with a cleaning tool.
4. Class it up (straighten it up) every day.
5. Claim it if it's yours.
6. Can it if it's trash or litter.

"FLEX" cleaning

For some reason many people wait until the weekend or some other time when they can "do the cleaning" all in one big push. Then they dread it coming (because it takes all that nice Saturday morning or Sunday afternoon). So they come to hate cleaning.

I love to clean, but even I am not willing to trade special times like the chance to be with kids doing things that are important to them, to visit the sick, help out at church or in the community, or simply enjoy some beautiful morning or golden afternoon—interrupt or lose a precious life experience—just to clean. The old business of "I'm afraid I can't go, I've got to stay home and clean" is out of my life. And sometimes my responsibilities on the job are too intense to allow me a chance to clean.

I don't clean (in sense of do scheduled chores) every day. Some days I do zero, and some weeks I only find thirty minutes to clean. Yet the next week I may spend a half a day or more cleaning and repairing things, without scheduling it or really interrupting anything. I'll never give up an important family or friend event, or even sleep, for cleaning. But I know it has to be done and so have my antennae always on the lookout for the times when it can be done conveniently, or could even include some socializing in the process.

I pounce on cleaning whenever it falls easily into my path of pursuit... and it does. Whenever I'm in the mood, I scratch or drop something less compelling and grab a vacuum or spray bottle. (Keeping your tools and supplies handy really helps here.)

Even if it's backed up a bit, most cleaning can usually wait until you find a convenient or "get to it" time. Cleaning isn't a matter of "musts" unless you make it that way.

If cleaning is done right, it takes little time and so the answer as to where it fits into your schedule is totally your call. Cleaning can't always be charted or scheduled because our 21st-century way of life often means fast changes and quick decisions, impulse following and instant reacting to all kinds of situations and opportunities like suddenly available trips, a special on TV, busy kids' schedules, calls to work, or caught in traffic.

Modern "Minute" Cleaning

In my grandmother's time women spent twelve of the sixteen waking hours cooking, washing, and cleaning. In my mother's era it was often divided into days: Monday all day was washday, Tuesday ironing, Thursday housecleaning, and so on. In the last couple of decades we were down to hours, one or two or three-hour slots to do the same. Now, with all of the other demands on us, we often have only **minutes**, fragments of time we find or take here and there to clean. That's fine, and we can do it.

Just think of the old "drip of water" mystery... tiny little drips of water, coming seconds or even minutes apart, will soon fill a large bucket. When you think about it, most cleaning "acts" can be done in seconds, and some of even the major ones in minutes—we don't really need days anymore. Just for fun, assuming our cleaning gear is handy, let's look at how long some common household tasks actually take.

YOU CAN:

dust a large picture in 3 seconds

close a door or a drawer in 2 seconds

remove a handprint/spot from the wall in 10 seconds

hang up an article of clothing (while it's in hand, while you're undressing) in 20 seconds

wipe off a kitchen counter in 25 seconds

wipe out a sink and polish the faucet in 33 seconds

wipe or squeegee down a shower after use in 35 seconds (naked, too!)

straighten out a piece of furniture in 10 seconds

clean a TV or computer screen in 8 seconds

wipe down the whole console in 30 seconds

vacuum an inside mat in 17 seconds

police a piece of litter on the lawn (coming or going) in 8 seconds

squeegee a window in 35 seconds (and a large picture window in 50)

ask for help in 1 second (and even do it while doing something else!)

LET'S GO ON NOW TO LOOK AT THE "MINUTE" LIST—YOU CAN:

make a bed in 2 minutes (or less)

vacuum an average room in 4 minutes

remove a fresh spot in 3 to 5 minutes

sweep the average floor in 3 minutes

clean a bathroom in 3 1/2 minutes (if you clean it regularly)

do two people's worth of dishes by hand in 3-4 minutes

put in a load of wash in 2 minutes (if it's been presorted and pretreated)

fold a dryerful of clothes in 5 or 6 minutes

clean the kitchen cabinet fronts in 9 minutes

clean a light fixture in 2 minutes

wash down a door (both sides) in 3 minutes

dustmop a floor in 2 minutes

Some people fit life in around housework, others like me for example fit all housework around life. I never use prime time to clean and maintain. I do it all in bits and snatches. I do it in one, two, and ten-minute time segments that might otherwise be wasted.

DO IT WHILE YOU'RE DOING SOMETHING ELSE!

A lot of "time fragment cleaning" can be done while you're doing something else. I always pick up and neaten up while I'm walking through or on my way somewhere. I always clean the area around the phone while I'm talking on it, always clean the car while the gas is pumping in, always clean the kitchen while things are cooking, always clean my pockets waiting in airports—you do lots of this too, I know—so just do a little more of it. My cleaning crews beat competitors because we never "wait" for wax to dry, crew to show, etc. We have a list of what needs to be done and we always keep moving because in the course of a day ten 5 or 6-minute "lulls" or twenty 3-minute "waits" add up to one hour, and that can account for a lot of cleaning.

If you use my quick professional methods you can clean two bathrooms while you're waiting for a tub to fill. You can clean a sink or dejunk the refrigerator while waiting for water to boil. And cleaning the light fixture when you have to get up there and change a bulb anyway eliminates a nuisance job later. All straightening up, all trash disposal, all dusting, all spot cleaning, and a lot of dejunking can be done while on the way to, or while doing something else.

If they just cleaned during commercials the average TV watcher would have 48 minutes of extra time a day. Jumping up and down 96 times would eliminate the need for exercise class, too, so there's another hour saved. You could clean your neighbor's house too, just for good measure—all in extra, unused, nonproductive time.

Get a portable phone (or a long cord on your phone), if you don't have one already, and you can do all kinds of cleaning while "visiting" with friends.

Play the bits game. Do it for at least a week and see what happens. Don't schedule or plan any cleaning—just slip it in whenever you see the chance. You'll never be the same (nor will your cleaning schedule). Focus on fun and living and do the cleaning on your way or in between—*I guarantee you'll run out of housework before you run out of bits and snatches of time!*

Here's a few fit-it-in favorites to get you started, or to add to your odd-moments repertoire—many of these tasks can be completed in the time span of a TV commercial break!

- load or unload the dishwasher
- clean out one drawer
- wipe out the microwave
- pretty up one appliance front
- clean up one small appliance
- de-smudge the kitchen cupboards

- quick-clean the inside of the refrigerator
- sponge down the high chair
- declutter the entryway or the stairs
- make a bed
- shine one window, mirror, or sliding glass door
- dustmop a floor
- dejunk the window sill or dressertop
- clean off the top and sides of something
- put the scattered tapes, records, magazines, or newspapers away
- hang up some flung clothes
- wipe down some switchplates or door frames or one door
- clean out the cat box
- shake out one rug
- wipe down or declutter one or two shelves
- remove all the cobwebs
- wash one room's curtains
- take out the trash

Another strategy many over-committed modern homemakers use to cope with cleaning is the "worst case" or "most crying need" method. They decide how much time they dare devote to cleaning each day or week or whatever, and use that time to tackle the cleaning chore or chores that most need doing or just can't wait any longer. (You could also call this the "triage" approach to cleaning!)

Cleaning after hours

A young career woman in one of my seminar audiences stood up and asked earnestly, "Do you have any secrets for those of us who have to do our cleaning at night these days?"

My answer to her was, "Welcome to the club. Ninety percent of all professional clean-

ing is done at night." Home cleaners, however, face the exact opposite situation of pro janitors cleaning quietly at night in empty offices. At home, most everyone's there in the evening and in the way or up to something—cooking, eating, watching TV, doing homework, or up to their elbows in some overdue messy project. Which means we can either 1) move 'em all to some out-of-the-way spot; 2) wait till they are asleep; 3) (the best choice) make them help, or at least straighten up the new layer of litter they just created before they head off to bed and leave us with the rest.

Cleaning right under, over, around and through them—if that's what you end up doing—may annoy them a little, especially when the vacuum snows up the TV. But at least they see you cleaning so they're less likely to grow up thinking that messes are dematerialized by invisible little elves.

We night cleaners are definitely at a disadvantage, since ambition doesn't peak in the p.m. for most of us, and there's no real substitute for the nice crisp militant feel of an early start on a sunny morning. And you can't beat daylight for actually seeing what you're doing. We also can't make much noise, unless we want to advertise our efforts, get even, or rouse Rover out back.

But night cleaning is not without its compensations:

- In the summer, it's cooler at night, so cleaning is often easier to face.
- Sunstreaks are no problem for us.
- There are less doorbell interruptions at night, though you still have be wary of the phone.
- Energy (to run washers, dryers, dishwashers, and the like) is more available during these "off peak" hours.
- After everyone else goes to bed, there's less tracking over wet floors and using of things before they're really ready. So wax gets a chance to dry, etc.
- When we finish something we can glory in the sensation that it will stay clean for at least six or eight whole hours!

- And right up there with the sheer sensual pleasure of crawling between clean sheets— is putting out the light in a clean house— and waking up to a clean house!

But as for secrets of better night cleaning, the only one is LIGHT—get all you can, or daylight will reveal much that you missed by the light of the moon.

This isn't easy, since ceiling fixtures went out of fashion and most lamps and light fixtures are designed to diffuse or focus light, not let it flood the room. So get yourself a clamp light with a sturdy 150 watt bulb and you'll have your own bright portable ceiling fixture. (If you resort to the old strategy of moving a lamp close and taking off the shade, you'll trip over it or drip on it and be sorry!)

Another aid here is a headlight on your upright vacuum—many models have these.

To assist visibility, too, you can sometimes use a cleaner that makes it easier to see where you've been and where you're going.

If you have to deep-clean an area at night, it helps if it's a place you've cleaned a lot previously. It's like driving a road you're familiar with after dark—at least you know where all the dips and curves and potholes and soft shoulders are.

Some things are unquestionably better candidates for night cleaning than others.

- Neatening, policing, or "straightening" things is an easy and rewarding evening activity. I always do this first and foremost.

- In brightly lit rooms like the kitchen and bathroom, you can usually wield your sponge or mop at will. Mood rooms like the living room are harder.

- Limited-area or portable undertakings like polishing silver or reorganizing a drawer are no problem—as long as you can marshal the will to do them at midnight.

- Avoid things like wall or ceiling washing, waxing, painting, or anything where thorough coverage is critical. It's too hard to see the skips or "holidays."

- Windows, in case you wondered, are difficult to do at night. Re-wipe as you will, streaks will always be revealed at sunrise. (Which is why many professional cleaning contracts forbid night window cleaning.)

- A good job of vacuuming is hard to do at night, too. And keep in mind that things take longer to dry at night when it's cooler and more humid.

- Dusting at night—unless the area in question has a lot of lamps, is a little like spreading lime by moonlight. You have to consciously cover every inch, rather than fly by eye as we usually do.

- Unless you're angry, dejunking is harder at night, without the aid of the cold light of day.

- And bed-making—sheet-changing especially—may be trickier at night—though any nurses' or self-defense training you may have will help out here.

How can I Clean Faster?

Speed in cleaning is possible and even fun and any of you "slow movers" who think you can't do a good job in a hurry, better think again because you can. Anything worth doing is worth doing fast! All you have to do is apply a couple of simple principles and you'll be able to clean not just faster but better and can even brag about it at the next block association meeting.

- **Learn from the pros.** If you want to be a champion at anything (cooking, golf, skiing, or cleaning) then go to the champions and learn what they know—what they use and how they go about it. I've written a dozen different cleaning books, including this one, to share the secrets of the cleaning professionals with home cleaners. If you have a cleaning service or professional maid come in, you can watch closely, too, and ask questions to learn the tricks of the trade. You can even pay close attention to how you speed through the place when company's coming and learn from it.

- **Race the clock** on every job of cleaning and go for the gold! It's challenge that makes life come alive. I do dishes five times faster (and better) than my wife or daughter because I'm always trying to beat my previous record when I dip those dinner plates in. So see how long it takes you to do a chore—and see if you can shave a few minutes off each time you do it. Before long

I guarantee you'll be considerably faster than before!

The sheer exhilaration of doing anything well will power you up, here, too.

- **Prepare well**—round up the right tools before the job begins so you won't have to break your stride to hunt up stuff.

- **Seek new tools and better cleaners** constantly. The right tool—in anything—can make all the difference between clomping along and cutting right through. And keep an eye on your inventory. There's no greater waste of time (and a good head of cleaning steam) than having to drop everything and run to the store because you've just discovered you're out of paper towels or vacuum bags.

- **Carry all your supplies** right along with you in a cleaning caddy (see p. 126).

- **Don't take breaks**, stop for snacks, or sit down while you work. Just hit it hard once you get started.

- **Do everything as you go**—don't backtrack.

- **Use both hands**—in dusting, sweeping, vacuuming, and whenever you can. One hand moves stuff out of the way while the other swoops through with the dustcloth, vacuum, etc. When you're wall washing, work with sponge in one hand, and towel in the other, and so on.

- **Don't be ashamed to do "skip" cleaning**—you don't have to do every square inch every time. If something isn't dirty, don't clean it.

- **Combine jobs** whenever you can—start one thing while you're finishing another, let one thing soak while you clean another, etc.

How can I ever get around to the deep cleaning?

Deep cleaning is all those things that "ought" to be done, but they don't have to be done this minute. They could wait, and as our lives get busier and busier—they do wait. We don't have weeks and often not even whole days or weekends to devote to deep cleaning anymore, so how do we manage to get it done?

- **Do a little every day or week**. One sure way to reduce the deep cleaning in the future is to increase your daily surface cleaning just a little—say five percent. *Things that are kept clean seldom need deep cleaning!* So sneak some little deep cleaning chore into every cleaning session: clean out one cupboard or one drawer, dust all the woodwork in one room, wash one set of curtains or one shelf of grimy knickknacks. You don't have to pick the job out ahead of time—in fact it helps to give yourself free rein here. But don't make it too ambitious, so it stays scarcely noticeable and doesn't derail your general cleaning agenda for the day. There are only so many corners and surfaces in a house, and if you keep chipping away at it you will make a dent.

- **Focus on one room or area** a month, or whatever, and do deep cleaning that needs to be done there whenever you get the chance.

- **Don't fail to act when the impulse strikes**. Deep cleaning energy is too rare, too fine, too exotic to ever be wasted. If the urge suddenly comes over you to dejunk the bulletin board, ditch all the outdated seed catalogs, sweep the unspeakable cellar or finally face up to the inside of the storage shed or refrigerator—don't let anything short of salaried employment or deathbed pledges get in your way. And if you get started and have a genuine desire to keep going, take the half-day of vacation you still have coming or postpone lunch with Aunt Lottie and keep on going.

- **Snatch those sudden bonanzas**: when the company can't make it, the concert is canceled, or your pingpong match is postponed (we're so overscheduled these days we never have "free" time unless it was originally allotted to something else). You've finally got it—don't waste it!

- **Plan a deep cleaning expedition**. This can be sometime when you do have a stretch of time—such as a long weekend in honor of a holiday you've never given a hoot about, and your beloved will be at the Bass Finals anyway. Recreation, after all, is a very personal thing—once we're over thirty we realize anything we want to do badly counts—and that even includes deep cleaning. Deep cleaning (the under, over, inside, behind and ignored portions of a house) can almost be fun once we actually get to it. Regular daily surface cleaning is the same old thing every day—here we get a chance to explore some forgotten region of our house!

- **Do it first**. Especially if it's only one thing on your list of To Dos for the day. Deep cleaning does take extra emotional and physical energy, so go to it before the sap evaporates or the adrenaline runs out.

- **Start with a garage sale**, a great incentive for deep cleaning. Once you dejunk, the all-out cleaning will be half done!

- **Corner yourself with commitment**—Such as taking the drapes down and sending them out to be cleaned. You know you'll want to get the rest done before those fresh, clean drapes return. Or invite someone you're in awe of to come stay for a weekend.

Deep cleaning checklist

Remember: Checklist means "checked." Not all of these things have to be done every month or six months or year or whatever, but they should be checked, to see if they need doing. You want to clean things when they're soiled, not when they're scheduled!

INTERIOR

✔ Clean all floor corners and edges

✔ Vacuum upholstery

✔ Deep-clean ("shampoo") upholstered furniture

✔ Wash other furniture

✔ Deep-clean ("shampoo") carpet

✔ Dust blinds

✔ Wash blinds

✔ Dust drapes

✔ Wash or dry clean drapes or curtains

✔ Clean light fixtures and lamps

✔ Dust/wash tops of tall furniture, exposed beams, rafters, and the like.

✔ Dust and decobweb all other missed places

✔ Wash woodwork

✔ Clean behind and under things

✔ Rewax heavy traffic areas of waxed floors

✔ Strip and refinish waxed floors

✔ Wash kitchen cabinets

✔ Clean out refrigerator

✔ Clean oven

✔ Degrease stove hood/exhaust fan

✔ Defrost and clean the freezer

✔ Deep clean the toilet bowl

✔ Remove any hardwater deposits or soap scum from other places

✔ Clean walls

✔ Touch up nicks in walls and woodwork

✔ Clean ceilings

✔ Wash all windows, including the hard-to-reach ones

✔ Wash window screens and sills

✔ Wash doors

✔ Wash door mats

✔ Wash/clean blankets

✔ Turn mattresses

✔ Clean or replace furnace and air conditioner filters

✔ Vacuum vents and ducts

✔ Clean/dejunk storage areas

EXTERIOR

✔ Wash and sanitize garbage cans and the garbage area

✔ Wash exterior of all windows

✔ Clean storm doors

✔ Clean house siding

✔ Clean roof gutters

✔ Clean/sweep chimney

✔ Check for damage or deterioration of house structure

✔ Trim trees and shrubs hitting the house

✔ Round up anything and everything broken—fix it or get rid of it

✔ Hose down the sidewalks, patios, and driveway to remove dirt and debris

- **Divide it up**. The pros can clean carpet, for example, faster, easier, and cheaper than you can, so let them do it. Call and schedule a carpet cleaning. It'll force you, again, to finish the cleaning before the carpet guys come.
- **Do it by degrees** if you must. Even the biggest job can be broken into steps or layers that can be tackled one by one. You can even clean a closet or an oven in stages if you have to. Even if you don't get as far as you'd planned by a given point, don't get discouraged or give up. If you keep on making progress you'll make it.
- **Don't try to do too much**. Don't pre-doom your deep cleaning project by running it head on with some other intensive activity. And don't bite off too big a piece for the time you have available.
- **Don't get deflected**. There's undone deep cleaning on every side, so no matter how littered the garage suddenly looks or how badly the ceiling fan blades beg to be dusted, stick with getting the bugs out of the light fixtures. Otherwise you'll have six things started and nothing really finished and end up down on deep cleaning.
- **Don't let things ever get so deep** that you have to dig out. "Cleaning as you go"—every day, all year round, can nearly eliminate deep cleaning—entirely (reread p. 21-23).
- If you're determined to do the **deep cleaning all at once**, you don't have to block out a whole week for it, or make an endless campaign out of it. If you have the carpets done by a professional and get the whole family plus maybe an in-law or two together for a day or a weekend, you should be able to do everything on your list.
- **Hire a pro** to do it—it's an entirely honorable way out. See Chapter Seven.
- **Before you start** that chore, are you sure you even need to do it? (See p. 10.)

Making a clean MOVE

We Americans move an average of fourteen times in our life. (Sure, some of us move only once or twice and others two dozen times or more, but it does average out to fourteen or fifteen times each.) Cleaning plays a big part in the whole spectrum of moving, and the cleaning of moving day brings some extra frustrations, too. To make the cleaning involved in moving easier on you and everyone else:

First

Save time and money! Deep cleaning, painting, repairs, wood floor sanding, and the like will go much faster and better if you do them before you move in or after you've moved out. We always end up doing things like cleaning the carpets after we get moved in. **Don't!** I know we're in a hurry both going and coming, but schedule the time to do an operation like this right. It'll only take **half the time** and cost less, too, if you do it when those rooms are empty!

Second

Be early, early! Late always means tension and trouble, hassle and panic and desperation and lost and broken things. Always start early! Nothing is worse than starting moving at noon and finishing at nine or ten when stores are closed and it's dark, no food available, and so on. Start at five or six in the morning and be done by two p.m. while you still have energy, friends, and a good attitude.

Third

Always triple the number of boxes and garbage bags you think you'll need and it will be just right. Nothing is worse than having to stop when you're really rolling to get more boxes. Having enough also prevents us from overloading containers or cramming things in the wrong size or shape of box.

Fourth

Get help! I know you hate to ask (and helpers will eat your lunch and drink all the pop), but the first move of any smart mover is to assemble some sturdy assistants. A hundred-pound item is reduced to a handleable fifty pounds with just one extra helper.

Fifth

Have a "mover's tool kit" and keep it handy. Removing things (like nails, screws, and brackets), and taking things apart for moving or shipping is a big part of moving things out and then setting them up again. Doing it without quick access to a hammer, pliers, and a dozen other little tools will almost double the effort involved. Have a supply of felt tip markers, labels, and plenty of packing tape in there, too.

And never even think about moving without a sturdy pair of leather gloves and a dolly!

Sixth

Assemble your cleaning kit. The perfect, portable cleaning kit is a nice big Rubbermaid Roughneck storage container, filled with the following: three spray bottles (of all-purpose cleaner, glass cleaner, and disinfectant cleaner—see p. 123); six terry cleaning cloths (see p. 146); two rolls of paper towels; two sponges; and one nylon scrub sponge. I'd also bring a couple of buckets, a squeegee set, and a Scrubbee Doo floor tool (see p. 157). Toss in several good mats, too, for the doorways and moving things in and out—see p. 41.

Don't forget the kingpin of moving day cleaning—the vacuum cleaner! It should be the last thing loaded and the first thing unloaded at the new place. Too often it is buried and unavailable!

Making a house look good in a hurry

What can you do when you don't even have time to give the house a quick once-over? Such as when unexpected guests call from their car phone to let you know they'll be by in about twenty minutes?

This happens to every one of us. Don't panic and don't just shovel the bulk of the junk quickly into the nearest closet.

1. First turn up all the lights! Yes, brighter not dimmer helps a dirty house look clean. There's a tendency to try to hide cobwebs, dust, and dropped popcorn by subduing the light, but the opposite is true. Darkness causes shadows, mystery, suspicion. Your place (even clean) will give guests a "cover up" feeling if it's darkened. Brightly lighted homes feel good and visitors feel better and they'll remember that nice feeling and forget the sweat socks or Tinkertoys sticking out from under the sofa.

2. Then clean yourself up—a little makeup or quick shave, new shirt or blouse or sweater. A quick upgrade of your appearance goes a long way toward making things seem under control—after all, they'll be seeing a lot more of you than they will of the house.

3. Enlist all the help you can, quick—but don't force or threaten anyone into it. They're likely to retaliate by saying something to the guest like, "Boy, if you don't believe in reincarnation, you should have seen this place a half-hour ago."

4. How small a part of the house can you confine the guests to? It'll help a lot if you can target your efforts. (There are some wise folks who keep one area of the house always clean, for company.)

   Weather permitting, you can stay on the porch, deck, or terrace, outside. Otherwise stick with the living room or kitchen, or at least the lower story. Close all the other doors and decide now what you're going to say when they ask for the "grand tour" of the house—and the kid with the messiest bedroom acts like he's going to take them up on it.

5. Cast your eye over the entrance area (porch, door, entryway, steps, even the sidewalk leading up to it). This is what gives that

all-important first impression and sets the tone for the whole abode. Remove any out-of-season ornaments and anything crooked or rusty, and scoop up all those chewed dog bones, broken toys, muddy boots, dirty doormats, grubby pet dishes, dead plants, and half-composted shopping flyers.

6. Dejunk—especially any empty food containers, strewn clothes, garbage, etc. Merely removing all the loose litter and repositioning everything out of place will do wonders. But do leave reading material and half-done projects out. They make you look industrious and intellectual and will give the guest a complex that will help keep their mind off the "wash me" etched in the dust on the TV screen. If nothing's out there already, spread your one-quarter-done quilt, the first draft of the family history, some seed catalogs, or the kids' salt-dough diorama of the moon out in the middle of the living room floor—"in progress" excuses the most unimaginable messes.

7. Floors—play a big part in an overall aura of cleanliness. So do squander a few minutes sweeping or vacuuming. If you're really rushed, you don't even have to haul out the vacuum—just handpick all the obvious stuff off the carpet.

8. Next hit the mirrors and glass doors and any picture windows or glass furniture tops within the target area. They look so good when they're sparkling clean, and so bad when they're streaked, handprinted, or spotted. You get a lot of mileage from a quick glass cleaning. (Do the outside of windows or glass doors, too, anywhere there's a view.)

9. If you don't have a dishwasher to stash undone dishes in, pile them in a sinkful of sudsy water. You can also leave a vacuum, dustcloth, and maybe a bottle of furniture polish out in plain sight. Explain when the guests first arrive how you were just in the middle of the weekly cleaning.

10. Run in the kitchen and prepare a fresh batch of lemonade in your prettiest pitcher.

They'll notice it more than anything else—just don't feed or refresh them too much or they'll have to use the bathroom. The bathroom, by the way, is the next place to hit quickly, if there's still time. Pull the shower curtain shut, hit the sink, faucets, and toilet, neaten up the towels. Even if they never visit the bathroom, the relaxation will show in your facial muscles and you'll be a better host or hostess.

Whatever you do, don't apologize for the condition of the house. When they ask "What's up?," take a deep breath and say "We've been rather busy between our jobs, our exercise program, our night classes at the college, our church and scout leadership activities and the time we like to devote to volunteer trail-building, historic landmark preservation, and voter registration. Plus we had to take a few hours out to make hot meals for a sick neighbor. We haven't used the living room for weeks, but we're really glad you happened by at the same time." (Be sure to find the TV knob and get the set turned off before you launch into this.)

An antidote for "perfect house" stress

If you need an antidote for "perfect house" stress (because company is coming), consider what one reader wrote to me—a woman who put into words what many overcommitted people are feeling today:

"If visitors are invited, it means I've asked them to share my living experience. I'd like them to enter my life for a little while and feel comfortable, and feel comfortable myself. I do want to sanitize my surroundings and lifestyle slightly so as not to shock them, but I want them to share my **life,** *not a perfect museum I don't actually live in."*

How to Make Cleaning Last Longer

When we have little time to clean, we want to make the most of our hard-won efforts to make the place look nice. To help make your "clean house" last longer:

- If you expect company, there are chores that can safely be done ahead of time (because they involve lightly or little-used parts of the house, for instance) and more "perishable" things to only do at the last minute. Don't do the latter too soon, or you'll be redoing them before the big day.

- Don't bother to do things like clean window and door glass right before you have children over to play with your child.

- When you manage to make the whole house look terrific, for a special occasion like the boss and her husband coming to dinner, make the most of that sparkling setting while it's still sparkling. Invite someone else over for an overdue visit.

- Once you do have the place clean, be extra vigilant to dispose of new clutter as soon as it appears—newspapers, junk mail, etc.

- Think "spot-cleaning" to keep up appearances after a big cleaning. Use a Dustbuster for the crumbs under the breakfast table or the stray cat litter on the stairs. Use this approach wherever you can in your home. A few quick swipes on your refrigerator shelves, for instance, can return the fridge to its just-cleaned splendor.

- Keep paper plates around for light meals, so there are no dishes to pile up when you're busy.

- Use the barbecue to cook more of your meals. If you have a gas grill, it's just as easy to use as your oven or stove, and the cleanup is much easier. Plus you have the added advantage of less fat in your meats.

- Do you have certain meals or recipes that always seem to spill over when you cook them? Why not put a cookie sheet or piece of aluminum foil beneath them before they blow their tops, so you can keep oven spills to a minimum, and keep your clean oven clean.

- Prepared casseroles are a great way to keep your kitchen looking good longer. No dirty pots and pans, the oven is all you use.

- Keep your entryways clean, including your garage. This will prevent dirt and soil from being tracked in to your house. Install good walkoff mats (see p. 41) inside and outside every entrance.

- You might even considering taking a tip from our Japanese friends, and have all family members remove their shoes at the door when they enter, especially if you have hardwood floors. This will keep your floor and carpets looking clean and new much longer. Keep slippers near the door for family members to put on.

- Apply soil retardant to carpet after you clean it.
- Keep furnace filters changed often to filter out airborne soil.
- Restrict craft projects and other messy undertakings to a back room, shop area, or basement.
- Make rules for your family to follow, such as "No food allowed in the living room" and "No leaning on the walls." Scofflaws can be sentenced to the appropriate cleaning measures for each infraction, i.e., cleaning the carpet, or scrubbing fingerprints off the walls.
- Spray bug-prone areas (garage corners, garage windows, screens, porch eaves, doors and windows near an exterior light, etc.) with bug spray. This will help prevent spiders and bugs from causing their usual mess.
- Keep the car in the garage, especially after it's been prettied up.

Let it go?
(ANOTHER APPROACH TO HANDLING THE NEW-CENTURY "TOO MUCH" OF HOUSEWORK)

When we're feeling the pressure of other priorities, decreased energy, and selective ambition, a spirit of "just let it go" seeps into our thinking. Why should we worry about cleaning, when there are more important things to do on all sides? And so housework goes lower on the list.

I'm the first to agree that "let it go" can be a good solution when our life's schedule intensifies (and it will). However we need to be careful of **what** we let go of. Anything we own, or are responsible for—be it places, possessions, plants, pets, or people—we must either tend, or face the consequences of not tending. Letting the required attention to something "go," ignoring it, let the time for it slip by, or reducing how often we do it, may not immediately or noticeably change its appearance or condition. But neglect means buildup, and eventually deterioration and damage, not

to mention a guilty conscience. All of this collects into that famous "backlog" to await us later, the care needed and problems that need to be solved much compounded by then.

If you have a big lawn, letting it go because you're too busy, have other priorities, or are too old to cope with it anymore, doesn't change the lawn's needs. It still needs to be cut, watered, weeded, and fertilized, or it will look bad, develop brown spots and bare spots, and grow up in crabgrass and dandelions.

What we sire we need to serve, and if we can't, **we need to change something.** If you took it on, you can take it off—reduce it, but not its care! Say you have doilies all over your furniture, and have always had them, because you love them. Your friends respect you as "queen of the doilies." But now that you have fifteen grandchildren, five dogs, a part-time job, and much less free time, doily upkeep has become next to impossible. Something has to go—your fuse, or the tender loving care you usually give those lacy little furniture finishers. Maybe what should really go is the doilies themselves. No doilies at all is better than dusty, wrinkled, soiled ones. Or maybe you should just keep (wash and starch and iron) two or three, in places where you'll often see and be delighted by them.

If you are at the "let go" point of life that's probably good. Time and circumstances are forcing you to a different level or focus of living. Maybe it's time to let part of the lawn go back to meadow, move, or hire all the mowing out. I encourage you to let the less significant go, just don't neglect the necessary, or it will reach a point of backlash—literally!

True, there are a few things in a house that won't be harmed or deteriorated by neglect. Some things (such as windows or other glass) can go twenty years without cleaning and still be okay. If dirty windows don't bother you or your neighbors, let them go. Carpeting, or any flooring, for that matter, is just the opposite. Neglect here will just accelerate wear. But if you are wealthy enough to afford frequent carpet replacement, carpets too can be a "let it go."

"Downsizing" is as applicable to the home as to big business!

CUTTING SQUARE FOOTAGE CUTS CLEANING

Cutting the square footage of our living quarters is another way to reduce cleaning. In a place to live we often confuse quantity with quality, and forget that as our life changes, so does our need for space, possessions, and furnishings. Many of us don't use our living quarters fully. We may have two or three empty or unused rooms, that we're not just cleaning but heating, insuring, and paying taxes on.

Stop and look at yourself and where you live today. You'll know in a minute if what I'm saying applies.

An oversized home can be a real handicap. We can spend so much time cleaning it, keeping it up, and maintaining it that we have no time to live in it, to enjoy the sumptuous setting we have created with great effort and expense. Life isn't measured by number of bedrooms, or size of lawn. A house is to live in, not for.

As I travel around the country and around the world, people everywhere tell me the same things. Every single person, without exception, who got rid of a huge place (because they couldn't handle it, or no longer needed it) said it was the most lifesaving thing they ever did. They missed the old place for about eleven minutes. So if too many "to-do's" are making your home life impractical or unbearable, consider this option for bringing things back into balance. Have the courage to cut down to what you really need, even if some might consider it small.

I'm in a seven-bedroom house myself and all of the kids are gone now. So my wife and I are modifying the house: converting two rooms to one to create more open space, shutting off other rooms, and narrowing and streamlining our living space. This in turn reduces the area we have to clean. When you don't have the time or the energy anymore, or it makes you sore to ride all around the North Forty, maybe it's time to sell it or reduce it to a nice ten or twenty. If you don't want to move or change homes, at least close off some little- or never-used areas. Think about it—it's one more way to outsmart housework.

Close off unused space:
We professional cleaning people know that unused space—under the deck, under the stairwell, or even a room you're not using, means wasted maintenance time and money and trouble. If unused areas are kept open and accessible they waste energy (such as heat and lights) and attract trash and clutter, as well as rodents and other unwelcome creatures. It adds up to unnecessary care and cleaning.

CHAPTER 4

The Best Way of All to Cut Cleaning

Prevent It!

This is the biggest and best of all cleaning secrets—eliminating the need for cleaning right up front. I'm talking about what you can do before you ever pick up a broom, get out a bottle of cleaner, or turn on the faucet. The prevention of cleaning—a necessary attitude for the new century.

What we might call Home Preventive Medicine focuses on the most intelligent of all home management approaches: THE FIRST PRINCIPLE OF EFFICIENT CLEANING AND REPAIR IS **NOT HAVING TO DO IT!**

Sound idealistic? Well it's pure reality and the easiest course to follow. Prevention is so much easier than restoration, recovery, and repair. Prevention saves us not just time and money, but lots of negative emotions such as stress, as well. It's also easier on the environment. Our goal should not just be getting better at cleaning, but simply eliminating it. One of the best ways to do this is to reduce the CAUSES of it.

How do we do it now?

Prevent those down-the-road problems

There are little things going on around the house all the time, that are vicious breeders of things breaking down later. Let's catch and fix them before they fail or cause a failure somewhere, and in this way eliminate, PREVENT, a big percentage of cleaning and repair. Some of the following you may have already figured out for yourself, others you may not have been aware of, or forgotten. Here are some down-the-road problems you can defuse right NOW!

Drain and pipe plugging

Overflows can really wreck a room, they aren't fun to deal with, either.

You should own a toilet plunger and enough good sense to keep all pipes and drains clean, clear, and working by watching what is flushed, tossed, or poured down there (i.e., no toy trucks, sanitary napkins, washcloths, toothpicks, combs, hair, grease, etc.) Many people worry about the clogging capacity of toilet paper, but it is designed to disintegrate and is rarely the culprit.

Forcing sticky doors and drawers

Forcing any door, window, or drawer that isn't sliding, closing, or opening easily will often cause damage. When something is operating stubbornly or not working at all, our inclination is to "put more weight on it" until it jams or breaks. The first thing to do in a situation like this is stop fighting "it." Then find the reason it isn't working and fix it, or report it to someone who can.

Faulty, broken, or missing things

A missing rubber bumper on a vacuum, for example, can ruin every door casing and baseboard in the place. Furniture with casters missing (which often means nails or screws in the legs rubbing the floor), faulty lamps that can cause fires, tools that damage, break, or discolor things are other examples. If it isn't working right stop using it NOW!

Food fallout

Food has great mess potential, so declaring certain parts of the house off limits for eating and drinking can really reduce our cleaning hours. See p. 45 for more on this.

Clean up spills promptly, before they have a chance to become stains. Food left anywhere compounds hourly into one of the biggest cleaning timetakers in the house. Don't leave food, food fragments, or drinks sitting on or under anything, especially not for long periods. Left food will rot and mold, create bad odors, stain surfaces, and attract insects and rodents. Left drinks will be spilled and create ring stains.

No two ways about it—confining or controlling where food is consumed cuts housework!

Saturday warrior cleaning

When something is left uncleaned for a long time, it takes more chemicals, moisture, and aggressiveness to remove the dirt and soil. This often results in damage to, or premature wear of, the object or surface. Things cared for regularly, instead of in a big marathon push, can be cleaned in half the time or less, and will last twice as long.

Smoking

Cigarettes, cigars, and pipes not only inflict almost unremovable odors, but deposit a yellow-brown film on ceilings, walls, windows, furniture, and other surfaces. Where there is smoking there are always stray ashes, and burns, too—permanent damage that causes a need for repair or replacement of furniture surfaces, bathroom fixtures, etc.

The obvious way to prevent all this is to limit smoking to a certain area, or not allow it in the house at all.

Junk and clutter

"Too much" is bad for our place as well as us. When there is too much stuff in a space it has to be stacked up, crammed in, shuffled around, and leaned against things—all of which will deteriorate a room fast. Even just sitting there, clutter often crushes things, shifts position, bumps heads and shins, and makes getting through or by hard or impossible. See Chapter Five for how to weed out the junk and clutter so you have room for, and can enjoy, your "good stuff."

Careless use of chemicals

Most household cleaning chemicals these days are safe if used where and for what they are intended. But often cleaners are used carelessly—in the wrong strength, or on the wrong thing. And things like bleach, acids, ammonia, and homemade cleaning brews can oxidize, discolor, degloss, and ruin surfaces, even in the hands of a professional cleaner. Don't leave any acid, for example, on fixtures for long. Rinse, rinse, rinse, and wipe dry with a terry cloth.

Rinse and "read the instructions" are magic words when it comes to preventing damage to household surfaces when cleaning.

Using abrasives to clean

Don't use powdered cleansers, steel wool, sandpaper, or harsh scrub pads to grind dirt off surfaces. Don't coat sinks and other surfaces with cleansing powder and then attack them with brisk rubbing. You can actually hear the results—a grinding abrasion that does remove stains and spots—along with the chrome or porcelain finish on the unit! Be careful with stiff brushes, too.

Most of the newer cleaners are designed to be mild and safe for surfaces, and they will work well without "elbow grease." A light pass over the surface with a white nylon scrub sponge or even a cloth dampened with the so-lution will generally do what you want done by way of cleaning.

If you must use powdered cleanser, steel wool, or an aggressive scrub pad (such as on old, worn, or badly stained surfaces), always use it wet. The water or cleaning solution will lubricate the surface so there is less chance of it being damaged.

Door blocking

Holding a door open by inserting a make-shift wedge on the hinge side will do fifty dollars worth of damage to a door instantly. Doors are delicately adjusted, and applying leverage to the hinge side will spring them. Then they rub, swing poorly, won't close, have to be forced, and things go downhill from there. NEVER wedge a door. Use a rubber-bottomed door stopper on the knob end of the door.

Reckless friends and visitors

What they do to our room or apartment, we have to answer for. Visitors to rental properties, particularly, seem to have a relaxed sense of responsibility. They can and will inflict damage, especially with spills, cigarette burns, misuse of tools and equipment, and thoughtlessly parked cars. It may take a while of dealing with the aftermath of visitor carelessness to give us the courage to carry this out, but what we need to do is make a set of rules for guests and visitors, and gracefully make them known to all upon arrival. (See Chapter Seven to minimize guest mess.)

Hanging things on places not designed for it

When we hang something on a thing or place not made for hanging (such as curtain rods, lamps, knobs, doors, or furniture), it is likely to cause warping, bending, sagging, and other problems. Then we have to pay for a repair, and find another place to hang the object anyway. So put those clothes right in the closet when you bring them back from the dry cleaner. And don't install heavy things like shelves (meant to hold even heavier things) on plain sheet rock walls.

Ignoring overflow

Anything with moisture in it—from flowerpots to fishtanks—should always have provision for leaks, drips, or overflow. Uncontained moisture means ring marks, rust, mildew, and other damage. Don't forget the drip potential of candles, either.

Storing outside equipment inside

Such as motorcycles, bicycles, sports equipment, and chain saws. Before we know it we have oil stains on the floor and gouges and gashes on furniture and woodwork.

That's why we are encouraged not to store our snowmobiles (or racehorses) in our rooms.

Windows left open

Open windows are wonderful if watched. But if we just go off and leave them, the weather can shift and a "leaning" rain can in no time not just drench the sills, but deteriorate the sheetrock, soak the carpet, warp wooden floors, and cause all kinds of opening and closing problems with the window later.

Dragging things

Such as appliances, furniture, and other heavy things. Dragging usually means drag marks, which may be impossible to remove.

WHAT RUINS CARPET?

Don't be a carpet "beat'le"—avoid these common abuses of carpets:

✔ **Not vacuuming it regularly.** This causes dirt and grit to accumulate at the base of the fibers and grind away at them.
✔ **Not having good mats** at all entrances to your home.
✔ **Glue, nail polish,** and other things that should never be used over carpet.
✔ **Pet pee and poop left undealt with.** Things like this don't just smell bad, they stain and bleach the carpet and the padding and floor beneath it.
✔ **Heavily colored foods and drinks** (such as Kool-Aid) spilled on it.
✔ **Leaving spills** of any kind instead of cleaning them up immediately.
✔ **Ignoring a flood** or anything else that saturates the carpet (toilet overflow, water from windows left open, sprinkler fallout).
✔ **Putting anything hot on it.** Most carpets nowadays are made of nylon and high heat will MELT the fibers.
✔ **Dragging very heavy things** across carpet, or letting them sit on it for any length of time.
✔ **No casters or felt protectors** on the legs of heavy furniture.
✔ **Cigarette burns.**
✔ **Chewing gum.**
✔ **Leaving drapes and curtains always open** so that the carpet is constantly exposed to direct sunlight.
✔ **Trying to shampoo** a carpet when you don't know what you are doing.
✔ **Scrubbing carpet** so vigorously that you mash or frizz the pile.

Tackle the tenth-time offenders

One sure way to reduce housework is to do something about the repeat offenders, the things that have to be cleaned up after again and again and again—the things that are always a mess. After you've raked up the droppings from the Mucho Sheddus Leafus plant or mopped up the slop from a too-tippy TV tray for the fiftieth or sixtieth time, for example, you can take the initiative and say, "How am I going to deal with this?" We can be eternal straighteners, or straighten things like this up in one fell swoop, forever—send them up the river or down the chute. So go through your home this week and note the things that you find yourself constantly fiddling with, cleaning after, or restoring to order. Stop now and correct the situation, to save yourself from dealing over and over with something, day after day, year after year, maybe even decade after decade!

Protect it!

Another means of housework prevention is simply looking ahead and protecting vulnerable objects or surfaces from the onslaught we know is coming.

Let's start with the #1 home protection and housework prevention tool, the doormat.

USE MATS

When I was lauding the advantages of doormats in one of my cleaning seminars once, a man jumped up in the audience and yelled, "I hate doormats, all they are is dirt catchers." I rest my case. What you catch at the door you won't have to clean out of the house.

Once you have mats you won't have to vacuum or shampoo your carpets as much, or sweep, scrub, strip, and wax your floors as often. Mats reduce dusting and keep clothes, drapes, and upholstery cleaner. Good mats will catch much of the grit and gravel before it gets in and scratches and wears out your floors. They'll pull off the soil and tar before it gets embedded in your carpet. And they absorb rainwater, slush, road salt, and mud. Mats save tons of cleaning time and energy, save cleaning supplies and wear and tear on your cleaning equipment as well as your home and its furnishings.

A good mat is like having a full-time ser-vant sitting in front of your door cleaning off the bottoms of people's feet as they enter—what a deal! Matting every entrance to your home correctly, and then taking some simple steps to service the mats, will do more to reduce dirt and dust in your home than me moving in and cleaning for you full time. Mats are a minor investment that will last for years and make a big difference in your life.

What's the best mat to use?

To do the job right, you need a professional-quality door mat or "walkoff" mat both inside and outside your doors.

For outside of doors, I like the tough artificial turf mats called Astroturf. When you step on a mat like these, those little plastic "grass blades" bend and move and scrape your feet, and then the dirt drops down inside the mat so it can't be tracked in by the next visitor. Astroturf mats come in many colors and they last and last, won't rust or rot, and are a snap to clean. I have them at every outside door of my homes, including the garage.

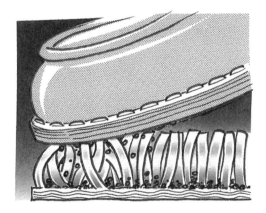

Astroturf mats are available at your local home improvement store or from the Cleaning Center (see p. 191). Go for 2'x3' or bigger—anything smaller is too easy to step right over. To do a good job of catching dirt, both inside and outside mats need to be at least four strides long.

Indoors use 2'x3' or 3'x4' commercial mats with a nylon or olefin carpet top and rubber back. These look nice and finish the job of drying and removing grit and soil from feet.

Keeping mats dust-hungry

To maintain outside mats: just shake them out well and hose them from time to time.

To maintain inside mats: 1. Keep them vacuumed. 2. Every so often take them outside and hose away the dirt. (If they're really dirty, you can scrub them with a brush dipped in all-purpose cleaner solution.) 3. Squeegee the water off with a floor squeegee, if you have one (see p. 157). Then hang them over an outside railing or whatever until completely dry before putting them back down. Never use when wet.

Every month or so, when I'm washing the car, I gather up the mats and wash them, too, after letting the car water drain off onto them. This goes fast and it's fun!

TAKE ADVANTAGE OF SOIL RETARDANTS AND SEALERS

We can protect many surfaces with waxes, coatings, finishes, paints, sealers, and soil retardants. You are familiar with most of these—now be sure to take advantage of them.

Protecting fabrics and carpeting

Products like Scotchgard give the fibers of fabrics and carpeting a clear protective coating that repels moisture and stains, and makes soil and spills easy to "release" from the surface if they do get on there. They also reduce lint shedding, and make dust and dry soil easier to remove. Soil retardants are available for everything from carpeting and upholstery to clothing.

✓ **Treat upholstery:** When the salesperson asks if you want soil retardant applied to that new piece of furniture you're buying, say yes. It costs something, but saves a lot of time and grief over time. Be sure to have it reapplied after deep cleaning (shampooing) of upholstery.

✓ **Treat carpet:** Most carpeting now comes pretreated with a soil repellent such as Scotchgard, however over time it gets cleaned or worn out of the carpet. Soil retardants should be reapplied after every major carpet cleaning.

✓ **Choose fabrics** with built-in stain protection for clothing and other fabric items that get hard use. If necessary, get yourself a spray can of Scotchgard or the like and do your own pretreating of things such as canvas duffle bags and fabric handbags, before they are put into service.

Protecting hard surfaces

✓ **Seal wood** to keep it from cracking, splitting, and absorbing stains, and make it easily cleanable (see p. 176). Wood sealers are available in glossy, semigloss, and matte finishes.

✓ **Seal concrete,** brick, stone, earth tile and other masonry, to keep it from absorbing dirt and stains, improve its appearance, and make it more cleanable. Masonry sealers will ease your cleaning chores on fireplaces, floors, and walls. You can get high gloss finishes, and ones you can hardly tell have been applied. Your local masonry dealer or DIY store can help you choose the right sealer for your masonry, interior or exterior.

✓ **Apply floor finish to other hard floors** such as sheet vinyl and tile to help protect the finish from wear, make soil and marks easier to remove, improve their appearance, and make them safer to walk on (**less** slippery!). See p. 158-160.

✓ **Seal almost anything**, to make it easier to clean, prevent soil penetration, help it shed dust and resist fingerprints, and enhance its appearance. A surface protector such as Beauty Seal (available from the Cleaning Center)—made of silicone and polymers—can be used on desktops, appliances, cars, boats, trailers, bikes, skis, vinyl upholstery, even eyeglasses and the inside of wastebaskets. Used on shower walls, shower doors, sinks, faucets, and bathroom trim, it will help prevent filming and hardwater deposits. On plastic laminate ("Formica") it renews the surface and helps prevent staining.

BE A COVER LOVER

We can also use covers to protect things.

Much housework is caused by failure to think ahead or consider the consequences. We're often so eager to get underway on something that we can't be bothered to lay down dropcloths or old newspapers, or move things out of the way before we start. We just launch right into some splattery or dust-producing activity.

But covering the area—tabletop, floor, or wall—before you start saves a lot of sweeping, vacuuming, washing, scrubbing, scraping, and refinishing! The ratio of time spent to clean up, compared to cover up, is about a hundred to one!

Likewise, anything left around loose or open will welcome the weather and visiting kids to get into it, along with all the dirt and dust. Put up, button up, or cover up what is used only occasionally. When you finish cleaning that seldom-used machine, why not put a dust cover over it, so you won't have to clean every knob and crevice again three months from now? Seldom-used appliances and recreational equipment, too, can be kept covered and/or out of the way.

CONVENIENCE: *Another key to reduced cleaning*

None of us are beyond yielding to convenience. Whatever is easier, handier, closer, quicker, will usually be the one we choose. Even the most disciplined person will grab a hunk of junk food or a place to gas up (even an expensive one) if it's "right there." Often we take second best because it's more convenient than the rest. **Availability can really make a difference in ability!** And this is as true in cleaning as anywhere.

• If a trash can is close by and easy to use, most of us will "can" it. If it takes some effort to locate a trash repository, that bottle or wrapper will be left right where it was emptied. Make sure you have trash containers everywhere you need them, even two in a room if it merits them. For example, lots of waste paper and wrappers and the like are generated around a bed, but one seldom sees a waste container there. So trash ends up in headboards, on dressertops, under the bed, and among the covers, instead.

• If a place to hang them is right there, most things will get hung up, by young or old. If the rack is around a corner or two, however, the garment or ball mitt lands on a couch, floor, or chair back.

• If a vacuum is in the vicinity (and a plug-in, too), even a lazy bugger will vacuum. If we have to find or go fetch what we need we'll wait—a day or week or two!

- If a cleaning tool or product takes any degree of effort or thinking to put to use, we'll stall. If we can just push a button or add water and be underway, we'll grab it and go for it.

A "household convenience audit" might be a good idea, to find the hot spots of inconvenience that bear on home care and cleaning, and correct them!

This will be the century of CONVENIENCE!

CLEAN HOUSE CHECKLIST	
Trash	There are trash cans and baskets everywhere we need them—big enough ones!
Tools	Everything we use often should have a clearly assigned and easily accessible place.
Closets	Contain only often-used things, and have open, easy-to-reach space for everything that is supposed to be in them.
Storage	Contains only genuinely useful or valuable things, and they are all boxed or containered, labeled, and findable.
Junk drawer (necessary!)	Is dejunked and up to date, with all needed items.
Mail	There is a designated spot to put mail and pick it up, to open mail, and dejunk it.
Wrapping and unwrapping	Designate a place to open packages and wrap and box things up, for shipping or birthday parties. Saves packaging and supplies strung all over the house, and is much more convenient.
Windows	Are reachable, openable, and unobstructed (so we can see out of them, and clean them).
Cleaning supplies	Are kept close to where they're needed, and they're fresh, full, labeled, refillable, liftable. Have cleaning caddies (see p. 126) everywhere you need them, and keep them fully armed.
Vacuums	And any necessary attachments are handy and in good working order, bags emptied. Own three vacuums if you have to (one for each story of the house), and make sure they all work.
Other cleaning equipment	Is in good repair, and reachable, accessible, simple to use or run.
Cleaning safety gear	Is handy and quickly findable.
Stain removal kit and stain chart*	Are handy for sudden spots and spills.
Cleaning standards and assignments	Are clearly established, and written down, posted, or passed on to everyone.
Furniture	Is easy to clean and move, so we can get under and behind it.
Covers	For anything that needs to be covered are easily accessible.
Guests	Have easy access to any cleaning materials they may need.

*See the back cover.

Controlling food and clothes

Isolating the cause is the first step toward making a problem go away. There are clearly two big areas we struggle with when it comes to cleaning: Food/eating and clothes. Most of us are overblessed and overwhelmed with these, and constantly complaining about one or the other. Food and clothes are the things we end up most often having to pick up, clean up, or clean around, in the form of litter, clutter, stains, and spills. You can cut a lot of cleaning time if you just make some efforts to *curb or control food and clothes.*

FOOD

Even the neatest eating is bound, sooner or later, to mean spills, stains, smears, crumbs, and grease marks to remove, and if there are kids eating in an area we will have at least three times as much of this to deal with. So:

1. Put some restrictions on where food is consumed. Keep food and drinks out of areas not designed for them. For example, cut out eating in bedrooms and cars. Allow eating and drinking only in rooms without carpet, or outdoors.
2. Add a family room off the kitchen (to save the rest of the house).

Another way to prevent food mess:

Intelligent use of disposals and compactors is great, but the very act of garbage generation is where you can really make a difference. I got tired of bringing home two sacks of groceries that created three sacks of garbage. Buying more wisely can really reduce trash and waste. One box of healthy oatmeal, for example, produces one-tenth the trash and ten times the nourishment of all those cellophaned and tinfoiled breakfast goodies, all those chips and sauces and dressings. A dish of beans costs very little, makes little garbage and little cleanup. The same is true of anything we buy that involves packaging. Smart intake can really cut down outtake and cleanup.

An experienced mother knows that wet cornflakes stick better than Super Glue... so keep them in the kitchen!

3. Keep the kitchen table clear, to help curb the urge to flop on the couch and eat.
4. Keep a small TV in the kitchen for those who can't face life (or lunchtime) without watching TV.
5. If someone insists on eating in a recliner or living room chair, throw a washable cover over it.
6. Make sure napkins or paper towels are always easily accessible.
7. Cut messy snacks such as chips and dips out of your diet (most of them aren't good for you, anyway).
8. Add more garbage cans.

9. Get rid of narrow-bottomed glasses and cups, and get sipper bottles for the little ones.
10. Put a dropcloth around the high chair.
11. Don't use a too-small bowl or dish, especially when serving messy foods.

CLOTHES

1. Dejunk (trash or give to Goodwill or whomever) everything that is worn out, the wrong size, out of style, or ugly. Or that you simply never wear.
2. Buy and own fewer.
3. This goes for shoes, too. Three or four pair of shoes is enough for anyone!
4. Create more places to hang clothes in more locations, such as home entrances, and the garage.
5. Buy better hangers, so things don't slip off onto the floor.
6. Pack away seasonal stuff, so you don't have to paw through parkas looking for a tennis skirt.

Laundry timesavers

An intelligent and preventive approach can help with our household chores themselves, too. The more common and frequently needed a cleaning operation, the more time we can save by preventive thinking. Laundry, for example, isn't the timetaker it once was. It's now more of a timing judgment, choosing when it will be done, and including the possibilities of what else you can do while you are at it. (Such as washing while you're cleaning something else, taking a bath, working in your home office, or watching your favorite TV programs.) It's better to do laundry while you are around, so that garments that have finished washing or drying are not left in the machine, multiplying the wrinkles, and wasting dryer electricity.

Here are some other ways to help cut the "nonstop chore" of laundry down to size.

• Laundry shouldn't be just one person's job, but a family operation. A family that soils together should toil together, to lighten the laundry load. Post an instruction sheet over the washer, designed with your family in mind. List key facts such as how much detergent to use, ABC's of sorting for washing, how many pairs of jeans should be washed in one load, etc. Make it easy for everyone to help out or do his or her own. Even children can do their own laundry, with proper instruction, by say the age of twelve.

• Things family members can do to help speed the laundering process: empty their own pockets, turn things right side out (or wrong side out if that's how they should be washed), unroll rolled-up cuffs or sleeves, and so on.

• Dirtier does matter! Often because we know something is soiled and on its way to the washer or dry cleaner, we toss it around, tromp on it, or leave it out somewhere. Which only gets it dirtier and gives the soil already on it a chance to set. When something is cleaning bound, hamper it, hang it up, or otherwise get it out of harm's way.

• Don't be afraid to use a dry cleaner for special or problem items that need to be washed. (See p. 74.) You'll save time, money, and heartaches, too.

• Make sure the washer and dryer are close to each other, to save steps.

"Laundry was always a big time consumer for me. Then I started eyeing each piece of laundry and determining not just whether it was truly dirty, but whether it deserved my time and effort to take care of it. I do less laundry now—I'm not forever washing towels, bathrobes, blankets, and unneeded or little-used clothing."

- Locating the washer and dryer as close as possible to where most laundry originates and has to be redistributed is a big time cutter. Too often the washing center is by the kitchen, at the opposite end of the house from the bedrooms, for example, and piles of clothes and linens have to be transported back and forth forever. Design your new place with the laundry center close to the dirty clothes center, or even move it now if you can.

- If you have a multistory house, or are planning your dream house, consider a laundry chute to deliver clothes to the laundry area speedily. Kids will love it!

- Have the detergent, spotter, and pocket fallout container at eye level right above the washer and dryer so that you can see and reach the right stuff easily from a standing position. Have a good-sized wastebasket near the washer and dryer for the amazing amount of packaging, dryer lint, and other trash generated in a laundry room.

- Make sure you always keep a backup supply of detergent, spotter, bleach, and fabric softener. There's nothing worse (or more timewasting) than running out at a crucial moment.

- Never just throw clothes in the utility room. The ideal is to have sorting bins for clothes, so clothes (white, light and dark colors, delicate fabrics, etc.) are sorted as they are hampered.

  If you don't have separate bins to help presort laundry, at least have one huge container in there to hold everything until you have time to separate things. Make sure anything dirty and wet is hung to dry if you don't have time to wash it now.

- Having a nice big folding surface (countertop or table) in the laundry room is a real help in seeing that laundry gets folded promptly.

  Each person you're washing clothes for should have their own (color coded?) basket which you fill with freshly washed and folded clothes. When full, each person puts his own away.

  Near your folding center, it's also helpful to have conveniently placed hooks to presort clean laundry hanging on hangers. Then hung clothes can be carried all together to the proper room, wardrobe, or closet.

- Socks are a pain to sort and match. It may be more efficient to put them all in a basket and match them up every second or third time you wash.

  Next time you buy socks, buy as many identical pairs as you can for each person. Then when you do laundry, all of their socks will match and this will cut down on sorting and hunting time.

- If possible, establish a regular time or times to wash. Too often we take the spontaneous approach—do it as we need it—and this not only puts us in a time bind but is seldom efficient from an environmental standpoint. A scheduled laundry time also eliminates the "hunt and seek" complaints of someone's clotheslessness.

- When in doubt, read the manufacturer's care labels, and believe them, NOW instead of later.

- Know what the different settings and cycles on your washing machine are. If something isn't real dirty, don't put it on long wash—it wastes water and electricity, as well as your time.

  Likewise, don't dry things that take a long time to dry (such as jeans) together with things that take a short time to dry (such as sheets).

- A clothesline in a laundry is a good idea. Pulling partially dried clothes out of the dryer and hanging them on hangers to finish drying is better than ironing, and reduces shrinkage, too.

- If most things today are laundered in the proper way, and smoothed out, folded, or hung up at the right time, they don't need to be ironed. In this day of fuss-free fabrics and cheap and convenient professional laundry service, ironing shirts is slave camp labor. Buy clothes that don't need it, and if you're insane enough to insist on one hundred percent cotton, send those shirts out to be ironed.

- When putting away linens, put the matching pillowcases in the final fold of each sheet, so they are easily available. You can do this with other matching things, too, such as towels and face cloths.

Reducing holiday "hangovers"

HANDLING THE FESTIVE FALLOUT, OR CONFETTI CLEANING!

Holidays and other causes for celebration seem to be increasing every year, and celebrations create a unique cleaning challenge.

On holidays—every weekend can almost be counted in this, too—there is instantly more mess and clutter. We overcook, overeat, buy more new things, create more trash, spend more money more foolishly, have more mishaps, get less sleep, and (exhausted from the fun) **usually leave cleanup till later.** Holidays generally mean family and friends gathering, so add into this more people in the house and yard, more people going in and out, many more trips to the refrigerator, more spills, and other things that are hard on a house, including more taping, stapling, and gluing of things everywhere.

TO REDUCE HOLIDAY CLEANUP

1. Plan the festivities for parts of the house with expendable furniture and durable surfaces. Stifle the urge to show off: stay out of rooms packed with your prize possessions. Weather permitting, outside parties are a lot easier on the interior decoration, even if it will mean making a few provisions for wind or rain, and a few napkins blowing over to the neighbors.
2. Making sure you have good mats inside and outside all entrances really helps.
3. Add more waste containers in prominent places. You can gather up and store them afterwards. Otherwise, if a partier needs to get rid of something, it'll end up on a windowsill, under a cushion, or in the shrubs.
4. Add protective covers for things wherever it makes sense and can be done discreetly.
5. To keep down cigarette mess and burns, one of the big hazards of party giving, provide plenty of ashtrays, designate a single area such as a porch for the purpose, or set out tastefully worded "no smoking" signs.
6. As noted earlier, food has phenomenal mess potential. How it is served has a bearing on this, and buffet is about the worst. Offering people food this way is just asking them to walk all over the house with it. Where there are plates being carried around and balanced on knees there will be dropping and spilling and smearing. Plus a lot of excess food lying around because guests took more than they could handle.

Far better to have all the eating done in one place at one time on the surface actually designed for it—a table. If you must serve elsewhere, make everyone sit down first and bring the food to them, and provide some surface steadier than the human lap to set things on.

7. Give some thought to the menu itself in terms of its mess potential. Be wary, for instance, of scatterables like chips and popcorn, anything that crumbs easily, foods few will eat but all will leave around,

toothpicks that will be left everywhere, nuts in the shell, etc. And remember that red or orange sauces and beverages make some of the worst stains. For children, consider getting a supply of the paper cups that have lids with holes in them for a straw.

8. To reduce white rings on furniture, provide plenty of coasters, and whenever possible, serve beverages in paper cups, which are less prone to the condensation that worsens this problem.

9. Check and make sure fireplace dampers are clear. People often stuff wads of wrapping paper and empty boxes in a seldom-used fireplace and light it, only to find (after every smoke alarm is screeching) that the damper was closed.

10. When it comes to decorations, remember that what goes up must come down, tape goes on easier than it comes off, and crepe paper stains when it's wet. It's also easy, wise, and economical to avoid litter-creating party entertainments like confetti and firecrackers.

11. Finally, don't leave it all for the morning. No matter how beat you are, try to at least get all the spills up, the dishes to the sink, and precariously placed things put away before you collapse—most stains only set and worsen with time.

The key to avoiding home party hangovers is the key word PREVENTION. Making merry doesn't have to make a mess!

Cleaning when you aren't there

When we're going away, for a day or longer, we take precautions to keep our home safe and secure while we're gone. The following will save us cleaning headaches when we get back, as well:

- Check the stove, faucets, heaters, and small appliances to make sure nothing is left on.
- Close all interior doors so that if a fire should start in a room, it might choke itself out.
- Flush toilets.
- Take all garbage out.
- Don't leave any dirty laundry to generate foul odors.
- Don't leave fruit or other food out to attract insects and rodents.
- Pull the drapes to save sun rot of carpets and upholstery.
- Set the heating or cooling systems to suit the circumstances. Frozen and burst pipes mean flood damage—a nightmare of destruction and extra cleaning.
- Bear in mind that pets left alone inside for extended periods can and will cause mess and damage.
- If you'll be gone for an extended time, unplug all unused appliances and turn off the water supply to automatic washers to prevent flooding in case the hoses should burst.

Break those mess-making habits!

This last way to prevent housework is getting pretty personal, but the fact is that every single one of us does dumb things that create unnecessary work for ourselves—things that don't just cause, but *multiply* housework.

When mess-making manners and habits disappear, so does the mess. Simple behavior change can outperform the greatest tools and techniques, or any other cleaning magic. Just breaking a few mess-making habits will ease our housework routine more than anything else around.

CONTROLLING THE HABITS THAT CREATE CLEANING

Let's look at some instant housework eliminators here.

Latch the hatch

We can save a big chunk of cleaning and household care time if we just put lids back on, and close drawers, doors, and windows when we should. Close it now and there's nothing to it—leave it open, and it spills, rain, flies, moths, or mice get in, the prize animal gets out, heads get bumped, etc.

Put those caps back on now, too. It takes exactly the same amount of time to do it now as later, except by then the cap will have rolled down the drain or down the hall and the tube will have oozed out all over.

Kill the spills

The less spills, the less stains and the less cleanup!

- Leave nothing around that can spill or be spilled if you aren't there watching it every minute. Never set things where they're sure to get knocked over.
- Dry spills can make just as much mess as wet spills (maybe more), which means pay attention when you're dipping out a few cups of flour or sugar. For less Cheerios on the kitchen table and floor, make sure kids have deep bowls for cereal and that they don't fill them to the top.
- Overfilling anything (tub, bucket, sink, or bowl) is sure to mean drips and spills, whether you're pouring or carrying.

Pours we deplore

When it comes to that simple act of pouring, we're usually in a big hurry, or not really paying attention. For less spills when pouring:

- Don't pour too fast, and stop well before you reach the top of the glass or container.
- Hold things over the sink, or place them in the sink, if necessary, before pouring.
- Children who think they're big enough to pour, but aren't, should be gently demoted to the audience.
- Don't pour Kool-Aid or other strong-colored liquids over countertops—it stains them.
- If you have pitchers or carafes that seem to always pour crooked, replace them!

Dam those drips!

- Don't carry dripping things across the floor or carpet—if it's wet, and you must move it somewhere, put it in a tub or bucket.
- Don't throw things with liquid in them (such as partly drunk cups of takeout beverages) into the garbage can.
- There's many a drip between the pot or punchbowl and the ladle! So ladle things out on an easily washable surface (not over the tablecloth), and put someone dependable in control of the ladle. Set the cup or jar you're ladling into in a bowl first, if necessary.

Sawdust Savvy

Construction, craft projects, repairs, and workbench activities should take place in a clearly designated area where surfaces can't be damaged and fallout can be contained. Designate special "craft shirts" for yourself and the kids, to cover your good clothes when crafting, and keep the Spray and Wash handy!

Stop dropping!

The clothes you dropped right where you changed—you still have to spend the minute it would have taken to hang them up then—plus now, the time to de-wrinkle and de-lint them.

Don't put it down—put it away!

When something is already in hand we can put it in its rightful place much more quickly and efficiently than if we toss it somewhere and then have to find it and pick it up again later.

Picking up after yourself is the single most timesaving thing you can do. It took me a while, but I finally discovered that if I put my wrenches, my fishing equipment, and my baseball gear away, when it came time to work or play I could do it right away. I didn't have to hunt or rummage.

Don't put it down—put it away!

If you open it, close it
If you turn it on, turn it off
If you unlock it, lock it
If you borrow it, return it
If you're done with it, put it back
If you make a mess, clean it up
If you don't know where it goes, ask!

Don't forget the wet!

Don't leave wet things around... anywhere! Leaving wet towels or wet clothes lying somewhere, or draped over things, will cause mildew, rust, musty smells, stains, discoloration and peeling of finishes, and worse.

Stash the trash

It may take an extra five minutes now to put the garbage where the coons or the neighbor's ten-pound tomcat can't get to it.

But that's much faster and more pleasant than collecting broken eggshells, chicken bones, stained papers, sticky boxes, oily cans, soggy Kleenex, and coffee-ground-filled orange halves from all over the lawn and driveway. And then having to re-bag and re-haul all this.

Auto motto

Never leave anything (groceries, trash, coolers, sports equipment, etc.) in a vehicle after a trip. When you get out, it gets out. A sentence of "later" always sours something.

Attack the stack

Piles will always get spread around, ruined, or plundered. Pile to sort, but never to store, especially in the open!

Route the "out"

Anything left out, be it a puzzle or a bag of potato chips, will get spread all over, and have to be cleaned up or cleaned around.

For a cleaner home on the range

Many unnecessary messes are committed on the range top.

- Don't put pots and pans on to cook at too high a heat—this will splatter the whole surrounding area, cause the contents to boil over or burn, and blacken if not ruin the pot, too. (If it doesn't start a fire!)

- A spoon rest for the stirring or tasting spoon will help avoid sticky spots and little puddles on the range and counter.
- Don't use the range top as a food preparation and peeling area.

Cease the grease

Most kitchens have some kind of exhaust fan to remove cooking fumes, and all we have to do is flip a switch to use it. When we don't bother to do that, greasy smoke spreads over the kitchen, if not the whole house.

Fridge wisdom

Packages of meat and poultry that are just removed from grocery bags or the freezer and set on refrigerator shelves are likely to leak blood and other liquids over everything below them. Put such things in something leak-proof—bag, pan, or plastic container—before you put them in the fridge.

Wipe the bottom of "sticky jars" like pickles after use, before putting them back away, to avoid "sticky rings" in the refrigerator.

Make sure any bottles stored flat—such as wine or jumbo pop bottles—are well corked or capped before you turn them horizontal.

Dish demerits

- Leaving your dirty dishes on the table, or anywhere in the house.
- Leaving the sink a mess after you use it.

Shoe boo-boos

- Tracking in mud and dirt in waffle-sole shoes, boots, and sneakers.
- Wearing shoes that make black heel marks everywhere.
- Leaving your shoes wherever you pulled or kicked them off. (Shoes left lying right where they were shed can be dangerous, too, if someone trips over them in the dark.)

Untargeted tooth care

Flossing teeth—although important—will never be an Olympic event. Hold your head down when you floss or brush your teeth, and any spatters will end up in the sink instead of on the mirror.

Sins of "setting"

- Taking cups of coffee, bowls of chili, or whatever somewhere and leaving behind what will become an encrusted plate, moldy cup, or scummy bowl.
- Leaving empty or part-empty beverage cans anywhere.
- Setting the paint lid down somewhere "just for a minute."
- Putting cups and glasses on wood furniture without coasters, which leaves an ugly (if not impossible to remove) white ring.
- Taking out a load of laundry and setting it, mountain high, on top of the dryer or washer instead of folding things up and putting them away.
- Setting unwrapped gum anywhere!

Bathroom blunders

- Not putting the shower curtain inside the tub before you shower or bathe, so the floor and rug get soaked.
- Spraying hairspray not just on your locks, but everywhere.
- (Men only) Failing to aim... at the toilet.

Stain makers

- Not bothering put on a bib or apron, or old clothes before starting something messy.
- Wiping your hands on your clothes while cooking, etc.
- Not cleaning the grease or paint off your hands before walking into the house and handling everything in sight.

Cleaning-day carelessness

Even our very efforts to clean are often sabotaged by carelessness.

If a floor or area is really dusty and dirty, for example, don't sweep in big wide strokes or whisk briskly with a whiskbroom. You'll spread dust and dirt everywhere. Other dumb things we do on cleaning day:

- Using a dirty dustcloth or dishcloth.
- Washing something big and fuzzy in with a load of lint-catchers.
- Not emptying pockets before tossing things in the hamper or washer.
- Throwing dirty laundry on top of clean laundry.
- Not checking for spots that need to be pre-treated.
- Carrying dripping bleach bottles or bleach solutions over carpeting/splashing them on our clothes
- Setting wet bottles of bowl cleaner and other strong chemicals down on susceptible surfaces.
- Leaning against the sink while doing dishes.

Become more conscious!

So much of the mess-making we do each day is a matter of simple oblivion. We come in, plop down in a chair, have a pop, leave the can, read a paper, leave pieces of it all over, take off our shoes, and a sock sneaks under the edge of the chair, open an envelope, and one of the enclosures escapes, unwrap a piece of candy, and the wrapper drifts away, peel an orange, and a piece of peel eludes us, some of the juice from the orange gets on the end table, and creates a sticky spot, and so on.

We can save ourselves a world of work by simply **becoming more conscious** of what we do, and helping other family members to do the same.

Remember:
Cleaning can be reduced more by ***behavior change*** *than anything else—what doesn't get dirtied or abused doesn't require care!*

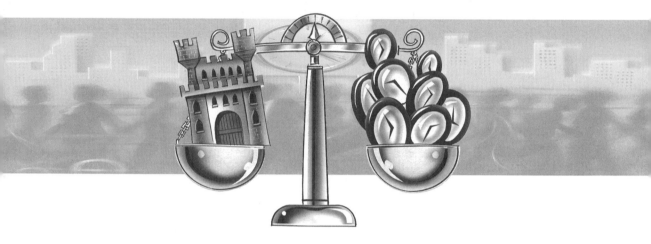

CHAPTER 5

Too Much = Too Much Time Cleaning

Regardless of how skilled we get in modern cleaning techniques, how good the 21st-century products are, or even how much help we get, we are bound to spend too much time cleaning if we have **too much**. Too much of even good stuff can still be bad when it comes to cleaning.

My office received a call one day, for example, from the number one national health magazine, which wanted a TV segment relating cleaning to health, done by me with one of the nation's top models. They flew me to Hollywood the night before and arranged for me to stay in the prestigious hotel where we were to film. When I signed for the room I noticed the cost of it was $950 (that's for one night, folks!). I wondered as I rode up the ornate elevator what a room could be like to make it worth almost a thousand dollars a night. I soon found out. This was the most prime example of overkill ever! There was so much furniture in there, getting across the room was like running through the Forty-Niner defen-

sive line. There were fake flowers and statuettes and other decorations all over the place. There were sixteen fancy lamps and lights of all kinds, yet I kid you not, to read the room service menu I had to go to the window of the room and hold that elegant little booklet up so that I could read it in the blinking light from the bar and grille next door. The bed had six or eight different sizes and styles of pillows, and the bedspread was silk and didn't have to be removed before sleeping because it slid off anyway. The bath towels were so big and so thick, they were honestly unusable (the face cloth was about right for a bath). The shower hardware was so elaborate I couldn't figure out how to turn it on. And so on.

Every day we see homes (maybe even our own!) that come close to this. Homes loaded with too much... the unneeded... the unnecessary.

TOO NICE CAN BE NASTY TO CLEAN

Be careful not to get things so "nice" (decorated) that they become nasty to clean. You may like to have trinkets, whatnots, and little goose crafts all over the place, but when they become a burden of care and cleaning time, sucking life from you rather than doing anything for you, it's time for a garage sale.

What we need to remember here is:

Everything that is in our home (or around it, if we have a home with grounds), we have to:

pay for
store
tend
protect
insure
inspect
use
CLEAN AND CARE FOR!

CUT YOUR HOUSEWORK IN HALF: GET RID OF JUNK AND CLUTTER!

I've done four top-selling books on the subject of junk and clutter, and the bottom line as it relates to cleaning is: "You can't clean it until you can find it." That goes for closets, counters, drawers, floors, garages, and yards. You can't deck the halls with boughs of holly until you clear the decks! At least forty percent of all cleaning time is wasted on junk and clutter—that "too much" in, and around the house and yard and office. And in our storage units! I know you agree with me because most of you are groaning and sighing about the burden of junk even as I write this.

What is junk? All that "stuff" you aren't using, don't really want, don't enjoy, and don't have room for. Much of what we call cleaning is junk tending—not just dusting and polishing things, but keeping track of them, storing them, insuring them, protecting, organizing and reorganizing them, repositioning them.

Cluttered rooms take ten times as long to clean, because we have to move so much out of the way to do anything, and then move it all back when we're done. And all those extra objects add up to hundreds of times the amount of surface to clean. You also need many more kinds of equipment and supplies to clean them.

Junk wastes our time and makes us inefficient, steals our love and affection, and stops us from getting to the things we really care about in life. It boggles our minds as well as our storage areas.

Head out to those junk havens:
closets
drawers
shelves
desks
lockers
medicine cabinets
purses
attics
basements
porches
backyards
storage bins
garages
car trunks
sheds

Tackle the top troublemakers:
clothes
papers
sentimental stuff
gadgets
grooming aids
hobby and sports junk
excess furniture
gifts and souvenirs
toys
scraps
containers and packaging
stuff to be fixed or finished someday

Dejunk—trash it, trade it, tromp it, give it away, sell it—but get rid of it. It'll be the greatest housework-reducing move you ever make. The formula is easy:

Don't love anything that can't love you back. If something doesn't enhance your life then get rid of it. When? Now, today. I can promise that dejunking will change your life (and housework schedule) more than any other single thing you can do.

Let's take a closer look at a few of the biggies now:

1. **Furniture**. Most of us have twenty-five percent more furniture than we need or use. We have it for looks, not utility, but still it catches soil, harbors dust, has to be cleaned around, over, and under. It makes the place crowded and hard to move around in, or do anything in. It takes away all of our open space, too. Eliminate unneeded and unused furniture and your place will look and feel better!

2. **Toys**. Grownups and children's toys. Kids and men between them have about seventy-five percent more toys than anyone could ever need or use. We use them as pacifiers, and gain new ones faster than we break or lose the old, resulting in overload and overtime when it comes to picking up and cleaning up. Child and adult toys are all over, inside the house, outside the house, and in the garage! In closets, drawers, under the beds, and on the walls. What we need is less toys and more places to keep them out of the way!

3. **Bathroom burdening**. Bathrooms should be one of the simplest, easiest to clean, and most strictly functional places in the house, yet often we see them filled with art, magazines, gadgets, frilly lamps, and other fancy trimmings. Any decoration or covering on or near the toilet, for example, is super unsanitary—it will only hold odor and look awful before long. And let's not even talk about medicine cabinets.

4. **Knickknacks**. There are knickknack (souvenir) stores in Alaska that will sell you moose poop. Yes, recovered moose droppings, when varnished and given wire legs and plastic wings, are called moose-quitos. Some knickknacks are wonderful, others are just no-longer-delightful shelf fillers. (Note, folks, your kids are copying you with their McDonald's collection.)

6. **Paper**. The average person now handles at least 300 sheets (pages) of paper per day, between magazines, catalogs, flyers, newspapers, notes, bills, junk mail, faxes, school papers, and computer printouts. In five days, if all this is not processed or recycled, a family of five can have over 7,000 pages of paper stacked, tossed, or stashed around. If they go a month without a paper riddance program, they'll have 45,000 pages. That's discouragement, a mess, and lots of cleaning headaches. **One day** is too long to keep useless paper!

7. **Entertainment/office tools and toys.** Only a few of these were found in homes in

earlier years. Now computer and entertainment electronics and their appendages are everywhere. Not only does the unit itself take up space, but the accompanying printers, scanners, tapes, disks, accessory speakers, paper, electric cords, etc. The instant obsolescence of these items and our reluctance to get rid of the old when we "upgrade" is burying us, taking up too much of our space, and often quadrupling our cleaning and care time.

Order helps cut clutter

Think a minute of the word "order." Order means neat, trim, and uncluttered. Order says it's lined up, sorted, arranged, regulated, coordinated. With order we can cut clutter and the confusion and agony that often goes with it.

Let's look at some ways to accomplish this:

1. **Assigned place:** In the armed forces, for instance, everything you, or the platoon or squad have, has a place. The tools are always in the toolbox, the locker always at the foot of the bed, clothes on right side, boots on top or whatever. This is a standard that once established becomes a behavior that is carried out automatically. So you NEVER HAVE TO HUNT for something.

A high percentage of home litter is caused by lack of official places to park things—a lack of racks, hangers, hooks, shelves, cupboards, etc. This is something you can do something about **today.**

Most of those "misplaced" items in a home are really "no place" items. Everything in our homes has to fit or go someplace. If something is just there in a corner, on the floor, or leaning up against something, it will almost inevitably be litter or need constant straightening up. When something has no place, no one can put it back where it belongs, so they just put it down—wherever.

You say, "Well, every member of this family has drawers, yet socks are on the floor; we have trash cans, yet rubbish is left out; there is a toolbox but tools are everywhere." This may be true, but go look at the drawers, the trash cans, the toolbox—you are very likely to find them full, or in a poor location.

2. **Separate the active and the passive.** This is a superb principle for me and it will be for you—establishing two different categories of things, in our living areas and surroundings at home and at work. Keep only the truly active things right with or around you, the things you use constantly or often. The passive stuff—things that might be important but are used only once in a while, put elsewhere—store them.

Having everything we need and use often in a clear and convenient place is wonderful. Having our "can't do withouts" mixed in with all that other "stuff" we sometimes or never use, it is a pain, a slowdown, and an invitation to tossing and piling and accepting a mess. Why leave our winter clothes in the closet when we use them only three or four months a year? A fifteen-minute move to storage reduces the mass we have to face (and fumble through) daily.

3. **Get rid of the nonfunctioning**. Broken and nonfunctioning things always end up just... around... they don't work so we don't care. Put things like this in their place (the trash, or the repair bin) and watch the results.

Reducing clutter will cut more housework time and chores and give us more freedom, than any other move we can make, bar none!

CHAPTER 6

Do Your Housework With a Hammer!

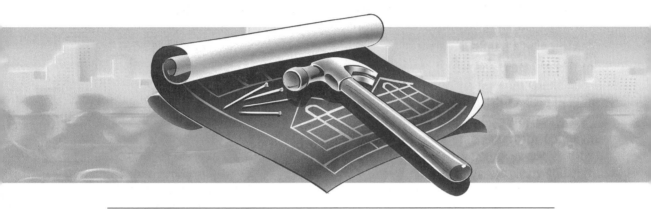

Can you clean with a hammer or a pencil? You bet you can!

Women figured this out hundreds of years ago, and men, who have usually been the ones designing and building dwellings, are finally listening (maybe because they're getting a little more involved in the housecleaning itself these days). This is one of the easiest, most economical, and emotionally sound ways to cut cleaning—the most modern way. I'm talking about DESIGNING AND BUILDING CLEANING OUT of your life forever—it can be done and you can do it.

In twenty-five years of public appearances, on TV, radio, and at my cleaning seminars across the country, many cleaning questions and suggestions have come forth from my audiences. One day I got an unusual one... "Do you realize, Don, that men build houses that are very hard to maintain? As a result we have to wrestle every day with things that aren't just dirty, but difficult or impossible to clean."

As time passed I got this comment or something like it more and more frequently, from sharp and intelligent women. Being one of those masculine builders (I built two large homes entirely myself, learned how to do so and then wired and plumbed them, etc.), I was offended at first that some woman would have the nerve to tell me, big Don, with a well-used genuine leather carpenter's belt and four well-worn masonry trowels, that men didn't know how to build. But after I thought about it a while I realized that those women were right— not just a little right, but right on. So instead of skipping over that remark and going on to one I agreed with, I began asking things like, "Well, how would you do it better, and what would you do?" Not only did I listen, but I collected all the ideas from those who really use and tend a house, and care for the children in it. We really don't **live** in a house until we take care of it and all its needs and problems.

To those wonderful women who raised their hands and called me stupid, I owe an important part of my life and enterprises—they got me thinking and gave me a new goal in my books, media appearances, my cleaning company, and my products: the idea of not just cleaning better and more economically but **reducing or eliminating** it, and the wear and tear on our homes, ourselves, and the environment. They gave me a whole new approach: conquer cleaning by designing it out. I realized that every time you eliminate an unnecessary timetaker, you save doing that job forever—it's gone.

I was working for the world's largest company then, the Bell System, doing contract cleaning of thousands of their buildings, and when I spoke at training sessions and conventions (to their architects and engineers) I passed on those women's wisdom. "Why don't you guys build things so we don't have to clean them as much, so we can cut care time, depreciation, and energy and chemical use by a third, or even a half?" They said "Great idea, how do we do it?" So I taught them what the women had taught me, and ended up a design consultant for one of their three million square foot buildings. They'd budgeted 120 people a night to clean it; I told them if the cleaning was done right and a few design modifications were made, that building could be cleaned with 65 people. So they built it that way and we did clean it with 65. This means that in the last twenty years, the savings in the cost of cleaning labor alone were more than five million dollars. Then think of the environmental impact, the savings of hot water, chemicals, lights, depreciation, and replacement of things. Immeasurable millions. All because a few brave, intelligent homemakers were finally heard.

By this time I had a sizable collection of maintenance-freeing concepts and my daughter was designing kitchens and other home interior spaces. In 1986 we teamed up to do a book called *Make Your House Do the Housework*. It's sold many thousands of copies, been featured by book clubs, and gone on to a revised and updated edition. It's also generated many calls and letters from readers, with more ideas of what they did to cut their cleaning time and costs, some of which I will share with you here.

After the book's success, it was clear that we needed to build a model low-maintenance house. I didn't think many of you would come to McCammon, Idaho to see it or to Skagway, Alaska, or Bozeman, Montana (my own favorite places). So my wife and I picked one of the most beautiful spots in the world (where they filmed *Jurassic Park* and *South Pacific*), the island of Kauai in Hawaii. We bought four acres there and after ten years of planning and working on it in a slow, steady, thoughtful way, we have a model low-maintenance home and you are invited to come see it.

Our model low-maintenance home will blow you away. It's a carefully thought out composite of many of the best ideas over the years for making our lives and our cleaning chores easier.

After reading *Make Your House Do the Housework* or visiting our Hawaii home, hundreds of people in the U.S. have now built low-maintenance homes. Our model home has also had visits from media people, architects, and engineers from around the world. They've come to look and after they say "wow" they've gone on to think of ways to apply this concept to their own situations.

Now before you say, "But our house is already done..." or "I can't afford it," here is the beauty of doing your housework with a hammer. Eighty percent of the high-maintenance items in our homes are things we replace regularly like paint, drapes, carpet, fixtures, faucets, appliances, and furniture. Whenever you make a change or remodel, you can make a few maintenance-freeing moves, and cut time and expense out of your cleaning schedule.

I can't take the space in this book to give you the whole show, but here is a tiny taste to get you started, and you can take it from there if you are serious about reducing your life's maintenance load.

Because you may not get a chance to hit Hawaii and drop by for a tour, here is a quick idea of some of the things we did to make our own home low maintenance.

SOME BIG AND LITTLE THINGS WE DID IN OUR HAWAII HOME TO MAKE IT "MAINTAIN ITSELF"

Masonry for maintenance freedom The basic structure of all three floors of the house—walls, floors, decks, and columns—is made of one hundred percent masonry, 250 yards of concrete. Concrete can be made attractive, and it's strong, enduring, soundproof, fireproof, pest resistant, and childproof. There are many other forms of masonry with the same merits, and many new finishes and paints for masonry that last indefinitely.

Eaves We extended the overhangs from a generous three feet to a thoroughly protective five feet, shielding a large portion of the house from direct sun and other weather damage, and eliminating the need for rain gutters.

Large overhangs like this, because they reduce "splashback," also cut down on the need for cleaning of exterior windows and house siding.

Roof Our roof is concrete tile, underlayed with roof felt, for a roof that will last not just twenty or thirty years, but a century. The roof caps are cemented on, and every tile is clipped to the roof with stainless steel anchors, just in case 200-mph-wind hurricanes pay us another visit. The roof is pitched steeply enough to flush off debris and self-clean.

Runoff control The roof and walks are designed to catch and utilize the runoff of rain wherever possible to water the lawns and fruit trees and other plantings, and fill the pools. The same is true of the water from the floor drains in the garages and parking pads. Thus runoff becomes a plus instead of a problem.

Rock The house entrance on the ground floor has columns made of lava rock and moss rock, native to the island. These are beautiful and maintenance free—they won't show nicks, scrapes, yard machine abuse, or bug stains, and they'll never need paint, stain, or repair.

Exterior doors Most of the exterior doors are either sliding glass or vinyl clad. The front door is frameless, made of strong decorative glass like the doors on commercial buildings, and eight feet high, rather than the usual less than seven.

Glass We used as much of this as possible in the house, including floor-to-ceiling windows, because glass is a true low-maintenance material. It never rusts, rots, or needs to be painted. It provides exterior light for free, and if you use a squeegee, you can clean all of your windows in a few minutes with a few cents worth of dish detergent. We also used glass on the inside office door and for the railing of the three-story circular stairways (instead of hundreds of wood spindles to collect dust and damage).

Skylights Are used to take advantage of natural light and minimize use of electricity, even in the bathrooms. There is a large, slanted, oval, six-foot skylight over the staircase in the center of the house for permanent lighting. The skylights are frosted, to let in light but camouflage dust and dirt, and we can let the rain clean them.

Carefree ceilings On the top floor we used dropped ceilings of 2'x2' acoustical tile, which absorbs sound, doesn't need painting, and is inexpensive and easy to replace. Koa wood, a native Hawaiian wood, on these same ceilings put the beauty of this attractive material where it was safe from damage and would require little upkeep. The ceilings in the rest of the house are a combination of Koa wood and a small amount of painted, plastered Densi-glass. Densi-glass is not susceptible to mildew and moisture damage like gypsum sheetrock, and it also resists nicks and gouges better.

Ceiling mounted We put many of the things usually mounted on walls, such as lights and speakers, on the ceilings, out of harm's way.

Floors The floors in the main house and the patio floors are made of granite tile with a narrow grout line. The tiles are a medium tone (not dark or light) with plenty of pattern to camouflage dirt. They always look good, even with eighteen grandkids and hundreds of other visitors tromping on them. The floors upstairs are carpet, to muffle sound, and for extra comfort and softness, especially for bare feet. The floors of utility areas such as the shop and garage are made of sealed concrete, which makes them good-looking, easy to clean, and resistant to stains.

Baseboards are either carpet or stained wood. No painting upkeep here.

Decks Most of our decks are made of concrete, or concrete covered with granite or other tile. This makes them weather and damage resistant, and they require next to no maintenance—forever. They also blend the outside with the inside for a clean, consistent look in the living areas.

Stairs The stairways in the house are made of steel and solid concrete built in a spiral pattern to reduce the danger of falls. These staircases are capable of holding up to seventy people for a family picture, and have no creak or sag problems. They can be vacuumed in minutes with a built-in vacuum located near them.

Railings All of the interior railings are made of koa wood and glass, elegant and low maintenance.

Interior doors There are only as many of these as truly necessary to insure privacy. The rest of the house is a "walk through" open space because doors get—and show—a lot of wear and abuse. Doors also require a lot of adjustment, repair, and other maintenance. Doors get dusty and dirty, too, take up a lot of space, and are visual clutter.

Lighting is all built in. This reduces dusting, fixture cleaning, dead bug cleanup, and clutter, and eliminates knocked over lamps. The lighting is designed for low cost and high output. All of the lighting of the house and grounds is computer controlled from a central location, making turn-on and shutdown quick and easy.

Drapes are used instead of blinds. Overall we felt that drapes served the purpose of window covering best, because they are easy to clean, need little dusting, and have few mechanical breakdowns.

Furniture has simple lines and durable surfaces in basic neutral colors. Beds, side tables, and dressers are built into the floor or wall, reducing the area that needs to be cleaned.

Sound systems Sound system speakers and intercoms are set into the ceilings to reduce damage and dusting and eliminate knocked over speakers.

Storage There is plenty of it, right where it's needed. The tools are all kept in a tool shop adjacent to the garage, not in the garage, and there is high, dry storage for things like holiday decorations. All storage is in plastic or fiberglass drawers or bins, not cardboard boxes.

Decorations We used wall murals and large windows to bring in the natural beauty of the outdoors (a decoration that is ever-changing and doesn't need dusting!). Most other decor is suspended or hung.

"Brag wall" We designed a big 8'x6' wall display of pictures, souvenirs, quilts, and other family things. This is like a "living history" exhibit in a museum and it's one of the most popular spots in the house (visitors love it). It is lighted and enclosed in glass and is easily cleaned and added to.

Countertops are made of seamless solid surfacing (see p. 63) in attractive "camouflaging" patterns for the lowest maintenance counter possible.

Faucets are of a simple, easy-to-clean, one-piece design.

Soap dishes and the like, and small appliances are suspended.

Showers and tub areas are "walk in," so they don't need shower doors or shower curtains. The showers are extra spacious and the entrances large enough for a wheelchair.

There is an outdoor shower located by the entrance to the garage. This washes off beach and yard debris, helping to keep sand and soil outside.

Tile grout lines We made them 1/16th of an inch instead of 1/4 inch or 3/8, to reduce staining and the other maintenance headaches of grout. We also used colored grout, to camouflage soil and stains. Most of our tile is 12"x12" granite.

Quieter plumbing Plastic pipes are like a microphone broadcasting bathroom activities. We used cast iron pipes, instead, in the walls and floors, to eliminate that flushing sound.

Toilets All of the toilets are wall hung, with no exposed tanks or other unnecessary china to clean.

Trash chute An 18"x18" chute for dry trash in the center of the house moves trash from the upper stories of the house instantly to a basement depository. This saves time, eliminates delay, and keeps walls, stairs, and doors from being beat up by trash carried in and out the old way. One cabinet in the kitchen opens to a garbage chute, so there is no garbage can in the kitchen and no daily chore of garbage removal.

Two laundry centers Because we have many guests, we have an upstairs and a downstairs washer and dryer. This saves many steps, eliminates the transporting of clothes (loaded with sand) up and down stairs, and keeps the walls and doors from being beat up by baskets and boxes. The appliances here are among the most water-saving and energy-efficient around.

Extra sinks of "janitor" size in the garage and laundry room provide a place to wash oversize or awkward items.

Kitchen Has no exposed handles, knobs, or other hardware to hinder cleaning, and collect grease and soil. The kitchen table and chairs are suspended, which eliminates that forest of legs on the floor to clean around. The kitchen cabinets are extra tall, to make use of all possible storage room. The kitchen floor space is small and concentrated for faster cleaning.

Garages Our garages are wider and longer than the standard, so they can be converted into large sleeping or activity rooms. We also use them for indoor recreation such as table tennis and quilting. The walls are finished with fiberglass and the garages have automatic doors, built-in vacuums, sinks, and not one single tool, machine (other than the car), or piece of junk stored in them.

Recreation area Is built around the house, to keep vigorous play pastimes outside.

Maintenance center The house has a fully equipped workshop, repair center, and yard tool center, to make home maintenance easy and convenient.

How about your own low-maintenance home now?

Consider the following when you're choosing a furnishing, design, or material for your home:

✔ Do you really need this?

✔ How hard or easy will it be to clean?

✔ How long will it stay clean?

✔ What kind of equipment and chemicals will you need to clean it? And how much?

✔ How often will you need to service it (clean, repaint, or repair it)?

✔ How accessible is it, how easy will it be to reach it to clean it? Will special equipment be needed?

✔ How will you **feel** about caring for and cleaning it? (Love every moment of it, or soon find it a drag?)

✔ How safe/hazardous are the operations needed to clean and maintain it, for you and the environment?

✔ How soon will the cleaning operations depreciate it (wear it out)?

✔ Aesthetics: Not just how does it look now, but how will it look after much use and many cleanings.

✔ What will the replacement or repair cost be when it wears out or breaks down?

✔ How "datable" is it? Generally, the better quality and simpler something is, the longer it stays in style.

SOME MAINTENANCE–LESSENING PRODUCTS AND SURFACES TO CONSIDER

There are new things coming out all the time, so keep your eyes open. There are surfaces being developed, for example, with antimicrobial agents incorporated right into them,

for use in places that need frequent "germ killer" cleaning. Here are some other products that have become available or been improved in recent years to make your home more maintenance-free.

1. Solid surfacing. In the mid-1900s a thin veneer of plastic laminate called "Formica" was developed for countertops and the like. It was stain resistant, sanitary, easy to clean, attractive, reasonable, and lasted up to thirty years.

In recent years manufacturers have taken this type of material a giant step further, into a new composite called solid surfacing, bearing such names as Gibraltar, Avonite, and Corian. Unlike the laminates of the past, it is seamless and not just a surface coating or veneer, but solid all the way through. This makes it strong, longlasting, extra good-looking, and even possible to repair. Surface scars and damage such as cigarette burns can be sanded away with extra-fine sandpaper, and then the surface polished back to good as new. Nothing penetrates or stains solid surfacing and you have to work hard to damage it. It is still expensive but if you can swing it you will appreciate it every day you live with it. It comes in natural stone-like patterns which are attractive and nondating. The sinks of solid surfacing for either kitchen or bath are formed as part of the counter, so there are no rims or edges to worry about.

You can buy vanity tops ready made of solid surfacing at many DIY stores. Kits for showers are available from Wilsonart or you can custom make your own shower interior. Once you put this product in you will never (and I mean never) have to replace it. Solid surfacing is used for sinks, countertops, the inside of showers, and window sills among other places.

2. Laminate floors and baseboards. Floors and baseboards are some of the highest maintenance items in a home, so you really want products that are low maintenance here.

Floors and baseboards are available now that look like wood or marble, but they are really a hard laminate.

This ultramodern flooring (Pergo and Wilsonart are two leading brands) is another improved version of the laminate that has served us so long and well on our kitchen counters. Pergo, for example, is made up of several layers (a layer of tough space-age resin called melamine over a decorative layer, over a layer of moisture-resistant wood), and the result is superior looks, durability, and ease of cleaning. Only one-third of an inch thick, Pergo planks can be applied right over existing hard-surface floors, and they come in a variety of attractive designs.

This is the first truly "no wax" floor—earlier "no wax floors" did, after time and wear, eventually need a finish applied to them to keep them bright and shiny. The surface of laminate floors, on the other hand, is so strong, dense, and tight it keeps its handsome sheen indefinitely. You never need or want to use a wax or floor polish on them. The hard, compact surface of these floors will resist most soils, and what does stick to them can be removed with a cloth or mop only lightly dampened in plain warm water.

Laminate flooring also resists fading, stains, and damage—even high heels and cigarette burns. I was at a home show once where the salesperson was offering $100 to anyone who could hurt it. People were beating it with high heels and trying to scratch it with all manner of things and they couldn't. The demonstrator took a power sander to it and it took something like 10,000 rotations to break down the surface, so you can imagine how it would hold up for you.

Laminates seem to be an answer to that question I get constantly: "What kind of floor should I put in for ease of care and cleaning?" As much as we want to love vinyl flooring, it looks bad after a few years if you use it hard and any damage can't really be repaired attractively. When it comes to floors you really have three choices—wood, tile, or laminate—if you want a floor that will last and look good. Both wood and tile have drawbacks in that tile is cold and hard and wood gets damaged

and is not waterproof.

Matching laminate baseboards are also available for laminate floors, which again cannot be easily damaged and never need painting. Take a look at your baseboards right now—how do they look? Baseboards are nearly always in need of care or repair. They are a high-maintenance necessity, but with laminate you can make them low maintenance.

3. New approaches to painted walls. Faux painting, suede finish, sponging, ragging, and stippling are all names for some newer approaches to wall painting. These techniques make for a low-maintenance wall because they don't show every little mark or smudge. They have a textured look, but are much easier to clean than textured finishes. These kinds of wall painting also put a nice acrylic surface on the wall which washes well and protects the surface. You can have a lot of fun applying a finish like these if you are a do-it-yourselfer, or a professional painter can do it for you.

4. Vinyl windows and sills. Once you have these you won't need to paint windows anymore. Vinyl windows look freshly painted forever and need little upkeep. Vinyl windowsills also eliminate the need for painting sills, which because of all the moisture that collects here, need painting often.

Better yet than vinyl (but more expensive) are the solid surface sills mentioned above. Vinyl is the next best thing.

5. Built-in vacuums. This is a vacuum with a motor and collection tank mounted in a utility area of the house, and PVC pipe run from here to key locations all over the house. This means that by simply attaching a hose to a wall outlet, you can vacuum anywhere quickly and quietly. Built-in or central vacs also don't redistribute dust back into the air like many conventional vacuums do.

The convenience of a built-in makes us much more likely to vacuum as often as we should, and to remove dirt from hard-surface floors instead of tromping it into the finish or spreading it around with a broom. A built-in makes it easy to get the dirt out of corners where brooms and dustmops cannot. It pulls dirt and dust down from high places where you would otherwise have to dust first and then pick up the dust from the floor (two steps). And on tile floors the vacuum easily removes all the elusive dust and dirt in the grooves of the grout.

Living with and without a built-in vac is like the difference between day and night. Built-in or "central" vacs cost from $600-$1500, and you can learn a little more about them on p. 135.

6. Self-contained gas fireplaces. With one of these you can get the look and feel of a fireplace without the smoke, soot, airborne dirt, ashes, and wood mess of a real fireplace. You won't need a chimney, either. Gas fireplaces are also more efficient and lose far less of the heat they produce, so all the way around this is a maintenance-freeing way to go.

7. Metal with an "aged" finish for handrails, light fixtures, furniture, curtain rods, etc. This is an attractive look and it's low maintenance. It doesn't show dust, doesn't need painting, and is very hard to damage.

8. Stainless steel appliances. If you think these look too utilitarian, let them grow on you. Stainless steel is corrosion resistant, durable, easy to sanitize, and in today's designs looks rich and again timeless. Appliance trends change from white, to black, to almond about every five years or so. Stainless steel is forever and is simply the easiest to clean. White enamel is the next best thing and black is the worst—it shows every smudge and speck of dust.

9. Smooth ceramic cooktops. This is a biggie. Kitchen cleaning has become much easier since these tops appeared. They are available on electric stoves only, but basically they allow you to wipe the stove top up just like a counter. These tops are available on ranges and built-in cooktops and are a must for a low-maintenance kitchen. You have to

be crazy to go back to coils!

10. Radiant heat. This is heat that comes into your home by hot water pushed through tubes in the floor. There is no forced air and thus much less flying dust in the air. Radiant heat is much cleaner and will cut your heating bills in half. It does cost about thirty percent more to install than standard forced air, but those who have it are glad they do. Just think—no dirty cold air returns!

11. Wide-slat vinyl blinds. We've had the good old wood blinds for a while now, and the aluminum mini blinds that I hope will go extinct soon. Wood blinds warp and the surface breaks down over time, and the little aluminum blinds are delicate, hard to clean, and attract dust like mad. If we must have blinds (and they still do serve a purpose), there are vinyl blinds now with sturdy slats two or three inches wide. This means slats that are much harder to damage and easier to dust and clean. These usually have a simulated wood finish—the surface on them is washable and moisture won't cause them to warp or peel. All in all, I would choose drapes or these to cover your windows.

12. Leather furniture. Yes, leather! Its surface is tough and durable and repels almost anything as long as it has a good aniline surface. That's the key. Raw leather is a nightmare to keep clean, but when leather is cured and finished the aniline is applied. This holds the color and makes the surface soil and moisture resistant. Most little spills can be wiped off and over the years you will see—compared to a chair or sofa upholstered in fabric—that leather holds up better and longer.

13. Home exteriors can be much more maintenance free, with the vinyl or aluminum siding, aluminum eaves, vinyl windows, synthetic stucco, and brick and rock siding, real and synthetic, available now. There is simply no need for painting or staining the exterior of your home anymore. All the surfaces out there can be covered with materials that need little or no upkeep.

IMPORTANT ADVICE FOR YOUR OWN HOME DESIGNS

Here are three important pieces of advice for your own home designs, now.

1. Be bold. Come up with what you want, and what fits you, your family, your activities, and your setting.

2. Go looking. New low-maintenance materials and products come out every year, so do your homework and see what's out there for you.

3. Don't cave in! There are in life and building the standard, generic, time-tested patterns and methods that I agree are often smart to follow. Some standardization is wise—some conventions make real sense and we don't necessarily want to have to reinvent the wheel. On the other hand, we are all different, and adding and adjusting things to suit your own unique lifestyle is exactly what you want to do. Here are just a few of the hundreds of bold and novel ideas readers have shared with me.

- One man built a stage in his family room and he said it was the best thing he ever put in a house. The kids used it constantly. It kept them entertained, reduced mess and litter in the rest of the house, and did wonders to develop budding talents.

- I know a number of people who have, at little extra cost, added a nice food storage area to their home that is easy to clean and sanitize and has clever storage mechanisms such as shelves that help keep track of how long the stored products have been there.

- Fancy molding in a home is nice until it's damaged, which often happens, and then it becomes a hard-to-repair eyesore. One woman put hers all up high, so you could enjoy looking at it, while it got little or no damage.

- Another put stained glass in her entryway window, so it let light through without ever showing a streak, handprint, or flyspeck.

- A woman built a climbing wall on the outside of her fireplace chimney. It kept all the teens busy and made a wonderful family and neighborhood fun center (and is about the best use of one of those worthless fireplaces I've ever heard of).

- Another woman built her entire exterior deck of the new "Trex" plastic composite material. It was easy to clean, resistant to damage, and would never need to be treated or stained.

- Another woman eliminated those "backing out of the garage" woes and worries by putting garage doors on both ends of her garage, so cars could just drive right through in a circle. The extra door didn't cost much more than a plain wall would have, and it saved time and damage to vehicles, and reduced the chances of backing over a child or a pet. And it kept the garage from getting junked up!

I think you're getting the idea. Remember, every change or adjustment you make will benefit you over and over, thousands of times over a lifetime, so don't underestimate the impact of a simple little thing like changing to a single-lever faucet instead of the old double handles. Especially for things that are heavily used, the savings in cleaning time (and replacement cost) over twenty or thirty years add up to significant improvements in life quality.

That third bit of advice, "don't cave in," is an important one, too. We all have our plans and dreams and special requests when building, but the peer pressure in this department is tremendous, from the Home Glamorous magazines who show us how they think things should be, to contractors telling us that "nobody does that," to loan officers who say they won't finance anything that is too different.

Remember, this is your house and your time and money, and the physical, emotional, and economic effects of where and how you live are a big, BIG factor in life.

So stick to your guns and do what's good for you, not what everyone else is doing, or is cheap or convenient right now, or the hottest thing at the home show or DIY store. Save and further develop all of those insights and flashes of inspiration, those "I shoulds," "I'd like to's," or "I'm going to's" that have come to you during frustrated cleaning sessions and exhausting maintenance efforts. At least some of these ideas, no one else has ever thought of.

Make a list of what is important to *you* by way of reducing cleaning and care time. Put it in priority order with the most important first. If you can't afford it all, be sure to do what matters most to you.

Once you start your move toward maintenance freedom, I encourage you to pick up *Make Your House Do the Housework*, a step-by-step guide to applying maintenance-freeing design to every room in your home. You'll find it in your bookstore or library, or you can order it by mail. Send $14.99 plus $3 shipping to Make Your House, PO Box 700, Pocatello ID 83204. It has some excellent basics and lots of ideas, but its real value will be in stimulating you to come up with fifty more of your own!

The following is a little sampling from "Make Your House":

SOME TIME ROBBERS TO AVOID

- **Floor coverings with indented or embossed designs** (such as synthetic slate). Floors like these may look great, but recessed surfaces are hard to sweep and wash, and will gradually fill with dirt and wax.
- **Indoor-outdoor carpet.** It shows every crumb or speck of lint. It's hard to vacuum and adds zero plushness to a home.
- **Highly textured walls and ceilings**. They are a dust and cobweb paradise and are hard to clean and paint.
- **Unfinished wood.** Looks nice and rustic, but once it's soiled, you've had it. Wood should always be sealed with a resinous or polyurethane finish.
- **Fancy hardware.** This is hard to clean and provides breeding grounds for germs.
- **Extremely high ceilings.** Although impressive, they're hard to maintain and energy-wasteful.
- **Multi-surface furniture and finishes** Every surface needs maintenance—so the less kinds of surface the better. Walls or furnishings, for example, made of many different materials take more time and types of equipment to clean.
- **Very dark and light colors.** Colors like these—in furniture, floors, carpet, or countertops—require more daily upkeep than medium-colored items with some pattern. Dark colors, especially, show dust, lint, and spots—everything!
- **Decoration do-dads** When it comes to wall hangings, for example, one nice big picture sure beats thirty-two dusty little ones (and cheats spiders out of bases).

Here are some principles of maintenance-freeing design to keep in mind

Camouflage it:	Choose colors and textures in flooring, wall coverings, and furniture that hide and downplay the dirt, fallout, and spills till you have a chance to go after them. Get an orange couch if you have an orange cat.
Suspend it:	If you can get it up off the floor or counter, do so—it'll take up less space, won't collect dirt under it, can't be moved out of place, and won't get in your way when you're cleaning. Suspend or wall mount small appliances, tables, chairs, lamps, coat racks, and so on.
Build it in:	Built-in furniture and appliances, for example, save not only space but bumps and grazes on you and the furnishings, and eliminate a lot of sides, backs, and underneaths to clean. You can get built-in furniture at a cabinet store.
Keep it simple:	The less details and decorations, the less curves, joints, grooves, edges, and ledges, the fewer kinds of materials something is made of, the easier it will be to clean, and keep clean. And the less equipment and supplies you'll need to do it. A louvered or elaborately paneled door, for example, will take much longer to clean than a simple, smooth door.

Choose the smooth:	Anything with an uneven, indented, or relief-design surface—from floor covering to countertop material to wall covering—is going to accumulate dirt faster and be harder to clean.
Keep it in reach— your reach:	Forget about what's standard or usual or customary. Make sure things aren't too high or too low or inaccessible—for you.
Foil airborne grease and soil:	This quiet aerial invasion is one of the biggest mess-makers we have to contend with. Choose heating, cooking, and ventilation systems accordingly, and consider an electrostatic air cleaner.
Avoid high-maintenance materials:	Anything that needs constant polishing or servicing, that stains or damages easily, or shows every grain of sand or speck of lint immediately.

Cleaning faster and more efficiently is fine, but why not go one better and simply ELIMINATE all the cleaning you can? Build, remodel, and design it out.

*Anything that is too high or low to reach easily, or hard to clean because of its color, surface, design, or composition, will add a lot to your daily and weekly cleaning chores. Uncleanable grout, for example, cannot be made to look good no matter how long you work away at it. Grand ballroom-style chandeliers take days to clean, even for the experts. Own things that are easy to live with—**cut cleaning at the source.***

CHAPTER 7

Other Hands That Can Help

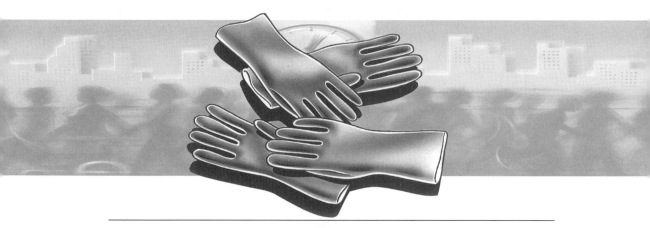

> *When there's too much to do, remember that you don't have to do it all yourself.* The mess is seldom all made by you, and it shouldn't be all yours to clean. For decades now it's been a mission of mine to enlist everyone—young, old, male, female—on the cleaning roster.

Get some help from your mate

I saw a cartoon once that showed a woman on the phone, husband in the utility room in the background, and she was panting, "Hello, Channel 2 Action News? My husband's doing laundry!" This sort of thing is unfortunately funny because it's so true. In all of the speaking, teaching, personal appearances, and one-on-one counseling sessions on home cleaning I did in the 1970s and 1980s, almost one hundred percent of the clients, audiences, and customers I dealt with were... you guessed it... women.

It is working: at least thirty percent of my audiences now are men. I don't know if they're fully converted yet, but they are there looking wise and nodding and checking out the professional cleaning gear.

If you are old enough to mess up, you are old enough to clean up. Age, sex, education, or occupation doesn't exempt you, nor whether you are rich or poor. It's true that for far too long women have borne the brunt of the domestic duties, even after they entered the work force and spent as many hours a week at the office or factory as men. I believe the solution to this is not confrontation and demonstration, but education and example.

In fact, I'm changing the title of my 100,000-copy seller, *Who Says It's A Woman's Job to Clean?* to *How to Make Women Love You... Do the Cleaning.* I wrote this book "for men and boys only," in hopes it would make them as enthusiastic about the toilet bowl (cleaning it!) as the Super Bowl. It's a fun and motivational little book on why and how to clean, starting with your own messes.

I don't mean to get on the soapbox on this subject, but if we are going to manage to do the housework as well as everything we now have to do, a more equal sharing of the cleaning chores is one big, obvious answer. Here's a few little excerpts from "Who Says" to get you started:

- Today men and women do much the same kinds of work outside the home. It only makes sense that we share the same kinds of work *inside* the home, too.

- Men can't do it? Consider the fact that eighty percent of all of the professional cleaning companies in this country are owned and operated by men. And of the cleaning chores they undertake to do, fifty percent or more are performed by men.

- Forget those expensive courses in surviving desert disasters or Himalayan hardship. Unless you're rich, unemployed, or extraordinarily unlucky, you have about a thousand-to-one chance of ever putting them to use. Learn to clean, on the other hand, and you'll learn the real survival skills of modern life. Knowing how to take care of yourself in your everyday environment is a skill *nobody* should be without.

- The cure to the "housework" problem will come from one basic thing: each of us being aware and considerate enough to take care of our own junk and mess.

- Housecleaning can be a chance to work together with the family toward a common goal. What you learn about compromise and cooperation here will carry over into other areas of your relationships. Sit down together with your mate or all the household members and decide what the cleaning priorities are, and who can help out with what.

- The single biggest reason people don't help with cleaning is because they don't know what to do or how to do it. So post your family's cleaning policies or standards, make a list of what needs to be done, write up or give directions on how to do it— whatever you need to do to remove this stumbling block.

- Actually **ask** people (nicely) to straighten and clean their own mess, instead of moaning and groaning and muttering incomprehensible phrases at them. Taking a little time to raise an awareness or change a habit can mean a lifetime of not having to pick up or hang up behind a careless clutterer.

- In the housework arena, if you're worrying about each household member doing his or her exact share, forget it. We don't split work and expect everyone to do his or her share—we all work together to get it done. If one finishes first, he helps the others so they can get it all done faster and do something else together. It doesn't matter who did it last time; all that counts is that we end up with and enjoy a clean, neat setting. So just jump in and do it. DON'T KEEP SCORE!

If you need more guidance in this area, write to me for a copy of *Who Says It's a Woman's Job to Clean?* Send a check for $6 + $3 shipping to: Who Says, PO Box 700, Pocatello ID 83204; or call 888-748-3535.

At a cleaning seminar a few years ago, a woman picked up a copy of this book, walked up to my wife and asked earnestly, "If I buy this, will it really help my husband clean?"

My wife opened the book, pointed to some of the most popular parts, and said, "Mrs. Walker, there are over a hundred short lessons for your husband in this book, and encouragements to start helping with the household chores. But if he reads the whole thing and only does one single job, even a little thing like turn his socks or underwear right side out... if he learns or does only that one thing from the whole book, and does it the rest of his life... that's at least 10,000 times that *you* won't have to do it!" (Mrs. Walker proceeded to buy six books, one for each of her sons-in-law!)

The new-century cleaning constitution: All people clean equally!

(For how to get some help from any youngsters in your household, see Chapter Eight.)

Trade help with someone!

When you have no time to clean, you can also look outside your household for help, in a pinch, or even on a regular basis.

I've had hundreds of readers tell me stories of how they used "many hands" to lighten work. Here's a few to get you thinking!

"My neighbor and I traded work in an emergency. She needed help cleaning her house for unexpected visitors, so I spent an entire day helping her clean. A few days later, she helped me all day. We enjoyed each other's company, caught up on gossip, listened to our soap operas, and got double the work done."

"Several years ago, a friend of mine had a death in her family, and her home was the most centrally located for all of the out-of-town relatives to stay. In a panic, she called me for help. She and I and her sister cleaned that entire house in five hours (that was actually fifteen hours of nonstop cleaning!) In return the two of them came to my house several weeks later and cleaned in preparation for a Tupperware party I had planned. My house

was never so clean, and we ended up at her sister's house cleaning a couple of months later."

"When my daughter was thirteen she wanted to have a party with a dozen or so friends. I put it off as long as possible, then I made an agreement with her. If she and her friends would clean the house thoroughly, she could have the party. Within the hour, six of her friends showed up at the door ready to go to work. I gave them a list of what needed to be done, everything they needed to do the jobs, and supervised them. They actually did a good job, and had a ball doing it. They turned the stereo up as loud as it would go and danced around as they went, all the while cleaning their little fingers to the bone. They even cleaned up after the party! I got a nice clean house and it didn't cost me any more than a few party snacks and drinks."

"My daughter was an active girl scout who earned many merit badges for different accomplishments. One of those badges required doing a housework project for an older citizen. Guess who the older citizen was? The entire troop showed up at my house one weekend. I'd filled a bucket with slips of paper listing different jobs that had to be done, like 'wash off the cabinet fronts.' With sixteen girls, by time two hours were up I had to think up more things for them to do. By the end of the day my house was so spotless you could eat off of any of the floors. We laughed, sang songs, and generally had a wonderful time. I fixed a big pot of chili and we ended the day with a bowl of soup."

Think about what needs to be done, and who might be in a position to do it, and you'll find your own ingenious ways to get help when you're in over your head.

Minimize guest mess
(THE CLEANING WE INVITE!)

In century 2000 we'll have more guests than ever—stopping by, staying overnight, and sometimes seeming to have moved right in!

We like company so much we usually over-look the added cleaning burden this creates. Whether made by welcome grandkids or less eagerly awaited others, "guest mess" is an area we need to "clean up" now. We love to have people come by, and most visitors leave a good feeling, but many also unthinkingly leave a mess. Crumbs and spills, dirty dishes, crumpled napkins and candy wrappers, ciga-rette butts, magazines and videotapes and towels strewn about, toys scattered every-where, the list goes on and on. When all this is left for one or two people to clean up, it can erode the afterglow of a pleasant visit.

The biggest problem is us, not them. Ninety percent of guests will usually ask, "Is there anything I can do to help?" And ninety per-cent of we hosts are as quick to say, "Oh no, you just relax, I'll take care of it."

Why do we do this? Are we crazy? We refuse their help and then spend hours, even days restoring, redoing, and tidying up behind

them—not a good thing for either us or our enthusiasm for future visitors. We all have more to do than we can handle now; we don't need any more to tend. If company doesn't pitch in, we will begin to plan for... less com-pany, and that isn't much fun.

When guests ask if they can help, my lips have finally quit saying "no" and my finger points to the tools and supplies. When the Queen of England or President of the U.S. stays at my house, even they are going to be encouraged to clean their rooms! Getting guests to help clean up their own mess isn't really an option any more.

Quietly introduce the standard around your home and yard, "Anyone old enough to make a mess is old enough to clean it up." You tell adults, your kids tell their peers. You'll be amazed how the idea will catch on after you apply it for a while. Your guests will actu-ally enjoy their stay more if they help out, because PEOPLE FEEL GOOD WHEN THEY CONTRIBUTE! Doing work together can be a real social and bonding experience, even more so than shared play. So:

1. Bring out some mess savers before guests arrive, such as a stack of paper cups at every faucet; an extra roll of paper towels on the kitchen counter, maybe one in the bathroom too; and if there are toddlers, boxes of wet-wipes upstairs and down.

2. If you give them some gentle hints that you expect them to help out, and make it easy for them to do so, most people will cooper-ate (and that even includes kids). Inform guests when they arrive where the sheets, towels, trash cans, etc., are. Travel-ers always are in need of laundry services, so it's nice to say at bed-time, "There's detergent and fabric softener in the laundry room if you have some things you'd like to throw in, so help yourself." You could even add, "Stick the towels in if you need to fill out a load." My mother-in-law even set out sheets on the day of departure for her guests to switch on the bed—she had the right idea, and people loved to come to her house and thought she was the most gracious of hostesses.

3. Keeping cleaning tools in plain sight helps, too. Hands go to a handy broom or vacuum (we put a built-in central vac in our house in Hawaii, and there is a hose and wand in every room, including the guest bedrooms).

Put a scrub sponge on the edge of the tub and the sink, and a caddy of basic cleaning supplies on a shelf in the bath-room guests are using. Include things like a dustcloth or duster, spray bottle of all-purpose cleaner, and a couple of terry cleaning towels. Ordinary cleanup aside, there'll always be spills and accidents, nosebleeds, cut fingers, and maybe even a bit of upchuck on the carpet. Most people will be grateful for the opportunity to clean up their own messes, if you have the supplies handy for them.

4. When someone offers to help, take them up on it. When visitors volunteer to do the dishes, make the beds, or help straighten up before they leave, let them!

5. A little good example goes a long way here. If you act like you don't care, others (even ordinarily neat people) simply won't worry about leaving a mess. When you get up from the table, scrape and rinse your own plate and load it into the dishwasher, and your guests will get the cue to follow suit.

6. Tiny (and tastefully worded) signs in the right places don't hurt if you have a lot of guests. In our guest house we post the daily and weekly maintenance duties for all to read.

7. Come right out and ask for help if necessary once or twice and you'll get it—and you won't have to ask next time. After a meal you can just say "Who'd like to rinse? load? wipe the table? while I clear the leftovers?" After all, everyone cheerfully clears off their own table at McDonald's, because it's expected. People love to help and if you ask in a good-natured way and express some real thanks when they're through, you'll always get more help than you ask for.

8. "Not knowing where anything goes" is always a big hindrance to the helping process. So make sure it's easy to see where to put the trash, trays, toys, and so on. Have a rack or other clearly designated area for reading materials, and wastebaskets out in plain sight, so guests know where to put things.

9. Policing: Before they leave, ask people (especially people with kids) to help pick up and straighten up. It's amazing how much faster "pick up and put back" can be done by five people than by one person (you). Have your guests make a quick scouting trip through the place for forgotten toys, books, coats, gloves, and the like, too. Things like this can otherwise cause a big housekeeping burden—two or three long distance calls, frantic searches of the premises, another trip back or a $10 trip to the post office.

10. Again, always thank people profusely when they do help out and leave the place nice. They'll do even better next trip.

Remember, at least three quarters of guest mess can be eliminated by the simple word "Okay!" Say YES when a guest asks if he can help, and join in this big but important change in a centuries-old tradition. A wonderful side benefit from this is that you'll enjoy having company—family or other guests—more than ever, and you can't beat that!

Make more and better use of dry cleaners

Using dry cleaners intelligently is another big way to help yourself when you have no time to clean. Making your favorite dry cleaner an important partner in home care is a smart and profitable move. Dry cleaners work hard to help us and earn what they charge. Their facilities and equipment are better than ever, in terms of both quality and environmental impact. And the pricing is low when you weigh the alternatives.

I get many calls and letters from people struggling with a spot, stain, or soiling problem. They spend stress-filled hours on it and $10 worth of solvents and solutions, when a professional dry cleaner could take care of it perfectly in minutes for half the price.

Dry cleaners using steam guns, professional solvents, and other smart methods can even save things that seem ruined. They can also anticipate problems and damage and advise wisely—when you're taking something in or picking it up, they often offer all kinds of helpful information. They are always happy to give us good counsel about our clothes and cleaning.

Dry cleaners can also take care of those "niceties" of cleaning that we hate to give up, but just don't fit into our schedule any more, such as washing, starching, and ironing cotton shirts, linen tablecloths, or the six sets of ruffled muslin curtains for the little windows on the porch. They can help us with things we simply don't know how to clean, too, such as a handsome shower curtain hand-painted in acrylic. The dry cleaner's price for things like this is usually far less than it would cost us to take the time to do them ourselves, and saves us the dangers of experimentation, especially with valuable or one-of-a kind objects.

Now here are some things we can do to help both the dry cleaner and ourselves:

1. Don't delay the inevitable

When something needs cleaning, do it NOW! Waiting allows stains and soil to set and encourages further abuse of the item in question, like hauling it around for a week in the car, letting the dog sleep on it, leaving it in the sun or rain, or tromping over it where it lays on the floor. Lots of simple dry cleaning jobs have been complicated by delay and abuse.

2. If you don't know, leave it alone

If you don't know or are not sure if you can clean something yourself, leave it alone before you bring it in. Trying everything from hairspray to WD-40 on it doesn't enhance the dry cleaner's chances with an item.

3. Be nice

Because spills and spots are pretty negative discoveries, we have a tendency not just to delay doing anything about them, but to take some of our hostility out on the dry cleaner when we do get around to taking a problem item in. Don't do it!

4. Be honest about what happened

If you know what the stain or soil is, or what happened to the article in question, explaining this to the dry cleaner will greatly aid the cleaning process.

5. Remember the sensitivity of some fabrics

The machines in dry cleaning establishments are computer intelligent, and their solvents are the safest possible, but they are not miniature healing chapels. Dry cleaners are very aware of the problems of cleaning leather, silk, suede, and other items that may fade, shrink, or run. Dry cleaners seldom make mistakes, so if you have a seriously soiled "iffy" item, ask them what the cleaning alternatives might be.

P.S. I always tip my dry cleaners. I believe they work as hard as waiters, cab drivers, and bellboys. (And the results mean more to us!)

Get professional help with the cleaning

Cleaning and cooking are the big ones that can really get a homemaker down, especially if she or he is trying to cope with the other needs and demands of a family plus an outside job. The explosion of fast food restaurants has taken some pressure off the feeding end, but not everyone realizes the cleaning indus-

try has also provided a giant home relief valve.

This is the day when professionals can often do things cheaper, faster, and better than we can, from fixing our hair to fixing our car, from booking our flights to doing the mending. So why not cleaning?

When and if circumstances merit it, and you can afford it, **go for it!**

There are times when hiring a pro cleaner is a good option, maybe the only one:

❑ When your job, schedule, or family size makes it impossible to do all the housework. (Eighty percent of two-income families will hire a cleaning service by the early 21st century.)

❑ A cleaning job is too high, too big, too special, or you just don't have the knowledge to do it.

❑ When illness, physical impairment, age, or allergies don't allow you to clean.

❑ Renting or finding the equipment to do something will cost more than hiring someone to do it.

In the early days of my cleaning business I remember a married couple without children who called us every year to clean their house from top to bottom—wash every wall, shampoo the carpet and upholstery, strip and wax the floors, clean all the windows and screens, and so on. I was always surprised, as they were both young and able, and it was an easy house to clean. One year as the husband was writing out the check to pay us (our price was $180—this was back in the good old days). I asked him, "Why don't you do this yourself?"

"We figured it out," he said. "We both have good jobs, but leave at seven a.m., and come home at six. We want our nights, weekends, and vacation clear of work. If we did all this cleaning it would take us three or four full days and by the time we rented the equipment to clean the carpet and figured out how to wash the walls in the stairway, etc., we'd have more than $280 worth of our own time and plenty of hard work in the project. This way we save a hundred bucks plus you do it all better."

He had a point.

We rarely make our own bread, sew our own clothes, or churn our own butter anymore, so it's not unimaginable to get some outside help with the cleaning, too.

TYPES OF PRO CLEANERS

There are plenty of professional cleaners around, at least 80,000 companies in the US alone. But there is a difference in the types of pros you can hire to come and do your housework.

• **Maid services** Usually, you want a maid or maid service for daily or weekly light or keep-up cleaning—dusting, vacuuming, kitchen and bathroom cleaning, and the like. Maid services charge by the hour (usually in the range of $20-25 an hour) or by the visit. They often won't do heavy housework like shampooing carpets or waxing floors. They may do some of these "big jobs" for a special hourly rate, but usually they just scoot in and dust, vacuum, straighten, touch up, and go.

• **Housecleaning contractors** For once-in-a-while deep cleaning, such as wax stripping, wall washing, or windows, look for a housecleaning contractor. These are the heavy-duty dudes who do the big, heavy jobs that often call for big, heavy equipment. Call pro cleaners when you have big, onetime, or seasonal jobs.

- **Specialty cleaners** There are also specialty firms who do nothing but carpet and upholstery, blinds, or on-location drapery cleaning.

FRANCHISE OR INDEPENDENT?

If it's maid work you're after, should you contract with one of the mushrooming maid services, or seek out and hire an independent?

Advantages of a franchised service

- Franchised services are usually more professional, and costly. They usually send two to four people to clean, which means a quick in and out.
- If one cleaner gets sick or quits, they send someone else—the work still gets done.
- The company has the hassle of finding, hiring and training (and retaining) maids.
- You don't have to worry about Social Security deductions, taxes, or insurance coverage on the cleaners.
- They bring their own cleaning equipment and supplies (and lunch).
- They'll be supervised by a trained crew leader.

Disadvantages of a franchise

- You probably won't get the same worker each time, won't get the individualized attention your own maid might give.
- Maid franchises offer set services—and may simply refuse special or unusual requests. Extra services, such as windows, laundry, oven cleaning, or dishes, will probably mean extra charges.

Cons and pros of independents

- Independents are more likely to send one person, who may not be professionally trained.
- Independents don't always have adequate Worker's Compensation and liability insurance, and are often not bonded.

- Independents are usually more affordable, and offer the advantage of always having the same person or persons in your home.
- You have a better chance to get to know a small independent cleaner, and they come to know your personal cleaning needs and preferences.
- A small independent operation may have more to gain—or lose—by pleasing or not pleasing you.

Think about what the services offered will be worth to you, not only in terms of cost but in terms of time freed for other things. How many hours of maid service, how many times a week or month, does your household need to keep chores from backing up and to keep things looking good? How many big, tough jobs could you let a professional do instead, to give you time for a long-awaited mini-vacation or some other R & R with the family?

You may decide that since you and your family can do the same work for nothing, you'd rather spend the time than the money, after all. Doing it yourself will eliminate lots of arranging and key-handling and home life interruptions.

CHOOSING WHO

You can find cleaning companies in the Yellow Pages, in newspapers, in classified ads, and on bulletin boards everywhere. There are lots of good contract cleaners and maid services out there. But the cleaning business also has a high turnover rate and a high failure rate. This means there are new, inexperienced people entering the industry all the time. So how do you get the best people, job, and price out of the hundreds of choices available? Here are some things to check out before you choose or hire:

1. **Experience**: Ask how long they've been in business. Generally anyone who's survived more than five years in the industry is pretty capable, or they wouldn't still be around. If they've been in business less than two years, think twice about it.

2. **References:** Ask for references—and check them out. Don't just believe all the claims in the ad or the brochure. Get three to five references and call them. This **is** worth your time, because you'll be selecting someone who may be doing your work for the next decade, or you may be risking an $800 couch or chair. If they ruin it, it's your problem. Workmanship isn't insurable; you'd have to sue.

3. **Referrals:** You can also ask four or five friends who use professionals for cleaning how they like them. Some of them may have some horror stories of incompetents loose in their house, but when they tell you who they picked for permanent help, and why— that's who to call first.

4. **Do shop around**, to get a good price. Ask several firms to give you price quotes. Don't let price be your only guide, though—you want someone you like and trust.

5. **Insurance:** Be sure to check on the prospective cleaner's insurance coverage. Are they carrying professional liability insurance, in case there's an accident, they burn the house down, break the front window, or have a fight and wound each other? Remember, it's all going on in your house and you are responsible if they don't have their own insurance coverage. You are also responsible for avoidable hazards in your home, so make sure Ferocious Fido is safely out of the way for the day.

6. **Cleaning technique:** Ask for their input and opinion on any challenging chores or special cleaning problems in the areas you want cleaned. You can gauge what they know pretty quick by the way they answer.

7. **Equipment:** If someone doesn't have equipment and wants to use yours, I'd get a little nervous. Personal maids and friends might get by with this approach, but professionals, never. If they don't have the tools, chances are they don't know how to use them properly, either.

Pro cleaning costs sampler:

Window cleaning, depending upon size and accessibility of the windows, costs from 3 to 8 cents per square foot of glass area.

Shampooing a carpet without reapplying stain repellent costs about 15 to 25 cents per square foot of carpeted area.

Stripping and waxing floors is around 20 cents per square foot of floor area.

Washing walls and cleaning woodwork is about 12 cents per square foot of wall area.

Cleaning ceilings costs about 17 cents per square foot of ceiling area.

MAKING THE DEAL

Once you've chosen the company or individual you'd like to do your work:

1. **Get a firm price:** For big, onetime jobs or other work by pro cleaners, get a firm price (or bid) for the job, not an "estimate." A real pro knows what they can do work for and how long it will take. Rough estimates and by the hour can really end up costing you. If a pro can't tell you exactly how much, I

wouldn't use him.

With a bid, you know in advance what you are in for. Bids are often quoted in terms of square feet (to be cleaned, shampooed, stripped, whatever). Bids need to be written, and **signed**.

For maid work an hourly rate is the best deal for a homemaker—you're getting what you pay for. Services like a flat fee so they can work faster, cut corners, and boost their profit on the job. And as for tipping, most residential maids only expect a tip if they do something extra or maybe at Christmas.

2. **Outline the job/duties:** Make a complete list of what you want done. Don't leave this part to them, or they'll pick the fast, easy, profitable jobs and leave the tough ones for you. Then have them give you a detailed outline of the work to be performed, and where (what room or rooms or area) on official company letterhead stationery. For maid work especially, leave no doubt as to exactly what they will do and what your expectations are!

Most pro/client problems result from misunderstandings of what is to be done and when. "I thought that was/wasn't included" is the single biggest stumbling block in keeping everyone happy. Once you get the outline of the job, read it carefully with the other members of your household to make sure it's what you want and expect. This alone will prevent at least of half of the potential problems.

A written and signed contract is a good idea, too. Most professional services have a proposal form which lists the tasks to be performed and the price of each. It becomes a binding agreement when you sign the acceptance portion.

3. **Clarify the scheduling,** or when they will do the work. This is a big one. You need to say exactly when you want the crew to come, both the day and the time, and know not just when they'll start but when they'll finish. Otherwise you may irritate the street

sweeper because the cleaner's van is parked in the wrong place at the wrong time, or the cleaners may arrive at 2:30 when your daughter's graduation party starts at 3:00. Tell them which door to use and make sure the arrangements for how they will get in and out are clear, even if you expect to be home. Sudden emergencies, like a sick child or pet, have the habit of popping just when the cleaner is due.

4. **Staff:** Ask who will actually **do** the job—will it be the person whose name is on the business card, or the wonderful friendly voice on the phone? Or will the job get farmed out to three thugs and two grade-school dropouts who'll be smoking, swearing, and kicking your cat around? Ask for the boss if it's a small operation, you'll generally get the best. Ask that they send uniformed personnel, if possible.

5. **Make your own rules known:** Whatever they may be. Such as no eating, drinking, smoking, using phones, or snooping on the job!

6. **How to pay: Never** pay in advance. Ninety percent or more of the job will be labor, so there is no need to pay ahead. Anyone who asks for or needs prepayment, I'd avoid. Pay when the work's complete, and done to your satisfaction. Always pay by check or credit card, so that you have a clear record of payment, and get a written re-

ceipt. Make the check to their business name to avoid the "nanny tax."

A FEW LAST POINTERS ABOUT THE PROS

- **Try a trial run.** Hire a maid service on a one-shot, trial basis to begin with. You might get a dud the first couple of times, but before long you should find someone reliable who works at a reasonable rate. When you find somebody good, talk to him or her about returning weekly, monthly, or whatever. You need service you can count on, and if those you hire know they're getting regular work, they can give you a better price.

- **Prepare!** Nothing is worse (and more negatively affects both a pro cleaner's productivity and your reputation) than asking someone to clean a place that is so cluttered the cleaners can't find the floor or walls to clean them, or even a place to set down their vacuum! This doesn't mean clean the house before they come to clean it, but clutter and stray belongings should be up and out of the way. Only you know where most of this goes.

- **Inform the neighbors:** It's a good idea to let neighbors know who, what, and when, so they won't report your cleaners as burglars. Amazing how a good neighbor (like some sort of long-distance supervisor) helps you get a good job, even if you are home.

- **Kids and pets:** Kids and animals are a distraction to professional cleaners. Remove any pets from the areas in question, and as for the kids, a good movie will save you money here.

- **Getting your money's worth/a good job:** You know approximately how long it takes you to do most household tasks, and a pro should be faster. If they take too long, something's wrong.

  As for quality control, use your common sense. It's best not to stand over them and watch them as they work, but you'll definitely want to inspect the job afterward and make sure it's up to snuff.

Any dissatisfaction must be noted NOW, not later. If you don't like something the maid or cleaner has done, tell her what you're unhappy with and why, and ask her to redo it. (It usually only takes once.) You may want to establish a time frame with your cleaners for callbacks.

- **Satisfaction guaranteed?** As much as I love my profession and my fellow cleaners, all of us don't do perfect work. If you happen to be ultra fussy, we may not satisfy you. We are human and use the same tools and techniques you do (or can). We just have one thing going for us—**experience**—to do things faster and often cheaper.

Most cleaners can and will respond to what you expect... demand it and you'll get it.

- **Pros are expert cleaners, not miracle workers:** Pros don't (can't) solve all your household problems, they just clean. The procrastination, clutter, wear, damage, and buildup you hand them to deal with can make a job cost more, or they may not be able to cope with it.

- **Security:** As for that nagging worry, security—janitors and maids are among the most honest people around, simply because we know that if anything is missing we will be the #1 suspect. So we don't steal (at least 99.9 percent of us don't). In thirty years of nonstop travel, leaving money, cameras, watches, and all kinds of valuable things in motel rooms, I've never had a single thing missing. The same is true at my office. Stealing is one of the least common complaints we get as a cleaning company, and when the cleaner is accused, before long the accusing party usually finds the item where they hid it.

  To put your mind at rest, I suggest a couple of preventives here.

a) Point out and make the cleaners aware of your concern for valuable objects in your home, and for that matter all the contents. Ask in advance about bonding and insurance of the workers and exactly who will be working for you. This will go a long way toward preventing problems.

b) See that any personal and confidential things and all money and valuables are tucked away out of sight before the cleaners come. Any item that is extremely costly or you are otherwise very concerned about, I would remove to a secure place, or cover. We pros don't want the risk, either. Don't have cleaning people clean very valuable or sentimental things.

- Don't forget to treat your cleaners the way you treat anybody you want loyalty and cooperation from: give them your respect, treat them like equals, make them feel important, and recognize their efforts and accomplishments.

Having your own trusted maid or handyman is hard to beat. Trust, loyalty, and dependability are worth nurturing. Your relationship with your cleaner is just as important as your rapport with your hairdresser!

How soon can I expect a robot to help out?

Everyone says that robots sophisticated enough to perform basic household chores are in the near future (whenever that is). We've certainly made strides in that direction. We're already seeing homes with central systems management computers that regulate the functioning of everything in the house, from heating and cooling to entertainment systems.

These built-in "brains" can be programmed and instructed by keypad, by voice command, or by telephone from another location. The obvious next step is appliances controlled by voice alone, which will even be able to answer you and ask questions if they need to. Washing machines, dishwashers, and cooking and food processing appliances able to make routine operating decisions on their own should be common before long.

We've already got robots that can clean swimming pools, shear sheep, fight fires, deliver mail, dive in deep water, and handle toxic wastes. Surely they can make one to tackle the green hairies in the refrigerator. After all, there are 1001 other computerized household items being researched and developed right now. And not long ago, a "personal computer" would have taken up an entire room of the house—today it's a typewriter-size machine in the corner many of us think of as our right arm!

But when it comes to a robot to do our housework there are still some hard-to-solve problems involved:

1. The initial cost and upkeep of such a creature. Though no one knows just what the price tag will read, household robots are foreseen as being extremely costly, both in terms of initial purchase and maintenance expense. For the next decade, at least, making some design changes in your home

(see Chapter Six) will reduce cleaning more cost-effectively than "Robot waiting."

2. Much of cleaning is a "value judgment," and lots of the unexpected is involved. A cleaning robot would need to be able to make all kinds of decisions. It would have to be capable of seeing crayon scribbles on the wall and removing them, leaving the wall intact. Or picking up clothes and identifying whether they're clean or dirty, or telling the dog dish on the floor from the one the resident couch potato left there.

Interestingly enough, some of the most mundane chores require the most sophisticated robotics. You and I have always known the finesse it takes to get around and under with a 24-pound roaring vacuum, without clipping, bumping, or smashing into things or slurping up anything you didn't intend to. Robotic floor scrubbers and vacuum cleaners already exist to do large unobstructed areas like supermarket aisles and corridors, but they're like a bull in a china shop for a crowded room.

Major strides will have to be made in artificial intelligence, visual acuity, and manual dexterity of existing machines before they can do a lot of the stuff you and I can do while daydreaming!

3. The design of homes and their contents would have to be standardized for full efficiency, and I doubt that we independent Americans will want perfectly matching Star Wars wardrobes and washrooms for some time yet.

The possibility of robots lightening our housework load is a genuine one, and in century 2000 we're sure to see some of it, starting perhaps with robots cleaning large commercial and industrial areas where there are repetitive tasks to be done and unobstructed areas to work in. But I wouldn't count on the day coming too soon where there will be a fourth entry into the family: husband, wife, children, and Robby the housecare robot.

However the chemical and engineering advances already available on the home cleaning front—easier to clean interior and exterior materials, disinfectants that can now be incorporated into household surfaces and cleaning tools, dust control filters, better than ever stain-resistant coatings—if tapped and used, will all but eliminate the need for that fourth member of the family.

Look at cleaning machines, for example. These mechanical servants have already taken a great deal of the drudgery out of housework, and if we choose and use them wisely, they can free us up even more. Look over your present cleaning arsenal and the real needs of your home and family today, and consider a central vacuum, electrostatic air cleaner, dishwasher, home extractor, pressure washer, garbage disposal, or compactor—whatever cleaning machinery will make the work go better and faster and make your life easier. It'll do more to brighten your life than expensive seldom-used "toys."

Keep dreaming of a robot to do all the laundry, cooking, and cleaning, as well as baby-sit, balance the checkbook, write our thank-you notes, water the lawn, watch the house, and feed the parakeet. A robot capable of taking out the trash, washing the mini blinds, organizing the closet, and—yes— matching the socks! A governess, butler, and maid all wrapped up in one. For today's harried homemakers, it sounds almost too good to be true, but we'll probably live to see it. In reality, it'll probably be like everything else—getting the model with all the options you want will put you two hundred percent over budget!

CHAPTER 8

The Big One:

Getting KIDS to Help Clean

When you think about it, this is probably the most important topic in this book. It has a great deal to do with how much cleaning will need to be done in your home over the years, as well as what our young people will be like later in life.

THE LAST FRONTIER OF HOME LEARNING

In earlier years most of us lived in rural settings, and everyone in the family had to lend a hand to help the family survive. Children, too, had many jobs and assignments. Gone are the days of "doing the chores"—carrying water, gathering eggs or firewood, feeding the animals, working in the fields or the garden, doing the wash (most kids today don't even know what a clothesline is). Now few kids get to see a farm or are assigned a chore, so cleaning up after themselves and others is one of the few "schools of life" left.

Cleaning is one of the last opportunities children have around the house to learn per-

sonal responsibility, and help the family cope with the daily demands of living. The new century finds most things done for us—we have automatic sprinklers, rototillers, leaf blowers, snow blowers, dishwashers, washers and dryers, power saws and power screwdrivers, and remote controls to tune the TV. We hardly have to turn a hand to get along just fine—automation has eliminated hundreds of duties we once had to share with our children, and the skills and principles that went with them. The several-mile walk to school in the old days is now a luxury car or bus ride insulated from the weather. Things open by themselves, cook by themselves, and mind themselves, so where can a child find the satisfaction of doing something that needs to be done and feeling good about it afterward? Teaching kids to clean at home is even a chance to instill a work ethic—no one else is doing it!

The home is the first and finest classroom.

Learning to clean may even be more critical than reading, writing, and arithmetic, because if the only thing a kid knows when he graduates from high school is: "I am responsible for myself and my own life," he will succeed. If instead our children come from families where mother, dad, maids, nannies, or janitors always cleaned up after them, then we have expertly and completely taught them that they are not responsible for their messes. Most will carry this concept into the rest of their lives. So if they go on to mess themselves up at college, in their career, or in marriage—scholastically, socially, financially, or emotionally—we shouldn't be surprised.

CLEANING: A KEY TO PERSONAL SUCCESS

Kids cleaning is not an option or a nicety. It's a necessity. If children don't learn, it'll plague them the rest of their lives. They never will figure out what is wrong, always be blaming their problems on others or waiting for someone else to take care of them and their property—relying on lawyers, bankers, parents, spouses, ministers, the government, or someone else to step in and pick up after them or "clean up" things. No college class at Harvard or Yale can teach our children management and discipline if we have allowed them a lifetime of doing nothing. Learning to clean after yourself is a prime key to personal success.

My friend Gladys Allen once said about talented kids: "What good is a concert violinist if he can't fold towels?" Our first response might be that we'd take such an exceptional talent over cleaning, but inability to look after yourself affects every area of a person's life, eventually. Knowing how to take care of yourself in your everyday environment is a skill no one should be without—it's even more important than knowing how to entertain yourself!

If we allow and accept sloppy standards and poor cleanliness habits in our children, at home or wherever else they may go, we'll have guaranteed carryover into their writing, speaking, driving, playing, working, money handling, and relationships with others. Somewhere down the line, **how they clean will be how they live**. Does that make it seem important enough, enough of a priority, that they learn to clean?

WHAT ARE OUR GOALS HERE?

Before we launch into the effort to get kids to clean, let's take a minute to put our goals here in perspective.

1. **A home is to live in, not live for.** We sometimes pay more attention to the decor than to the young people present. Kids use and appreciate a home more than most adults. As we grow older our home often becomes more a matter of vanity, necessity, and financial burden. But kids love homes, so let them use them to grow and do! If we had more fingerprints on the walls at home, we'd have less on the police blotters downtown.

2. **There is nothing wrong with making a mess.** If kids are going to learn to build, overhaul, sew, paint, invent, whittle, or wrestle, do anything a person does, they are going to create some kind of mess. Mess is creativity's constant shadow. Cooking, bathing, having pets, and pursuing projects, all mean messes. Making messes is no crime. It's part of life and often the bigger the mess, the bigger the blessing. The problem is not in making a mess, but in leaving it behind for someone else.

SEARCHING FOR THE SECRETS OF "HOW"

I know as well as you do that convincing kids to clean isn't easy. It's a hard sell. I wouldn't believe anyone who said they had all the answers for getting kids of any age to be interested in cleaning.

Not only have I raised a big family, but I also had foster children, and young guests from other countries (we had eight teenagers in the house at once). Plus numerous youth parties, sleep-overs, and camp-outs. And I now have eighteen grandchildren that sometimes storm the house at once. I've given presentations on cleaning to kids in grade schools and high schools from Alaska to Cincinnati. I've lived and actively researched this subject, because I knew it was one that would help families everywhere.

For decades now I've gathered opinions, anecdotes, options, stories, solutions, and studies on this subject. I have files full of articles from magazines, and interviews with child psychologists. I've held contests for the best ideas on "How I get my kids to clean," and read all the books written on the topic. I've checked with home extension offices from Texas to North Carolina, and listened to every idea and incentive around, from M&M's to Mary Poppins movies.

My "kids cleaning" research file was enormous. There was some good stuff here and there, but it was buried in a ton of words, theories, philosophies, and idealistic should's and shouldn't's.

To spare you plowing through all this, I've boiled it down into a few short, simple principles that can be easily implemented.

The three big answers:
EXAMPLE, REWARDS,
PREVENTIVE DESIGN

Almost any child can be encouraged to clean by one or more of these approaches.

EXAMPLE

The power of a father's example

When I charted the results of not only my own experience, but all of my interviews, and the thousands of "comment cards" from my cleaning seminar audiences, I did discover something that worked, that had both short and long range results, a high percentage of success. One great truth emerged: the biggest single influence for kids to clean their rooms is the father's example. Where the father did cleaning himself, or pitched in and worked with the rest of the family, kids would copy it.

Kids usually grow up believing cleaning is done for them by a WOMAN (Mom), and most parents (and books and articles) say to kids: "Help Mommy!," reinforcing the idea that the job of cleaning belongs to Mommy. When the father cleans, not to "help Mommy" but because something needs to be cleaned, it makes all the difference.

Our children imitate us

A parent in great desperation was questioning his junior high age child as to why his room and all his possessions were such a mess all the time. The kid (who had taken Introduction to Psychology and learned a few new words), wisely said: "Gee Dad, it must be either heredity or environment!" Right on!

The history of the ages leaves no doubt that children imitate the behavior and habits of their parents. Today the

majority of we parents are junkaholics who buy and tend "too much," showing our kids how to do this all too well. Control of our children starts with control of ourselves, so if we want them clean and clutter-free, then guess who has to live that way?

Most of the kids who don't and won't clean have never heard a positive word about it or ever been taught how to do it. We parents have become commanders, senders, delegators—we are much too important and overcommitted to do anything **with** our children. We say: "Go and wash the car!" "Go clean your room!" or "Go clean the yard!" over and over, when a simple "Let's wash the car!" "Let's clean the room!" "Let's do the yard!" will do it. Include yourself in the process—having Mom or Dad working with them is almost an irresistible attraction for a kid. Then motivation, instruction, and habit can all be developed at the same time—plus the work really gets done! And the togetherness is great!

The magic words are always, "Here, let me show you how."

Let the little ones see you clean

Many mothers of young children have asked me: "What do you do with kids when you clean?" One time-honored approach is to do most of the housework early or late while the little ones sleep. It's better, however, to have the child with you in a baby backpack or walker so he/she can watch you clean happily (fake it if you have to). This will set a pattern for both attitude and technique which the child will be anxious to imitate. At the toddler stage, you can buy them some toy cleaning equipment such as vacuum, mop, and broom, and let them pretend while you do the real thing.

Clean the community together

When our children were growing up and we all went camping or to a park, we would clean the place up before we left. They'd say: "Dad, but we didn't make this mess!" and I'd say: "Yes, but we can't leave America like this."

Take your kids on community cleanup day projects. It can have a profound effect on their attitude towards mess creation. After they police the litter from a street gutter or five-mile stretch of highway, their chances of chucking something out the window of a car are small. And this will carry over to their room, home, and yard.

"Okay, but what am I getting out of it?": REWARDS

As for the big bag of tricks for getting kids to clean, kids will outsmart you. They were conning you when they were three months old, at three years they have the upper hand, and by the time they're teenagers, they can out-manipulate you two to one.

A mother, for instance, told her son to wash his hands three times a day: "I'll give you a dollar if you do it!" He did it, but his hands were still dirty. How could this be? He ran in the bathroom, washed his hands, dried them, washed them again, dried them again, washed them once more, dried them once more—all within about two minutes! Having fulfilled his contract, then he went out to play and ended up with dirty hands!

Unfortunately, rewards are seldom thought through and followed through. Too many of them are at-the-moment inspirations, stop-gaps, or acts of desperation. If not handled properly, rewards turn into bribery, and soon you are not able to handle the demands.

But rewards can work. Every man has his price, and even more so with kids! Adults grow narrow and will jump through the hoop for money. Kids learn this by the time they're teenagers, but before that they are sensitive to rewards like praise, love, travel, time spent with them, a chance to go on a trip or work on the job with Mom or Dad. Rewards shouldn't just be a matter of "I do this and thus I get that (thing or object)." Whenever possible, they should be "I do this and that will happen to my life."

Tie cleaning in to what they want to be

Tying cleaning in to what they want to be is a strong (and clean!) motivation! Question: "What do you want to be when you grow up?" Answer: "A pilot, nurse, president, executive, athlete," etc. Then explain how being clean and neat carries over directly to being good on that job ("One of the things you notice about pilots is how neat and clean they are."). A big influence on my decision to be clean in my own life was a single sentence of my mother's. We were cleaning some vegetables once and she stopped and said: "One of the first things that attracted me to your father was the way

he always kept himself, his workplace, and his tool shop so clean!" That really registered because like most kids, I worshipped my father and wanted to be like him.

Point out the personal benefits of "clean"

It's okay to tell kids to do something because it "makes Mommy happy" or "makes Grandpa smile," but that's secondary to convincing them that their own actions can make things better, happier for themselves. Keep pointing out the personal benefits of clean:

1. "Notice you feel better."
2. "You can find things."
3. "Your toys stay nicer when they are clean and neat."
4. "People treat you better."
5. "Notice that when your room is clean we let you..."
6. "Notice..."

Keep those compliments coming

Never give one compliment for a clean room. Give ten compliments—during and after, over, and over, and over! Clean will then become a praise earned at any cost.

Reinforce the value of "clean"

Whenever you get a chance, reinforce the value of "clean." Never fail to point out ugly, messy, filthy, or disorderly things when you're driving or walking through the countryside, town, park, anywhere! When you see something like this, ask your kids to look at it and sadly say how bad it makes you, me, or anyone who passes by or lives there feel.

Likewise, the more you can point out the benefits and pleasures of cleanliness, the more positive carryover you'll get for kids to clean at home. When you're at a sharp, clean place like Disneyland or a beautiful park or a handsome hotel, say, "Look how clean this place is, isn't it great, doesn't it make you feel good?" Things like this are a powerful influence for kids to adopt "clean" as an ethic and behavior in their lives.

You'll feel better, in a clean room or clean shirt or clean yard.

You'll have more room to play.

You'll be less likely to get hurt and you won't get sick as much.

Everyone likes you more when you're clean.

It's a good way to get a better allowance, or to earn extra money.

When you grow up you'll be ahead—you'll already know how.

Some rewards that work

Threats are the most common and least effective tactic parents use to get children to be responsible. Instead of saying: "You must..." or "You better...," give them rewards or praise for jobs they do well.

- Give a little prize or treat to young children at the end of each cleaning session.

- Make a list (and keep it current as they grow), of the things they like or want most, their favorite things. This is a strong reward if you connect giving or getting these things with "clean."

- Have a kid list what they would like in exchange for a clean room.

- Some parents give their children play money or tokens for each chore done satisfactorily, and at the end of the week or month the kids can turn them in for a reward or privilege of their choice.

- My daughter Elizabeth has a great reward system for home care and cleaning. Her kids love to go to "Grandpa's farm" (my ranch), so she keeps a reward bottle where good behavior is rewarded by pennies or notes added to the jar. When the jar is full it's time again to go and visit Grandpa. The kids associate clean with fun times and are encouraged in the habit of cleaning and picking up.

- Kids love surprises. To celebrate the whole house being clean, go on a picnic!

- Giving your time, your undivided attention to them, is a supreme reward. Just about any kid would clean for a parent's time!

- Money as reward: Sometimes "filthy lucre" does do wonders for filthy rooms! Every time I visit my grandkids, I carry a handful of $1.00 bills, and do a room inspection. If a child's room is neat I leave a dollar on the bed; if not, no dollar. But if my wife and I are staying a while, I'll tell anyone who didn't pass muster that I'll be doing one more inspection before I go. Often the reason they didn't get the dollar the first time around has been rectified. Once in a while, when even the closet is clean and the toys are not only picked up, but lined up (and it's close to Christmas), I drop a $5.00 bill on that spread!

- Odd, but for someone else's money, have you ever noticed how a kid eight to eighteen will work? I've hired young people of all ages who clean and work for me like desperadoes, yet their parents tell me they won't or haven't turned a lick at home. There is a wedge into the problem here, so encourage (if not set up) cleaning jobs for your kids with other people. This gives them a chance to see clear-cut results in "the real world" from cleaning—it's not just the old business of "clean your room."

- Don't fail to remind kids of the time-honored custom: any money found on the floor or under cushions while cleaning is now the property of the industrious cleaner!

- Guests as reward: Another principle that works is to encourage your kids to invite and have their friends over, always and only **to a clean room**. This cleverly puts the pressure for a presentable "pad" on the visitor, and the kids aren't cleaning up their mess but rather preparing for a guest. It's always better to present a job in the light of positive "get to's" rather than negative "have to's." This not only keeps rooms cleaner but teaches consideration and respect for others. Don't let this turn negative by taking the wrong approach: "You can ask Harry over, but clean your room first!" Far better to say something like: "Have you got things ready for Harry yet?"

The best device for clearing a driveway of snow is a kid who wants to use the car!

PREVENTIVE DESIGN

Is the last of my "big three" secrets for helping children clean.

Preventive design simply means designing to reduce cleaning and maintenance. If something doesn't get dirtied or torn up then it won't need cleaned up.

You don't have to undertake a major building project to take advantage of preventive design. The majority of what we are cleaning and maintaining in a house is things like floor and wall coverings, window coverings, fixtures, and furniture—items that wear out over time and have to be replaced. By changing some of these to "low maintenance" choices the next time you change them, you can cut out considerable cleaning. The whole thrust here is to eliminate the need to police, fix, or clean. Design can do it!

I encourage you to use your own wisdom in the layout and decoration of your children's rooms. Don't just copy what you see in the "glamour home" magazines or you'll have a ticking time bomb on your hands. They have some good ideas for children's rooms and areas, but often overdo it (because people with one or no kids designed them). Use your own imagination and experience with what makes messes! To start your own list of low-maintenance ideas, here are some design features that have worked well for me and other parents:

Built in furniture.

1. **Build in.** When our children were young, my wife and I built a miniature stagecoach in their room. It was inexpensive and cut cleaning way down. Besides being a great place to play, it had a built-in clothes closet, toybox, and hamper, and two nearby built-in beds with storage drawers underneath. This really reduced the places (like under the bed or behind things) to litter or leave anything. In a later home we built inset places in the wall (instead of shelves sticking out) for hobbies, displays, posters, pin ups, and charming collectibles. This kept them out of the line of fire.

   When furnishings are built in they can't be disarranged or tipped over, and there are far fewer exposed edges and corners for kids to get hurt on. Audio and video equipment and computer workstations are excellent things to build in, too.

2. **Wall hang.** Anything you can get up off the floor, do it! When the place where something belongs is clearly established, easy to reach, and easy to use, it encourages things to be put back rather than strewn around. Brackets, hangers, clamps, pegboard, and the like can be easily "anchored" to any wall. What doesn't get down and

around doesn't get dirty or need to be picked up. Even hang the trash can on a wall bracket. It's easy to sweep or vacuum under, and it never gets tipped over.

3. **Use semigloss or high-gloss paints.** Surprising how many people use flat paint in action places. Grease, oil, ink, and crayon then become impossible to clean off. Use high-gloss latex enamel paint, so the bad stuff will bounce off or clean off easily. And use a high-quality brand, so you won't have to be repainting before the year is out.

4. **Durable, washable wall coverings.** For the walls in a child's room, vinyl wall covering, hardwood paneling, or even carpet or chalkboard (for one of the walls) might be a better choice than painted wallboard. You don't have to put coverings like these all the way up the wall, since the bottom half is what gets the hardest use.

5. **Use vinyl flooring.** Vinyl flooring (extra-soft cushioned vinyl is available) is better than carpet for young children, and for any child's room that will be exposed not just to the usual spots and spills, but heavy craft activity. Toys roll better on vinyl anyway! You can always go to carpet when the children are older. Half vinyl and half carpet can be a good idea in a child's room, too.

6. **Use low pile, tight weave carpet** when you do use carpet.

7. **Camouflage.** Yes, this is war so it's fair! The carpet and wall colors in a child's room should be capable of camouflaging dirt and disorder. This means they should match the potential fallout of food, drinks, dead frogs, glue/clay/craft mess, makeup, etc. A textured, multicolored carpet will show less soiling than a solid-color pastel. In a child eating area consider colors like gravy brown, butter yellow, spinach green, pizza red, and taco orange. Again, houses are made to live in, not live for. When decorating and choosing furnishings and accessories, do whatever you can to reduce the beating a place takes and the need to be constantly cleaning and straightening.

8. **Install a lower closet rod.** How many mothers tell kids and even toddlers to hang up clothes when the average clothes rod is 55 inches high or higher? Installing a lower rod will cost only a few dollars and save thousands of hours of time! When the kids grow up or you move, you can remove or replace the rod in minutes. (Even in adult closets, lower rods are handy for short clothing items.)

9. **Provide low, well-labeled drawers.** If you provide drawers for clothes or whatever that the little ones can reach, and label them boldly and attractively, there'll be fewer pajamas, mittens, and T-shirts strewn around.

10. **Oversize switchplates**: An inexpensive little adjustment that cuts spot cleaning and wall damage. Oversize switchplates present a bigger, harder surface to collect the constant abuse.

11. **Adequate waste receptacles**. I see the saddest trash containers in kids' rooms. They are too small, easy to tip over, hard to dump into, etc. Put a nice professional-quality plastic one in there.

12. **Use one blanket, not three.** Bed mess is inevitable. Smart parents use a single heavy blanket or comforter and one sheet instead of many layers of covers and spread. It makes bedmaking easy and encourages kids to do it.

13. **Give them a generous bulletin board.** If the gallery for greeting cards, souvenirs, school papers, messages, calendars, and photos is nice enough, that's where everyone will put them instead of pinning and taping them all over the walls (damaging the surface, then falling off later). You can buy a nice big bulletin board and a white- or chalk-board for drawing. It's worth it!

14. **Provide a "pocket" shelf.** Have you ever noticed there is no real place in a kid's room to put the some of the most important items

(and the stuff that always gets strewn): knapsacks, purses, bookbags, duffel bags, and pocket contents? These things always end up on the floor or the already crowded end table or dresser top, establishing a bad habit that carries on into adulthood. Design a generous-sized shelf with a lip so that pencils, marbles, and stray Tootsie Rolls won't fall off onto the floor.

15. A desk of their own. A desk is something most people don't get until they're about twenty-five, when most of us need one (if not two) all our lives! Kids need one, too—a place to write, draw, color, and put private stuff. The inside of a child desk might get a little junky, but all of those papers and pencils and rulers and markers are off the floors, walls, and out of your kitchen drawers. If I could do it over, I'd have bought all my kids a desk. It confines the action and the mess!

HANDS ON=HAPPY!

As for the nitty-gritty of teaching kids to clean, now:

How should we divide or assign the chores?

> *"There are many good ways to organize maintenance responsibilities, but I believe the real secret is not in the plan but in the attitude which is established."*
>
> —Sally Higley

By the age of ten there are few cleaning jobs girls or boys can't do as well or better than you. At eleven and twelve my daughters were working in resort condos as professional maids, doing the same duties the seasoned pros did and doing them well.

Make sure kids get to try everything. Someone said to me once, "As a child I was assigned to clean the wash basin. That's all I did. I was an expert wash basin cleaner and when I got married that's all I knew: how to clean wash basins." Let children use every tool and run every machine, expose them to all areas and types of cleaning. When kids see the big picture, they get a big view! (And a big capacity to clean.)

Do give children some choices of things to do. If they are given the chance to help decide what their responsibilities will be, they are more likely to carry them through to completion. Give them the pick of the litter—let them turn their hand to whatever turns them on. If they hate toilets, trade or clean them yourself, until you can persuade them otherwise.

The junior cleaning kit

Must we find and furnish scaled-down tools for our kid cleaners? Nope—a child can use most cleaning tools every bit as well as an adult. The simplicity of cleaning tools is wonderful when you think about it—brooms, vacuums, dustcloths, spray bottles, etc. Buckets can just be filled a little less full, squeegees can be ten-inch instead of sixteen inches, and most sponges or cleaning cloths have no need of "youngster adaptation." And one of the greatest decluttering tools ever invented, the clothes hanger, works well in all hands. Which brings up something we often forget—a great deal of cleaning is done with NO TOOLS! Picking up and putting away, replacing things, straightening and organizing them requires only a willing brain and two hands and feet.

It is even more important in child cleaning than usual to buy good sturdy equipment, in bright and attractive colors whenever possible. Experience over the years has taught me that if our cleaning gear is nice and new and pretty

and kept clean, it is more likely to be used. You could even consider personalized cleaning tools, with the names or monograms of the owners and users.

I've had reports that by making the purchase of a new vacuum as much of an occasion as the acquisition of a new pool or bike, the kids line up to get to use it. Kids love a vacuum with a headlight!

You could even make each child their own little cleaning kit, with a dustcloth and spray bottle of all-purpose cleaner and some cleaning cloths, for instance.

Show them how

You can make cleaning into a game or adventure for the youngest children. Give them a dustcloth or lambswool duster and let them race you in the job of dusting to a finish point. Young children love to vacuum with a small hand-held vacuum—let them go after the spilled potting soil or the crumbs under the kitchen table. They will also enjoy taking a wagon or toy shopping cart and going from room to room to pick up litter and left-behind things.

Try to stick with sessions of no more than ten or fifteen minutes so you hold their interest, and keep the "games" fresh so they don't get bored.

When you clean with children, be sure to allow extra time for training, and accept the fact that they aren't going to do things exactly as you would. Yes, you could do a better job in half the time, but you want and need to teach them how. Don't just do the job for them, out of frustration. Your persistence will pay off as cleaning becomes a habit for your kids.

Help your children learn the right way to do things, the techniques and fine points, so that the job won't have to be done over because it didn't come out as expected. That cuts out tons of negativity: "This isn't clean!" the parent said to a kid who thought she had done her best, undoing all the preceding encouragement.

Again, the magic word is: "Here, let me show you!"

"Cleaning class" may be discouraging at times, but don't give up. For a while, maybe even months or years, your children's cleaning help may have to be redone, or may be of little actual help to you. But your child is learning. As children get older, they can help a lot more and even do major jobs themselves. One way to speed this is to teach your older children one skill at a time and let them perfect it. Window cleaning, for example—teach it carefully to one of your children. From then on that is his or her job. He or she will become very good at it and will actually help you now.

As that child perfects the job of windows, move him to another chore, such a bathroom cleaning. After a while he will become good at that, and so on. After a few years a child will be good at a number of jobs, and the rest will fall into place.

Some "how-to" pointers:

- When children use a vacuum, an important thing to teach them is *not to vacuum up things that will injure or clog the machine!* And show them how to go back and forth with the machine so that it misses nothing.

- When dusting, teach them to dust top to bottom.

- When they're doing spray and wipe cleaning (see p. 144), make sure the cloth they're using stays clean. Give them a fresh one as needed.

- One of the most valuable things you can teach children—or adults for that matter—is how to catch and clean up their own "fallout," whether it be cookie crumbs, candy wrappers, empty pop cans, dropped sweatshirts, or scattered puzzle pieces.

Train one and let him train the others

Another approach is to train only one child to do a job—the oldest! If he/she can get one of the younger kids to do his job to the necessary specifications, more power to him. This means he has trained them to do it and probably will not be able to get them to do it for long without rewarding them in some way. As long as that reward is not as large as the one he is receiving for the completed job, this is a satisfactory arrangement that teaches him management skills. When the younger child does the job suitably without supervision, the job is added to his chart and I pay the reward to him instead of to the older child.

Find a way they can do it fast

Kids love **fast!** Provide a way for them to do whatever they can do faster—sweeping, spot cleaning, dishes, vacuuming, window cleaning, whatever. Reduce the time something takes and the chances of it being done become better!

Here is an important principle that too many of us with children miss. Try to eliminate big long stretches or marathons of cleaning, such as the big Saturday morning siege, where we do all the cleaning in one big block of time every week. We all get tired of this and come to dread it, and kids, with their limited attention span, get tired of it even sooner. Better to break the cleaning up into little daily installments, do one of the seven things each day instead of all seven on Saturday. You'll enjoy the work more, it'll be done better (because you aren't tired of cleaning), and you won't resent the cleaning because it's cheating you of whatever your favorite thing to do on Saturday morning is.

To help children (and adults) clean faster, there is an action-packed video *"Is There Life After Housework?"*—ninety entertaining and educational minutes on how to clean like the pros. Kids will watch it over and over. Send $19.95 + $2 shipping to Life After Housework Video, PO Box 700, Pocatello ID 83204, or call 888-748-3535.

Have some good answers ready

You'll always get comebacks to your commands to clean, like, "I don't have time," "it's

my room," "it's not my job," "I just did it," "I don't know how," "it doesn't look dirty to me," "Amy's room is worse than this!" "I have homework," "later," and the big stumper—"why?" So be prepared for this, because kids can come up with some good ones, and logical, too. They'll even quote you against yourself, brilliantly! And when they ask "why" and you say "just do it!" or "because I told you so" you lose. So think ahead and be ready!

Don't cave in at the cave!

When the kids' room looks like a yeti's cave (even our adult areas look like that sometimes when we get busy or behind), the time has come to put your foot down.

When there is a rule, a policy, a standard, or schedule (here is a real crossroads of our behavior patterns in life), we can either face it and follow it... or con and cry our way out of it. I've hired thousands of full grown, educated, and capable adults who still handle needs or unpleasant situations this latter way—by trying to get around them. I'll bet it all started in a childhood situation where the parent "caved in," or failed to stand firm in a rule or assignment. I've seen kids pout and sit in their room all day in defiance of the order to clean it. This is an important moment of education. Let them sit in there for two or three days if necessary until they DO clean it, and it will be the last time they try this tactic.

But most of us haven't the heart—those cries of woe over having to pick up a few pair of socks sock us right in the heart, and we rush in to help. We end doing it all (or most of it) and letting them run free. The lesson taught here? Stall and beg and whine and you'll be rescued! Don't do it, don't cave in. It will only take a few times of standing firm in the face of whatever, and they will get the message and the work will get done.

Teach the principle of "keep up" cleaning

We get so focused on "getting the room cleaned" we forget that "keeping it clean" is the other side of the overall success of child cleaning. Keeping a room up every morning or evening is only a bit of work, much easier to take than a big, long session of cleaning every so often. Once kids get the picture here they are converted to "keep-up" cleaning faster than most adults. Look at McDonald's—all manner and age of people eat there, and they all help keep the place neat and clean—even your own kids!—because it's expected, and the restaurant has made it easy to do.

THINGS NOT TO DO TO YOUNG CLEANERS

- DON'T CRITICIZE. You'll put out all sparks of "clean" if you ever belittle the level of cleanliness achieved by one of your little "newcomers to cleaning reach!" This is also the single surest way to discourage grownups from helping—by saying their work isn't satisfactory, especially in public. No matter how you word it, what it's really telling them is: they don't measure up.

When something isn't up to snuff or isn't done right, better than talking about it is to simply lead them through the redo. I've also found that letting youngsters "inspect" and comment on each other's cleaning jobs or rooms causes them to be a lot more careful about what they do in their own. (They learn a few things about what and how to clean in the process, too.)

- Don't say: "This is your room and you are solely responsible for it." This takes away your authority. They will counter by saying: "Well, if it's my room I can keep it the way I want!" You're dead when you delegate authority! Tell them instead: "This is one of the rooms in our house, and you are using it. You know how we keep our house, and how you have to keep this room."

- Hiding things left out or around and making kids "buy them back" with service or money teaches them manipulation, not cleaning! It's like that "cleaning deposit" on a rental or dorm room. If your deposit is ever deducted from (even if you deserve it), you'll make efforts to change colleges. Taking away privileges or money to get "clean" seldom works!

PERSIST!

You'll have to keep at it to make it work, so don't get discouraged in the teaching process. If you need a little inspiration here, consider Proverbs 22:6 in the Old Testament: "Train up a child in the way he should go: and when he is old, he will not depart from it."

It is worth the effort, so persist!

Eliminate the statement we've all made too many times: "It's much easier just to do it myself!" Keep convinced that it's worth any amount of time and effort to keep teaching kids to clean.

A checklist for the children

Children will do what is expected of them, usually more often than adults, if they know the what, why, where, when, and how of it. Make up your own little attractive (even cartoon illustrated!) checklist like the following for your children, that could be hung up in some conspicuous spot.

I heLp CleAN Our house!

1. I make my own bed.
2. I pick up and hang up my clothes.
3. I put dirty clothes in the hamper.
4. I pick up and put away my toys when I'm done with them for the day.
5. I scrape my plate after I eat and take it to the sink/dishwasher.
6. I take my own things out of the car after we go somewhere.
7. I put wrappers, etc., in the garbage (right away!) and empty cans and bottles in the recycle bin.
8. I dust.
9. I sweep/dustmop the floor.
10. I help vacuum.
11. I help fold clothes and do the laundry.
12. I help keep my pets clean.

Cleaning Safety for Children

Let's head off any chances of injury in our new world of child cleaning.

RULE #1: *Keep the curiosity factor in mind*

Kids are energetic and inquisitive and will find, reach, and try out anything, anywhere. They're all too likely to be wondering things like "Will the vacuum suck up water?" or "How much Windex does it take to kill an ant?" So bear this in mind when you do any assigning or instructing in cleaning.

RULE #2: *Be chemical safe*

This is the day of attractive packaging, and just about everything, including cleaning products of all kinds, has nice, bright labels that can lure kids to try or taste. Kids can figure out safety lids these days better than we can.

Get serious about safe storage. Keep bleach, bowl cleaners, and all garden and pest control chemicals in a high, hidden, or locked place. Bear in mind that big, heavy buckets or containers of even less dangerous things, falling or pulled down from a shelf, can crush or kill a child.

Kids can police an area by themselves, but clean with your children when they're using cleaning solutions. You mix the cleaning solutions for them, so you can be sure what goes in, the temperature of the water, and so on. Most household cleaning doesn't require strong chemicals, just "elbow grease."

Keep the child cleaning kit confined to safe water-based cleaners, such as all-purpose cleaner, that would not harm them even if they drank it or sprayed themselves with it. You can let kids use a spray bottle of disinfectant cleaner to clean the bathroom if you're there with them, but *you* do anything that involves the use of bowl cleaner—ALWAYS!

RULE #3: *Don't let kids climb to clean.*

They love ladders, ledges, and roof tops, but make "feet on the floor" the rule for your child cleaners. Don't ever let a child stand on a chair or anything to clean... period.

RULE #4: *Electric alert*

Teach children to stay well away from anything electrical with wet hands or water in any form. Make sure they understand **why,** so that it doesn't make them curious.

You can let them use extension handles on dusters indoors, but put an eight-foot limit on any extension handles outside the house, to avoid any run-ins with electrical wires. (Nobody can see the dirt on anything higher, anyway.)

RULE #5: *Adults only*

Many modern tools, from mowers and trimmers to electric knives and scissors, are not the old hand-operated variety. Most are power tools that you just plug in or push a button to start, or turn a key that a two-year old can figure out. Any power tools used for cleaning should be stored out of sight, locked up, or with the key removed.

Let children vacuum, but not change bags, belts, or anything where they might get their hands in the mechanics. Don't let very young children work with beater bar vacuums or power wands, and make sure children of any age know to keep their fingers well away from the working parts of same. A canister vacuum is safer for a small child than an upright.

RULE #6: *Glass safety*

All of that "window plunging" in movies and on TV can lead children to believe that glass is harmless. But falling through windows and other glass surfaces and getting cut while trying to pick up broken glass account for many injuries of children and teenagers, too. Make glass a no-no for your youngest cleaners.

RULE #7: *Dump the drowners*

Don't leave buckets full of water or cleaning solutions out around very young children. A small child can drown in a few inches of water. Keep toddlers away from automatic washers and dryers, too.

RULE #8: *Trash savvy*

Taking out the garbage is a good chore for children, but garbage in a wheeled plastic can or other secure and/or closed container is a better bet for this. Garbage in plastic bags alone can contain dangerous things like broken glass, sharp bones, and protruding metal things—plus kids will drag the bag and tear it, spilling garbage everywhere. Don't let kids snoop in garbage. Any trash-carrying to the road needs to be supervised.

RULE #9: *They're not toys*

Never let kids use cleaning gear to play with, such as using spray bottles for squirt guns, riding on vacuums, etc.

Don't give them any vacuum crevice tools or edge cleaner attachments to use unless they have a notch in them for safety and you are supervising. Kids can and will hold attachments like these up to their eye while the vacuum is running and serious damage can result.

SAFE CLEANING JOBS ANY CHILD CAN DO

Sweep
Mop
Make beds
Dust
Remove cobwebs

Put their dirty clothes in the hamper. You can also give each child in the family a different colored pillowcase to hang on the inside of his closet door, and use as a laundry bag for dirty clothes.

Sort and fold their own clothes after they've been washed and dried, and then put them away.

Help sort and match socks, fold washcloths and towels.

Sort things and put them in order (books, videotapes, toys, shoes, etc.) Sorting helps young children build their cognitive skills.

Sweeping or hosing off the patio or sidewalk.

Cutting Kiddie Clutter

With most children's rooms, clutter can be a bigger problem than cleaning.

The old "one doll or train for Christmas" was over in 1949. Kids today have at least 75 percent more toys (and other things) than they need. Working parents with guilty consciences and more money than brains will enroll and engulf their kids in all sorts of things, raising the clutter high water mark to record level in no time. We give kids things to compensate, regulate, and sedate them. Kids get even more gifts and things at divorce time or when parents are having trouble parenting. Even a fast food trip has become a fast junking one now!

The kids are at a real disadvantage when it comes to dejunking their rooms. They have us for an example. They've watched us and been taught by us to keep on getting stuff and stacking it on the shelf and under the bed, and when the drawers and containers (and garage and storage shed) are full, they've gone with us to get more drawers and containers! We've even reprimanded them for using perfectly good junk storage boxes to make pirate ships and hideouts!

You are the one who gave most of this to them, or encouraged them in it, and you are the parent, so you have the legal and moral right to reduce it, too! Most of us would agree on the following:

1. Kids need very little to be happy.
2. Except for the famous security blanket or favorite teddy bear, kids recover from the spiriting away of most things in about ten minutes.
3. Big clutterfests aren't necessary for every event in their lives (they don't need a major birthday party every year).
4. The less there is to scatter, the less gets scattered.
5. Kids are better than us at keeping memories without a whole shelf of mementos.

KNOWN AND PROVEN ROOM FILLERS AND HOUSE WRECKERS:

Anything with batteries

Cards of any kind—once opened they end up all over

Broken or wrapperless crayons

Anything they still have an old one of (now there are two ball mitts to tend, though they can only use one at a time)

Fast-food meals that contain a toy (that kids collect and soon tire of)

Food and drink in areas not designed for it (it is sure to be spilled, spattered, or scattered)

Pets that don't get enough attention

Stickers

Little statues or figurines

Cheap junky electronic toys (watches, calculators, radios)

Automated toys with broken or missing parts

Junk bunkers (elaborate toy "organizing" boxes or shelves, fire truck parking garages in which nothing is ever parked, etc. Things that tend to just collect and harbor more junk, or become clutter themselves.)

Prizes and giveaways (from stores, birthday parties, fairs, circuses, trips to the zoo, etc.)

Half-completed paper projects, such as half-used coloring books

Big stuff (such as tricycles or motorbikes) kept in their rooms. Don't store large things, outdoor equipment, or seldom used stuff in a kid's room. Take it to the garage—have a place in the garage for their stuff too, such as sports equipment. Otherwise kids use it for a short season and then it remains in their room kicking around, taking up room for the next nine months.

Cut the source!

Kiddie clutter cures

- Get rid of the stuff you saved for them! Most of this they would never want. I'd flush this away first... fast!
- Practice regular rotation (but make sure no kids are around when you do it, because

like us they will automatically cling to anything you want to take). Gather up the playthings that have fallen out of favor and box those babies and pack or hide them away for the next generation, or at least the next couple of months.

- Many parents have semiannual kid dejunking days: Before birthdays and before Christmas to clear out the old, the broken, and the outgrown, and make way for the new.

- From my daughter Laura: "We have a shelf for each child in the main part of the house, near the kitchen. This is "their shelf" and they know it. When I find something of theirs around the house I don't run it to their room or yell at them, I just put it on their shelf. When they lose something they know to go to their shelf first—it's often there. When they come in from school they put their homework, shoes, and so on, there. This has eliminated tons of clutter, and hours of hunting and distress over lost items. Once every few weeks we clean the shelf to the bone, throwing away useless things and putting away the rest."

- When your child's room gets overrun with junk, take the time to clean it out with him or her. While the two of you are sorting through and eliminating things that are broken or no longer of interest, try to remember what these things cost and help the child decide whether they were worth it. This may slow down the collection of other expensive, worthless things in the future.

- Make sure you give them a place. Many of us don't stop to think that a kid's room has to be his or her whole house. We only allow them one room, so it's really a combined sleeping and recreation area, living room, hobby shop, dining room, and storage area—no wonder it's cluttered. Make sure they have space and a clearly defined place to put it all—toys, clothes, games and books, computer stuff, art and craft supplies.

A FEW IDEAS HERE

Multipart playthings: Store in clear plastic sweater or shoe boxes or plastic dishpans on shelves, one for each set.

Toys in general: Put a toy box in every major play area, such as each kid's room and the family room. You could even use something that matches the decor in non-kid rooms, but if you do make sure it's fitted with special (safety) toy box hinges.

Stuffed animals: The nets (such as Pet Net and Teddy Bed) that you hang across the corner of the room do a good job of getting these hard-to-stack critters up and out of the way. If your child doesn't really play with stuffed animals, you could consider just getting rid of most of them.

Bathroom toys: A zippered net lingerie bag is great, with a suction cup on a hook stuck right through it. Or you can hang the bag over the faucet or shower head.

Children's hair accessories or any tiny things with great clutter potential: Little plastic chests with divided drawers, or a fishing tackle box or the like.

Schoolwork clutter: We can't just throw it all away, it's their precious handiwork. But if you let those papers just pile up or try to keep them all, you'll soon be buried.

Get a large plastic container for each child, and put their name on it. As those school papers, projects, report cards, and so on flow back from school, winnow them down to the better, more important, or interesting ones, and put them in the child's container. When the child grows up, give his container to him (after removing the dozen or whatever things that are most precious to you), so he can save what he still wants.

Books: Built-in bookcases with shelves divided into narrow (about twelve-inch) sections are best for holding up those skinny kid's books. Far better than bookends, which are forever falling over.

Art supplies: Crayons, markers, brushes, scissors, etc., fit neatly and compactly into one of those lazy-Susan-like artist's bins available at art-supply stores.

Is it mean to ask kids to clean?

Finally, let me dispel any hint of abuse or cruelty on our part in requiring kids to clean. Cleaning isn't hard, and it isn't an option in life, it's a necessity. Teaching children discipline isn't an act of revenge or way of torturing them, it is their only salvation in the 10,000-paths world of the new century. Those who cannot or will not obey the rules and control their own habits will not survive to be happy, productive adults. I've known hundreds of people who had to work or "do chores" at home when they were children, and even go through some tough times of not getting everything they wanted or thought they needed. All of them— one hundred percent of them—now look back at those early days with pleasure and thankfulness for what this did for them.

CHAPTER 9

Quick Cleaning Room By Room

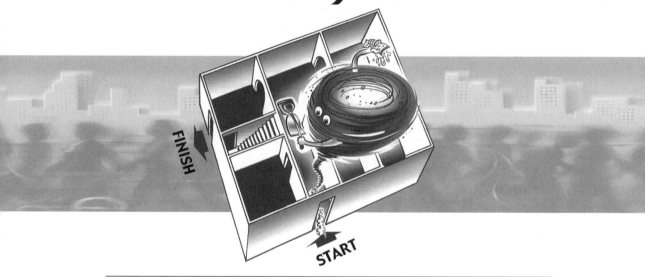

FINISH

START

We are all battling "too much" and "too busy" today, and the following can help you fit the necessary care of your dwelling into a tighter schedule. Here is how to clean your way quickly through the house, like the professionals do. The cleaning of every room can be reduced to a simple routine that only takes minutes. Our goal in this streamlined cleaning system is to go through the whole house in less than two hours and do a good job.

This trip through the house, alone or with one of the family, is fun and fast and easy and the house will look good afterward. Eventually there will come the time and need to pull out the stops and do some deeper cleaning. But if you keep the place up as you go, that will come at three- to five-year intervals, and not the old once-a-year spring cleaning bash.

Before we start, go get your cleaning kit and a pad of paper and pencil, to note any little repairs that need to be made or other things that need attention as you go along. If you don't write them down you'll forget them and end up fighting the aftermath someday when you're behind and busy. All kinds of inspirations and "should dos" will come into your mind while you're cleaning—almost as many as when you're taking a shower!

If you have any questions about the tools and techniques mentioned in this chapter, see the Quick Cleaning Guide (Chapter Ten).

The first thing to do

Is to make a quick trip through all of the parts of the house you intend to clean, and "police" and "trash" them. These are the pro terms for emptying the wastebaskets and picking up any litter or left-behind things, from ball mitts and schoolbooks to Grandpa's glasses.

Policing is important because you don't want to pick up any "big stuff" with your vacuum. It's also very inefficient to be running back and forth from every room, as you clean it, to put out-of-place things back where they belong.

To police, get a plastic laundry basket or big sturdy box and gather up all the stray clothes, tools, toys, and other belongings—anything you find in a room that doesn't belong there. Once you have all this together, you can sort it out once and then make one trip to the kids' room, the kitchen, the laundry room, the garage, or wherever, to put everything away.

To trash, get a large garbage container and go from room to room, dumping the smaller trash containers into it. Pick up any trash just lying around, too, such as empty pizza boxes, pop cans, or the cardboard box the new Nintendo game arrived in. Then make a single trip to your trash bin or whatever with all of the accumulated garbage.

If you police and trash first, a lot of the cleaning will already be done by the time you tackle the individual areas. And you can do both of these operations in about fifteen minutes if you hustle.

ENTRYWAYS

Let's start with the entryways. These are highly visible parts of a home that get hard use, with all of the coming and going. Entryways are a place it really pays to do quick regular cleaning.

1. Dust the doors, light fixtures, and any railings with a lambswool duster, catching any cobwebs. Remove any bugs from the light fixtures.

2. Spot-clean any marks on the walls, doors (especially the area around the handle), light switches, etc. Remove any marks on the windows and door glass with a spray bottle of glass cleaner.

3. Vacuum the inside mat or shake it outside far enough from the entry that the dirt won't get tracked back in. If the floor is carpeted, vacuum it while doing the matting.

4. If it's a hard surface floor, sweep or vacuum it. Get up all of that grit, sand, gravel, and other debris that otherwise will just get tracked through the house. If the floor is soiled, mop after sweeping or vacuuming.

You should be able to quick-clean an entryway in five to six minutes.

BEDROOMS

I like to do the bedrooms early on, because they're the easiest. Bedrooms are more personal territory and generally not as dirty as the rest of the house. They require little cleaning if you just train the occupants (including yourself!) to keep the clothes hung up.

1. Do the beds first so stuff won't fall in them as you dust. Hopefully the occupant has some pride and backbone, so the bed is already made and clothing hung up. If not, and you are stuck doing others' work, make the bed and hang up the clothes, taking the dirty ones to the laundry room immediately.

   Our goal here is to only walk around the bed once while making it. Start at the head of the bed and pull the sheet up to the desired area. Then go to the foot of the bed and tuck in the sheet. Go to one side, tuck in and straighten. Repeat on the other side. Straighten top blanket, pillow or sham, and you're done! Practice this and you'll get it!

2. Bedrooms can harbor a lot of clutter, so notice it and remove any that can be removed quickly.

3. Now dust, working from high to low. Get the cobwebs out of the corners, on the door frames, tops of doors, and drapes. Then the

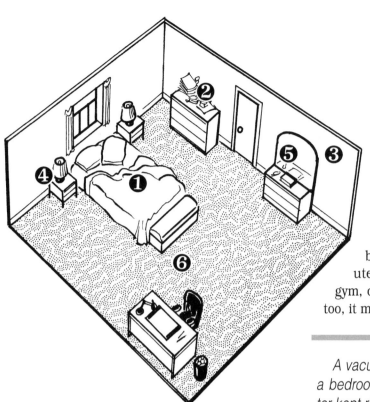

You should be able clean a bedroom in about eleven minutes, max. If you have a mini-gym, office, or sitting area in there, too, it may take a little longer.

A vacuum is the magic tool for a bedroom—often a small canister kept right in this room is worth it. It can do everything from dresser tops to floors to closets and drawers, even the daily fallout from footwear, and is sure death to the dust bunnies.

With a vacuum like this in one hand (carrying, not dragging it) and the vacuum's extension wand with a dust brush in the other, you can make an almost nonstop walk through the bedroom. Run the brush over the tops of the pictures, and down the drapes or curtains. Get the lampshades, the wall if it needs it, under the bed, around the headboard, and all the room corners. Don't forget to lightly vacuum the quilt or spread top—it gathers as much dust as the floor—and the windowsills where all those dead bugs are. I even hit the tops of the clothes hanging in the closet.

lamps or light fixtures, tops of mirrors, and the furniture tops. Dust right around any doilies or dresser scarves. As you dust down the wall to the floor get the bottoms of furniture and baseboards.

4. Straighten the headboard, nightstand, and dressing table as needed.

5. Use glass cleaner sprayed on a cleaning cloth to clean mirrors, telephones, and TV front, if any. Then use a spray bottle of all-purpose cleaner ("APC") to spot clean dresser tops and handles, the door frames, and any exercise equipment that might be in here.

6. The floor in here just needs a weekly cleaning.

Use a dustmop for hard floors.

For carpet, take a vacuum to the farthest corner of the room and vacuum your way out. Hit the traffic lanes and as far under the bed as you can reach.

LIVING ROOM

Living rooms are not used like they were in the past. Living rooms are becoming showrooms—mostly kept formal to impress, and for those special occasions of home entertaining that many of us are too busy to have any more. The living room usually has nice furniture and too many decorations, and the kids don't spend much time here these days.

Any fireplaces in modern living rooms are seldom lit, or they are largely self-cleaning gas fueled units.

Limited use means a limited need for cleaning. Daily policing of this room can often be eliminated. Weekly dusting and vacuuming is generally sufficient. People also eat less in here than before, so spot and spill cleanup is less of a problem.

Some caution is called for here when it comes to polishing furniture. Most living room furniture made in recent years is designed to hold out soils—the fabric is treated with soil retardant, and the wood has multiple coats of clear protective finish. So it doesn't need constant coats of "polish" of any kind.

FAMILY ROOM

Here is a room added to or off the kitchen that has largely replaced the old living room for home activities. This is where the "gang" hangs out, the center of between-meal eating, and of course our central entertainment center, complete with TV, video games, a home library, study area, fish tanks, and temporary pass-through "storage" of everything. The family room is used more hours a day than any other room, and gets more spots and spills than the rest of the house combined.

The thing to be careful of here is that the liberties allowed in the family room don't carry over to the rest of the house. This is an area that needs daily if not hourly policing and cleanup—a policy of "pick up and put away as you pass."

QUICK-CLEANING THE LIVING ROOM AND FAMILY ROOM

1. If you find any food here, take it to the kitchen immediately.
2. Then pick up and replace the things left out or down, such as magazines, tapes, and TV remotes.
3. Straighten chairs, recliners, cushions, framed pictures, and the like.
4. Now dust everything, working from top to bottom. Don't forget the tops of pictures, screens of TVs or computers, baseboards, and legs of furniture. If there are blinds on the windows be sure to dust them every so often with a lambswool duster.
5. Next, grab a spray bottle of APC and a terry cleaning cloth and hit the handprints on the walls, any on the furniture, and even the doorknobs and under the edges of tables and railings where you can't see the dirt and soil. Clean any spots on the carpet, too, especially in the area of recliners, TVs, and sound systems (see Spot Removal

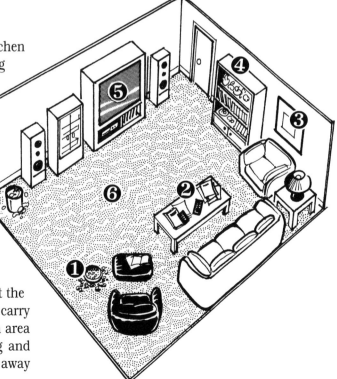

chart on the back cover). With glass cleaner, spot clean the windows and any other glass.

6. Now vacuum any upholstered furniture and then vacuum the carpets or sweep the floor of the living room/family room. When vacuuming, give the traffic areas a double or triple pass and just quickly zoom over the nontraffic areas. The edges and under and behind things don't have to be done more than once a month or so.

It shouldn't take more than ten or twelve minutes to do a living room, and fifteen minutes or so to do a family room, unless it has a lot of decorations.

Red relief: We pros used to say about stains, "If it's red, you're dead!" There is now (finally!) a stain remover especially for these toughest of all stains. You apply it generously to the cherry Kool-Aid or whatever spill, and lay a damp cloth over it. Then you set an iron heated to 300 degrees on it for twenty seconds, and by "heat exchange" it will pull out the stain. There are various brands of this product... I use one called Juice Out.

OFFICE

The office is a new room in many modern homes. Computers (notice the plural), printers, copiers, and faxes are almost as common in the home as in businesses today. Offices are created from spare bedrooms and remodelled basements and garages, as well as being built in as a bona fide part of many new homes, and they need cleaning, too. But it won't take you more than ten minutes, if you keep the clutter down. With the exception of the office equipment, cleaning a home office is no different than cleaning a bedroom.

1. Offices need dusting almost daily, because of all that paper dust and all those electronics. Just spend the time you would take to do the bed to dust or vacuum the equipment. Clean computer screens and the like with glass cleaner sprayed onto a clean soft cloth.

2. Now follow steps 2 through 6 as outlined under Bedrooms: remove obvious clutter, straighten furnishings, spot-clean glass and furnishings, dust the rest of the room, and dustmop or vacuum the floor.

3. Offices, at home and away, are filled with our modern clutter enemy #1: Paper. The deluge of modern communications will bury the best housekeeper if it is not controlled and kept cleared. A good way to do this is to sort through it all and divide it into four categories:

> **Out**—unneeded and unwanted things—recycle or trash them.

> **Route**—anything not yours or that might be of interest to others, move it out or on to them now.

> **Doubt**—if you're not quite sure what it is, or need to think about it or check on it further, drop it into a Doubt box. The unbendable rule of this box is that you work on it every single day until all of the doubts are resolved and it's empty, right down to the bare cardboard.

> **Sprout**—file anything that is truly worth saving—**now!**

HALL

Halls are the highways of our home, so we want to be sure to keep them clear of clutter (usually large objects that were on their way somewhere else). Our other main cleaning concern in halls is dirt and marks from passing hands and feet.

1. Dust top to bottom: ceilings, walls, cobwebs, wall decorations, light fixtures, door frames, any furniture, baseboards.

2. Spot clean to remove wall marks, and don't forget the door frames and light switches.

3. Clean glass on wall hangings, mirrors, and the like.

4. Vacuum or sweep the floor. When vacuuming, bear in mind that the whole hall is a traffic area! Before you start, sweep anything off the edges with a broom.

You should be able to hustle through a hallway in under five minutes.

KIDS' ROOMS

All of the ordinary housecleaning approaches can generally be applied to child-occupied domains, but there are some special things to be aware of here:

1. Children cover "their ground" more often and intensely than the average adult or teenager, so there are more sticky food smears, crumbs, crusts, spills, and other food mess here. Child areas need more spot-cleaning than the rest of the house, and need regular policing for food mess that will soon grow mold or mushrooms.

2. The other thing you can always count on in a child's room is plenty of black marks on walls and floor. Get these with a dampened white nylon scrub sponge—don't scrub too hard, though, or you'll take off more than you intended.

3. Anything that gets frequent hand or mouth contact (crib and playpen rails, high chair trays, etc.) needs to be washed and wiped dry. For this you want an all-purpose, not a disinfectant cleaner.

4. The heavily used parts of big toys like riding toys and plastic playhouses need cleaning, too. Most of these can be washed just like a countertop.

5. Floors that people not only walk on, but toddlers crawl, lay, and sit on, should be cleaned often, when the children are under three. Carpets should be spot-cleaned and shampooed as needed, and hard floors swept and mopped.

6. Periodically relieve the kids' rooms of outgrown and broken toys and toys that are out of favor, so there is at least a little clear space in here.

7. The rest of kids' room cleaning—pickup and putting away of all those toys, dusting, ordinary vacuuming or sweeping of the floor, floor mopping, and cleaning of any windows, you can and should leave to them (see Chapter Eight).

The time you spend in the kids' room will depend on how determined a delegator you are. If you get them to do what I've suggested above, you'll be out of there in ten minutes. Otherwise you'll probably spend twenty to thirty minutes in the junior jungle.

BATHROOMS

We have several bathrooms in each of our homes, and I generally do them all once I start on one of them. Most if not all of the materials you need to clean the bathroom should be under the sink in a caddy kept in each bathroom. Do this if you haven't already. Then all you need to take into the bathroom is your trash container. Always take a container around with you from room to room, don't run back and forth carrying trash containers to the garage. This is how we "trash" a commercial building. In containers that need a plastic liner (such as perhaps those in junior or senior citizens' rooms, or the craft room), I always drop three or four extra liners in the bottom of the can so that when the liner is full I can just pull it out instead of dumping it. An instant replacement is right there, saving a trip to the kitchen to get one.

If bathrooms are cleaned regularly, they can be cleaned in five minutes or less.

1. First dust the bathroom. Dust here before you vacuum or clean because any spray or moisture from cleaning that gets on the dust will "mud" it.

2. Take a good look at the floor. There are always bits of torn paper, lids, empty bottles, and other fallout from medications and cosmetics. A lot of the cosmetic maintenance stuff men and women use in a bathroom falls off the counter onto the floor, and finding it when you mop or vacuum isn't the best thing.

3. Spray a cloth with glass cleaner and wipe the mirror, and whisk any hair or whiskers out of the sink with a piece of damp toilet paper.

4. Now do the sink itself, the counter/vanity top, and the sink hardware, using a bottle of disinfectant cleaner to give things a light spray, then polishing them dry with the cleaning cloth. If you hit a bit of stubborn soil, use the nylon side of a white scrub sponge on it. Spray a little ahead of yourself, so the cleaner has a chance to dissolve the soil.

If disinfecting is a real concern, saturate the area or article well with disinfectant cleaner and leave it on for ten minutes before wiping it away.

5. Move to the tub and shower walls, and do them the same way.

6. When you reach the toilet, squirt some cleaner on your swab and swish it around the bowl. Then spray and buff the outside of the toilet (which is usually dirtier than the inside), working from top to bottom. Be sure to get all sides, as well as the seat and lid. Then wipe up around the bowl with your cleaning cloth, which is now damp with disinfectant cleaner, and put the cloth in the laundry.

7. Now spray and wipe the rest of the floor, and you're finished.

There is usually little deep cleaning needed in a bathroom, except for the old hardwater fight. You won't have a big hardwater fight in the bathroom if you do this quick cleanup process regularly. If you have a hardwater ring, stain, or buildup problem, see page 178.

When you're doing your quick regular cleaning this is not the time to dejunk, but remember bathrooms are another junk magnet in a house. So when you're doing your daily grooming and getting ready in here, dejunk something. Toss some empties or aged-out stuff as you go along and you'll never have to break your cleaning stride to dejunk. Stopping during the regular run-through to dejunk, fix, or find something can derail the most efficient cleaner.

FOR QUICKER TUB CLEANING:

The infamous tub "ring" (composed of soap scum, dirt, and hardwater minerals) that builds up in a tub will do so much faster in older or worn tubs, and is harder to remove from them. The key to quick tub cleaning is removal of the dirt while it's fresh, even while the bath water is still spiralling down the drain. A swipe around the sides of the tub with a white scrub sponge will generally loosen any dirt deposited there and allow it to be flushed away.

For a once-a-month approach, spray the entire inside of the tub with a good shower-scum remover like Showers-n-Stuff or liquid Comet Bathroom Cleaner, let it sit on there for five minutes or so, and then lightly scrub the surface while it's still wet with a white nylon scrub sponge. Add water from the tub spout as you scrub and the grime will float away. A touch with your fingertips will tell you when all the crud is gone!

A DELICATE SUBJECT...
BUT WE MEN HAVE TO DO BETTER

Alas, even here in the new century we are still faced with the problem of men and boys missing the toilet.

What can we do about this "overspray?"

1. Making men and boys conscious of this problem is what helps the most. And they should do all the toilet cleaning—period! This will give them some solid motivation not to miss. Give them the tools they need and show them how to do it, and inspect their work afterward. Teaching them how will eliminate, "Well, they won't do it right so I'll just do it myself."

2. Some housekeepers I know ask the males in the household to sit instead of stand. It eliminates the problem, and gives the guys an opportunity to tuck in their shirt once in a while!

3. When you spray-clean the toilet with disinfectant cleaner, spray it heavily, and leave the cleaner on there for several minutes, even as long as ten minutes. This will provide the "kill time" needed to destroy odor and the bacteria that cause it. After you wipe the cleaner off, spray these areas again lightly with the cleaner and allow it to dry on there. You can also use bacteria/enzyme cleaner (see p. 181) around the base of the toilet.

4. If you do the above and the bathroom still smells, make sure you've cleaned ALL of the possible problem areas, including not just the outside of the toilet and the floor nearby, but the walls and side of the tub if nearby, any baseboards nearby, the shower curtain, bath rug, baseboard heater, and the clever holder for spare rolls of toilet paper that sits beside the john....

5. If you've cleaned thoroughly and still have odor problems, a worn toilet bowl gasket may be leaking sewage into the subfloor. Have a plumber check it out.

6. Especially if you have this problem, hard flooring is what you want in bathrooms, not carpet!

LAUNDRY/UTILITY ROOM

I like to hit the laundry or utility room just before the kitchen, because if there is any backup of things to deal with or discover—lost or found, or ruined and hid—you'll find them here. I'd consider keeping a cleaning caddy of supplies in the utility room, too.

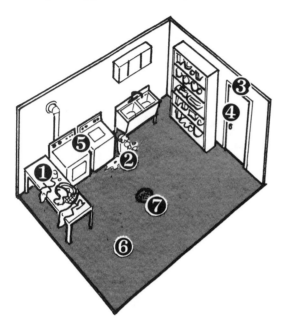

1. There is always plenty of clutter in a laundry room. Such as new products that didn't work, pocket fallout, questionable or on the way out things (worn-out apparel, odd pillowcases, ripped sheets, and so on). Get rid of anything that can be gotten rid of quickly.

   Do the same with any un-put-away clean laundry.

2. This room will have more spillage than any other—usually powdered detergents and bleaches. Vacuum up the latter thoroughly to avoid "mysterious" permanent white spots in carpeting.

3. Don't dust in here, because most of the dust is stuck on surfaces due to all the moisture in the air in a laundry room. Instead of dusting take a cleaning cloth dampened in APC solution and give things a quick wipedown—counter, tops of door and window casings, windowsills, etc.

4. You can count on the door handles and switchplate areas needing some spot cleaning. Do this with APC after wiping off all the "dustable" surfaces.

5. Use glass cleaner to polish up the appliance tops and fronts, and spot-clean any windows.

6. Now vacuum the floor if it's carpeted—there will be plenty of lint from washing or drying, no matter how good your venting system is. If it's a hard floor, sweep it and then mop it quickly if it needs it, so that if clean clothes fall down there they'll still be clean!

7. If there is a floor drain pour in a pint of disinfectant cleaner solution every so often, to keep the trap full of water and free of odor.

You should be able to quick-clean a utility room in ten minutes.

KITCHEN

On to the kitchen now. By now you should be on a roll, plus there is a food reward here if you're feeling the need of further energy.

The kitchen is always the last place I do, for several reasons. This is where we bring things to be cleaned or emptied, where we wash things out and fill buckets and spray bottles, rinse mops. It's also where we come for breaks and phone calls. If we clean it first someone (maybe even us) is sure to come in here while we're cleaning the rest of the house and dirty it.

Kitchens can look and seem intimidating, but the average kitchen can be cleaned in about twenty minutes.

QUICK KITCHEN CLEANING

1. The trash area has often been ignored. You emptied the trash earlier; now wipe the containers and the area around them, including the wall behind the can. There will usually be spots and smears here that need to be removed. A white nylon scrub sponge is great for this (wet it well first), as well as for getting up those little lumps of hardened food anywhere that were missed in

the hurry to get to work and school. If you come to a stubborn spot, wet it down or leave a damp sponge on it for a few minutes and you should be able to wipe it away.

To keep your kitchen "swabber" sweet-smelling:

We do a lot of wiping with a sponge or cloth in a kitchen—everything from cleaning off the table umpteen times a day to picking up spills, washing dishes, and wiping out the refrigerator. Ordinary sponges and dishcloths soon become sour-smelling and unsanitary. Take advantage of the sponges and scrub pads now made with built-in germ resistance. You can also put a sponge in the microwave for thirty seconds, or run it through the dishwasher, to sanitize it.

---

2. Now dust the high and low stuff in the kitchen (there is usually more overlooked high dust here). Insects love kitchens and cobwebs can appear overnight. Get the tops of things with a lambswool duster and then the window ledges. Don't forget the top of the fridge! For much of the kitchen a cloth dampened with dish detergent solution is the best duster. Buff dry right behind it with a clean, dry cloth.

3. Spray and wipe any spots or handprints on the stove, refrigerator, microwave, and cupboards. Don't forget the range hood, which is usually dusty if not greasy, and those smudge-collecting small appliances.

Now wipe the counter—starting at the back and moving canisters and the like out of the way. Wipe, then replace them as you go.

Clean ALL areas of the sink now, including around and behind the faucet(s) and corners and rims and ledges. Marks from pots and pans and the like can usually be removed with a wet white nylon scrub sponge. Avoid the use of powdered cleansers on sinks whenever possible.

Finish up with the tabletop and chair seats.

4. Windows right above a sink usually need attention. If you have large windows in the kitchen and they seem dirty overall, run some dish detergent solution into the sink so you can squeegee them off quickly. Otherwise just use a spray bottle of glass cleaner to remove the sink overspray, kid prints, and flyspecks.

5. The floor is the biggie here. You can't clean a kitchen floor too often. Sweep, vacuum, or dustmop the floor and then give it a damp mopping. I use the mini-mop head of a Scrubbee Doo (see p. 157), which can be rinsed in the sink in seconds. This is the easiest way to clean a kitchen floor in a hurry.

6. Now while the kitchen floor is drying, take out all of the accumulated trash, to be moved out to the street on trash day.

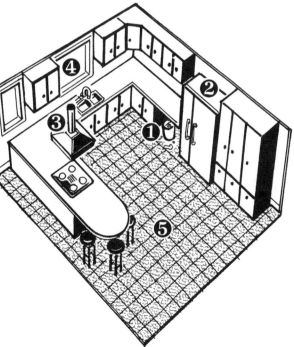

We're finished with our quick cleanup of the house now, and if you come and visit me at my low-maintenance home in Hawaii, and follow suit, you'll be able to do all this in far less time. Beating the cleaning clock is possible these days, especially if you remember the biggest success word in cleaning—NOW!

Quick-Cleaning Up, Down, and Outside

Not every home has an attic, basement, garage, or yard, but if you do have them, here is a concise guide to keeping them clean and clutter-free.

ATTIC

If you have one of these (which may be extinct before the end of the 21st century):

1. DEJUNK! Remember that forty percent of all housework is unnecessary work caused by junk and clutter.

   But do keep the memories! Spend a Sunday or two here and redistribute the worthwhile stuff to a better place—somewhere it will get used and viewed!

   Be careful what you decide to store here—most attics are hot, hot, HOT!

2. Decades worth of dust often collects in attics. Cleaning it up is a good project for a youngster anxious to earn some cash. First do all of the high dusting, including the rafters, any exposed insulation, and cobwebs (you want to **vacuum** up that dust, not just whisk it around).

3. Now do the mid-height and low dusting, and clean any windows with glass cleaner.

4. Vacuum or sweep last. Don't sweep with big, wide strokes if the room is really dirty—you'll just spread soil around.

5. To prevent pest problems, set off a "bug bomb" up here once a year.

BASEMENT

New basements—Modern engineering and building codes have eliminated most of the old basement problems. And if a basement is finished it can be cleaned the same, using the same tools and techniques, as the rest of the house. If it's an unfinished basement in a new house: seal the concrete floor to eliminate dust bleeding and allow easy cleaning. Then don't use this nice new space to store junk!

Old basements—Check walls for cracks and seepage. Arranging for more air circulation and light will retard mildew and the creepier varieties of insect. You can also install a dehumidifier if necessary. Cleaning the concrete floor well, and then sealing it, will eliminate the endless chore of sweeping up concrete dust.

BASEMENT BASICS:

1. Check out basements and other out-of-the-way storage areas in your regular cleaning route through the house, maybe not to do any cleaning, but strictly as a monitoring measure and security precaution. All kinds of things can go wrong in a basement or storage area—leaks, explosions of canned goods, thievery, college kids sneaking in more junk when we weren't looking, rodent and insect damage, snakes taking up residence, etc. Just because it's out of sight, don't let it be out of mind. Walk through areas like this and look and sniff and listen.

2. Get rid of all that old junk—anything you don't need or that has rotted, rusted, mildewed, and so on, into uselessness. Then store anything worthwhile you do store down here in nice plastic containers or closeable cupboards and shelves instead of old crumbly cardboard boxes.

3. Dust the basement from top to bottom with a sturdy canister or wet/dry vac.

4. Clean any windows with a spray bottle of glass cleaner. There are usually enough fly-specks and spider droppings on cellar windows to call for more than one spray and wipe.

5. Vacuum the floor, and mop it if necessary.

6. If you have a seldom-used drain in a basement or garage, put a bit of disinfectant cleaner into a half-bucket of water, and pour it down there, once a month or so. This will flush out and replace the old liquid in the drain. When drains sit unused for a while the water in the "s" trap (which is what keeps sewer odors from coming up into a room) turns rancid or evaporates, causing a bad smell.

GARAGE

Most houses built before the 1940's didn't have garages, and even in the 1950's many had only carports. But then suddenly the garage became as important as the house. Not as a place for the car, as first anticipated, but for the sleds, skis, mowers, bikes, trikes, hoses, garden tools, barbecue grills, lawn chairs, the workshop and the leftover construction stuff and unfinished projects and accumulated garage sale inventory, coming and going!

The garage became so important that designers and builders invented the two-car garage. Now there'd be a place for all of that and for the car, too... wrong again! More house overflow soon filled garage number two. As we move into the new century, three-car garages are everywhere and four-car garages not uncommon. Garage debris and house fallout is usually clogging them, too. Plus the garage is often he-man territory and that is usually a strike against it in the cleanliness department.

How can we achieve the "impossible dream" of a clean and neat garage?

1. I see no point in attempting to convince you that only cars belong in the garage, because all the above-mentioned home appendages have to go somewhere and the garage may be the most logical place. It's

okay to keep worthwhile things here, but not any useless, broken junk. Keeping the garage totally dejunked—keeping only "good stuff" in it—is the #1 secret of a low-maintenance garage that looks good and can be used for the things it was intended to be used for.

2. Hang up tools and equipment and everything else that can be hung here. Shelving is another good way to keep things off the floor. Open shelves, however, collect dust, and are not usually a thing of beauty to behold. For a bit of money and many years of blessings, find, make, or buy cabinets or shelving with doors or drawers—so that nothing you are storing shows. That alone will make garage storage much more serviceable and cut down cleaning. Anyplace a pile can be seen, people will pile more on it—even a workbench needs to be enclosed.

A few tools hung out in the open is fine, but paint, nails, rolls of wire, weed sprays, fertilizer, all that sloppy stuff needs to be out of sight.

3. Put dirt-, mud-, and grease-catching mats at both ends of the garage, where people come in from the outside and where they enter the house.

4. Seal the garage floor with clear concrete sealer. Sealing fills the pores of the floor, stops constant dust bleeding, and gives the floor a shiny finish. It will look wonderful, resist stains, and make dripped oil or dog doo easy to clean off. You'll also be able to sweep or dustmop the floor twice as fast.

5. Put a couple of sturdy trash containers in the garage, in handy places. Use the lidded type with a door that flips back after the trash goes in to keep out pets, rodents, and flies.

6. Have the tools and chemicals you need to clean the garage and the car right there, and easily accessible. This is a great place to keep big cleaning equipment and extra cleaning supplies for the house, too.

7. Don't leave the garage with bare 2x4's and other rough construction showing. Finish the walls and ceiling with sheetrock or tile and paint them with a good enamel and the garage will look and feel like another room in the house. It will be treated better and junked and dirtied less.

A garage will be easy to keep neat and clean if it's set up this way.

Cleaning our home on wheels

We spend hours a day in our vehicles, not just driving but eating, drinking, smoking, being entertained, sleeping, and working in them (many vehicles are mobile offices, complete with phones and faxes). The fallout from people and things, in such a restricted space—an average of 30 square feet—becomes visible much faster than a little dirt or clutter in a 3000 sq. ft. home!

Keeping a car clean inside and out will enhance its value even more than changing the oil faithfully. It also helps prevent accidents, not to mention what it does for our self-image!

KEEPING CAR INTERIORS CLEAN

THE TRASH—You can continue to be amazed how much trash is generated inside a vehicle, or commit yourself to keeping it removed. Clever little sacks and waste containers have been invented to collect car garbage, but they aren't big enough, and they don't stay put. Before long they themselves are part of the clutter.

The simple solution is to detrash your car every time you get out of it, whenever you make a stop, anywhere. This way there is only a handful of trash to gather up, and nothing will ever accumulate.

P.S. Only dejunk the car into a waste container—dumping litter onto a roadside or parking lot is worse than keeping it in there with you!

The DASH—and all its dials and knobs is a target for dust, so keep an electrostatic dustcloth in the glove box and use it regularly. Dust dashboards dry, not wet. If you wet-wipe a dusty dash you'll just create mud that's hard to get rid of. I use a tiny squirt of window cleaner on a clean cloth, after the dash is dusted.

HAND CONTACT AREAS—Clean the steering wheel and all handle areas regularly with a cloth dampened with APC—you'll find plenty of dirt and hand oil here.

SPOTS AND SPILLS—There more spills in cars than at parties or when you have kids over. Both the hard and soft surfaces in cars today are tough and resistant surfaces, and most things can be removed easily, if you do so **immediately.**

Carry a spray bottle of APC, a plastic scraper, and a couple of cleaning towels in the trunk of your car. When a spill happens, blot up or scrape off the worst of it, then spray the area with cleaning solution and blot dry. Take further measures when you get home if necessary.

Vinyl seatcovers and interior trim such as the plastic inside facing of the doors often get black marks and smudges. A white scrub sponge wet with APC will remove most of these, and any remaining ones can be dissolved with paint thinner or tar remover.

Car's best friend:

the vacuum—use it! OFTEN!

Car's worst enemy:

transporting things that should be hauled in a truck.

VACUUM—A vacuum cleaner used regularly is your vehicle's best friend. Feet and clothes pick up sand, dirt, mud, grass, gravel, and lint, and much of this is left behind in the car. Using the small upholstery head of a canister vac, do the floor and seats (and under the seats), moving slowly to give the vacuum time to pull out the grit and debris. Get out that seldom-used crevice tool and use it, too, because everything from M&M's to pine needles to crumbs and coins will find its way into nooks and crevices where the regular snout of a vacuum can't reach. Don't forget the rear window ledge and the trunk.

Anything you can take out of a car to clean it, such as the floor mats or car seats, do it!

ELIMINATING ODORS—Forget the perfume sprays and hanging strips meant to mask odors. Odors come from bacteria of some kind, such as the bacteria that will grow in spilled milk, or upchuck not promptly or properly cleaned up. Everything from dead mice to month-old lunches and long-deceased fishing worms have been found in vehicles, and things like pieces of dead possum from the roadway can get lodged under a car. So if you notice any bad odors take a good look around and find the **source** of the odor and eliminate it.

Removing entrenched smoke odor or the odor of longtime mildew growth can be difficult, and is best done by an expert who knows the right chemicals to use. Before you commit yourself to an expensive deodorizing method, however, let mother nature have a shot at it. Leave the doors open on a sunny, breezy day. You'll be amazed how much odor can be dispelled this way.

CLEANING CAR EXTERIORS

When you're washing the car by hand at home, there are some new and easier ways. There are car washing brushes out there now, for instance, with a five- or six-foot hollow handle that screws onto an ordinary garden hose. This means you can fill up a bucket with APC solution, dip the brush into the solution, and lightly scrub the entire car. Give the so-

lution a minute or two to work, and then, **while the surface is still wet,** switch on the water to whatever pressure you want and run over the whole car with the brush again. The bristles continue to scrub, and the water pouring out through the brush gives the car a good rinse. Best of all you are standing six or more feet back out of the way of splashes and puddles. The brush gets into all the cracks and crevices and ridges on a car body, and doesn't snag like cloths and sponges do.

Never wash a car in the hot sun—the solution will dry too quickly and leave streaks. Do it in the morning, late afternoon, or evening, or on a cloudy day.

If you want a perfect finish, a clean towel or chamois run over the car after the final rinse will leave it bright and shiny.

Car exterior checklist

WINDOWS—A quick-drying window cleaner like Windex and a cloth is best. This will quickly remove both the road film on the outside, and fingermarks on the inside of car windows.

When they're washing the whole car, most people use too much soap on windows and it leaves streaks behind when it dries. When a car window is wiped dry, it almost never streaks, as long as you use a clean cloth for the wiping.

MIRRORS—Whether you've sprayed window cleaner on them, or run the whole car through the wash, be sure to wipe mirrors dry with a clean cloth. Otherwise any streaks or residue will be all too apparent on that highly reflective surface!

HEAD AND TAIL LIGHTS—Be sure to give the headlight lenses, especially, a good scrub while you're washing the car exterior—dirty, bug-encrusted headlights can really cut down your night vision.

WHITEWALLS—Scrub them with APC solution and a nylon pad, and rinse well. For stubborn soil, a wet, soapy steel wool pad such as SOS works well, as do the bleaching cleaners sold for whitewalls.

VINYL TOPS—Find out the manufacturer's recommendation, or clean them like you do the rest of the car, just spend more time scrubbing and rinsing here. As the elements attack and dry out vinyl over time, it becomes porous, and thus more easily soiled and harder to clean.

After the top is clean, I'd visit the local auto parts place and get not just any old ordinary, but their best vinyl top restorer or coating. What products like these do is give a temporary, but valuable, new protective coating to the vinyl. A surface protectant such as Beauty Seal can also be used to give new life to old tops.

CHROME—When cleaning chrome, be careful to do nothing to harm that shining surface. So wet it well with APC, and leave it on there a minute or two to soften the bug bodies and the like. Do any scrubbing while the surface is wet with the solution (never dry, which might scratch it). Then rinse and buff dry with a cleaning cloth. Tar can be removed with paint thinner or tar remover.

The "chrome cleaners" widely available work well, but like all metal polishes they remove a little of the surface each time you use them. Overuse will eventually thin the chrome plating.

OTHER TRIM—Go easy when cleaning the aluminum trim on many cars today, or the trim that is actually plastic coated to look like metal. Don't use colored nylon scrub pads on any car surface except tires—they will scratch!

VANS—Today have lots of rugs and plush upholstery that can get grungy after months or years of active family use and hauling. Consider having a local carpet cleaner clean these professionally, for your next "spring vehicle cleanup."

FINAL PREVENTIVES:

Kids, eating and drinking on the move, and hauling things are the big three beaters-up of cars, but all three of these are also important to our enjoyment of life and often to our ability to get things done. So deciding on your own personal set of "do's and don'ts"—rules—is even more important for the car than it is for your home. Setting clear standards for what can and can't be done in the car is the easiest way to keep your rolling home as clean as you want or need it to be.

OUTSIDE CLEANING

When "housework" or "housecleaning" is mentioned, most of us immediately think of things inside the house. But what gets dirtier than things outside? And the outside of our home is at least a hundred times more visible to others!

So grab a "policing" basket or bucket and a broom and circle the outside of the house. It only takes a few minutes to pick up what's blown onto the lawn or into the bushes.

Now spot-sweep the porch and/or steps where needed, and sweep off the mats or empty the Astroturf onto the lawn (good nutrition for the lawn here!).

While you're at it, pull out those few weeds that sprang up in the sidewalk cracks and between the rosebushes. With the broom you can sweep down any cobwebs or hornets' nests out here. Be sure to write down any broken things you notice or repairs that need doing, or things that need to be checked out, just in case. Now return the broom and bucket to

the garage and dump the litter you've collected into a garbage container.

A QUICK APPROACH TO EXTERIOR CLEANING

I cleaned home exteriors professionally for thirty years, and our concerns here included:
1. The house itself—siding of all kinds, roofs and gutters, wooden trim, windows, shutters, chimneys, foundations
2. Steps and sidewalks
3. Patios and decks
4. Fences and railings of all kinds
5. Driveways
6. Storage buildings
7. Garages

These things had all kinds of soil on them: mud and sand, cobwebs and bug deposits, airborne and road-splattered dirt, smog and smoke, algae and mildew, hardwater stains, tree sap, bird nests and droppings, garden chemical overspray, old holiday decorations, and more.

During this time I invented scaffolding and ladder arrangements, and long-handled brush and sponge contraptions that would stagger your imagination. The costs, and risks of life and limb, were often considerable. It was hard work as well, and on things like stucco and brick soiled from drifting railroad diesel smoke or local manufacturing plants, it was almost impossible to do a good job. Worst of all, in that whole thirty years I don't think I ever made a profit!

Put the pressure on (and take some pressure off) cleaning!

If there is one new cleaning tool and method every homeowner should consider taking advantage of, it is pressure washing—that is, using water under pressure as an aid in cleaning. A pressure washer will cut your outdoor cleaning time and remove dirt and debris from exterior surfaces that have plagued you for years… if not a lifetime.

I do the outside of my own homes today, all three of them, with no scaffolding, no dangerous chemicals, and no help. I do it quickly and "dirt cheap" and the entire place looks great afterward. How do I do it? With a pressure washer. On all of the surfaces mentioned above, and other outside places, a pressure washer will remove about ninety percent of the soil. Some stubborn oily spots or graffiti may need pretreatment with chemical spotter from a janitorial store. And you may have to deal with those obsolete holiday decorations yourself. But for the rest, you can just hook that little unit up and pull the trigger!

Thirty years ago only service stations and a few other businesses had pressure washers. Ten years ago we pro cleaners had just found out how to use them to cut cleaning time and cost. Today pressure washers are more efficient and safer than ever, and made in sizes and strengths suitable for home use. They're available all over, and the price is down from the old $2000 range to $200+.

These little units are not much bigger or heavier than a briefcase. They attach by hose to an ordinary hose bib and plug into ordinary electrical outlets. They can be used without any cleaning chemicals and you don't need hot water—you just make an easy adjustment on a spray handle and water comes out of a nozzle with tremendous force, removing loose debris, surface deposits, and embedded dirt quickly and easily. My neighbor (in a part of Hawaii where it rains 400 inches a year) has a big brick garden fence facing the road. Every year it grows a fine crop of mildew. For her birthday one year (and to impress the neighbors with my cleaning skills), I cleaned

the wall with stiff nylon brushes, buckets of strong chemical solution, and three and a half hours of gut-hard labor. You know how difficult entrenched mildew is to remove.

The next year my brother-in-law, who had discovered home pressure washers, raved about them, bought me one, and brought it over to the Islands. This time it took fifteen minutes to clean the whole fence, perfectly! Even more amazing, no mildew came back for months. (Previously, even after cleaning with the meanest chemicals, it came back in weeks.)

You can teach yourself or one of your teenagers how to use a pressure washer in a few minutes. The rest is fun and you can clean almost any durable exterior surface this way. I've removed gum and algae from sidewalks, scraped ten years' worth of old paint off glass, cleaned rocks and brick so well I couldn't stand it. You can use a pressure washer to clean house siding, cars and boats, sidewalks, driveways, decks and patios, outdoor furniture, grills, pools, fences, garbage cans, pet cages (when the pet isn't home), and dog runs. I've even cleaned heavily soiled work clothes with them!

You will figure out another dozen good uses!

I hate to give the macho men around the house an excuse to buy any more tools, but this one comes before golf clubs, tennis rackets, guns, or computer games.

There are bigger and stronger units, but I'd start with a small one such as 1500 psi. You can get these at home and garden centers. Do get a good-quality unit, because a cheap pressure washer may leak when you're working with it.

Most pressure washers come with a detergent nozzle that can be used to prespray detergent on a surface for even more effective cleaning. If you use a detergent nozzle, clean it well afterward. When using a pressure washer with detergent, spray the solution on the surface with a wide spray and wait for five minutes. Then use overlapping high-pressure strokes to rinse.

When using a pressure washer:

- Use nonslip shoes and protective glasses—no bare feet!

- Connect the machine to an outlet with a ground fault circuit interrupter (GCI outlet). Don't touch the plug or the machine with wet hands.

- Keep a firm grasp on the washer at all times and pay attention to what you're doing with it. Never direct the spray at persons, animals, electric cords or wires, or toward yourself. Keep your fingers out of the water stream, too.

- Don't put the nozzle too close to what you're cleaning—this can cause peeling or chipping of the surface, or even blow out grout.

- Use caution when cleaning wood siding, painted, and soft surfaces. The high pressure water can chip paint and erode away parts of the surface!

- Don't overreach or stand on unstable supports—keep good balance and footing at all times.

- Put on the safety latch whenever you stop the machine.

- Never operate the machine with the spray tip removed.

- Inspect the hose each time before use—high pressure leaks can be dangerous.

- Don't run the machine dry—this can damage it. Clean the water filter and spray lance regularly to prevent blockage.

Room-by-room REVIEW
of basic cleaning and mess control measures

KITCHEN

1. Do dishes and clean up cooking equipment as soon as you're done with it/right after meals.
2. Clean up food and drink spills immediately to prevent stains, odors, and sticky floors.
3. Dump the garbage and get rid of any empties promptly.
4. Sweep and mop floor (as often as it needs it!)
5. Grease patrol: Have a spray bottle of light degreaser solution handy and spray and wipe cupboard handle areas and all hand contact spots as needed, or whenever you can't let go of the handles.
6. Clutter patrol: Dejunk and move out piles of mail, newspapers, and other paper clutter, and all other "in progress" projects that belong elsewhere.
7. Kitchens are the most efficient place to store cleaning supplies, as most cleaning is done from the kitchen out.
8. To reduce the need for cleanup: remember that this is not a place for clutter or hard-to-clean decorations.

LIVING ROOM/FAMILY ROOM

1. Remove all food fallout and left behind plates and glasses promptly.
2. Straighten the resident furnishings and return them to position.
3. Dust and neaten the TV/audio entertainment area and all its appendages.
4. Purge all those left-behind personal belongings.
5. Spot clean.
6. Now dust and vacuum as needed.

BATHROOMS

1. Use a spray bottle of disinfectant cleaner and a cleaning cloth to spray and wipe all often-used surfaces. (This will sanitize them, discourage odor, and keep things looking good.) Regular light cleaning of the bathroom is the best way to prevent unsightly mineral and scum accumulation.
2. Remove soiled things and empty trash promptly.
3. Leaving surfaces wet here will encourage mildew, and leave streaks and hardwater deposits after the water does evaporate away. So quickly squeegee down the shower walls after showering and use a towel to absorb any other loose moisture after showering, bathing, or cleaning. And turn on the exhaust fan after showering or bathing to help dry out the room.
4. Cleaning supplies here should be kept under the sink in a caddy.
5. Every month or so, deep clean the toilet with bowl cleaner.

BEDROOMS

1. Make bed each day immediately.
2. Put all clothes (worn, or freshly cleaned) away.
3. Keep dresser tops clean and clear.
4. Weekly or twice-monthly vacuuming is enough for most bedrooms.
5. Dust as needed.
6. Closets: dejunk them—make sure you use this precious space for only currently useful and needed things.

KIDS' ROOMS

1. Spot clean often.
2. Police and remove left behind food and other potentially damaging stuff.
3. Sanitize baby/toddler territory as needed.
4. Thin the toys periodically.
5. Leave the dusting, vacuuming, and toy pickup to the kids.

OFFICE

1. Keep paper organized and dejunked.
2. Keep work surfaces clean and clear.
3. Dust often, including all electronics.
4. Spot clean regularly.
5. Keep light fixtures clean.
6. Dustmop or vacuum floor.

UTILITY/LAUNDRY ROOM

1. Keep trash dumped and clutter under control.
2. Clean up spills promptly.
3. Use a damp cloth for dusting.
4. Keep laundry piling to a minimum, coming and going.
5. Pour some disinfectant cleaner solution in the floor drain every so often.

ENTRYWAYS

1. Sweep or vacuum often.
2. Have good mats here and keep them clean so they can do their job.
3. Dust and decobweb the light fixtures.
4. Every so often, wash the door and the threshold.

HALL

1. Spot clean to remove wall marks.
2. Vacuum regularly to control cow trails.
3. Keep hard surface floors swept.
4. Clean any glass or mirrors here.
5. Don't let clutter accumulate, or leave things out and in the way here.

BASEMENT

1. Carry on a continual decluttering campaign in the basement, and keep storage here to a minimum. Few things can be stored well in a basement, anyway.
2. Box up and label all those loose things. Plastic containers are a good storage choice for most (damp, damp) basements.
3. Make sure there is adequate air circulation down here, especially if you have anything stored in the basement.
4. Sweep regularly.
5. Dust and vacuum as needed. Be sure to include any ductwork or vents.

ATTIC

1. Don't let this become an overheated burial crypt for junk. Go through what you have here and move it to a better place or dispose of it.
2. Remove dust and cobwebs at least every so often.
3. Take pest control measures as necessary.

GARAGE

1. Keep oil and other spills off the floor. A tray of cat litter under leaky cars will catch and absorb oil drips. Seal the floor, if it's raw concrete. You'll be able to clean up spills in seconds and dust-mop the whole place in minutes.
2. Have good mats at garage entrances and exits and keep them clean. I keep an old vacuum in here for the purpose.
3. Hang up tools and equipment and everything else that can be hung here. Shelving and wall hanging are good ways to keep things off the floor.
4. Empty trash weekly.
5. Dejunk monthly.
6. Use a counter broom to whisk off horizontal surfaces.
7. Sweep as needed, with a push broom (or better yet, a dustmop, if the floor's been sealed).
8. Hose and scrub floor as needed.

PORCH AND PATIO

1. Have good exterior mats here, too, and keep them clean so they can do their job.
2. Police up all left-behind tools and toys (put them back where they belong!) regularly.
3. Do the same for left-behind clothes and towels.
4. Remove any broken or excess furniture here, and "temporarily stored" clutter.
5. Remove spilled or left-behind food that will encourage insects and other pests.
6. Spruce up flowerpots or planters (remove dead plants and leaves, prune, etc.) as needed.
7. Clean up any pet mess or clutter.

OUTSIDE

1. Pick up litter as you see it, coming and going. Police your entire grounds once or twice a month.
2. Provide sturdy, lidded trash cans where they're needed.
3. Keep steps and sidewalk swept and free of ice and snow.
4. Keep lawn and other greenery trimmed and neat.
5. Don't leave questionable stuff "stored" outside indefinitely—get rid of it!

CHAPTER 10

QUICK CLEANING GUIDE

To aid your campaign to spend less time cleaning, this chapter is a short course in cleaning the faster, easier, less expensive professional way. The following pages will explain the best and quickest way to do all of the basic cleaning operations in a home, and the tools and supplies you need to do them.

I've also included solutions to some of the cleaning problems I'm asked about most often (such as hardwater buildup, that monster mildew, and pet mess and stains), and ways to make housework easier on yourself.

Simplify your cleaning gear: another way to cut cleaning

In the early days of my professional cleaning operation, my crews and I would sometimes clean four homes a day, and occasionally we would have to open those cupboard doors under the kitchen sink. No matter how humble or upscale the home, that under-sink storage area usually looked like the cleaning aisle in the local supermarket... after a natural disaster, or like something unearthed in an archaeological dig. There it was, the cleaning cemetery of the house, the place where all the aged, deceased, nonworking, partly working, never tried, and mystery stuff was stored. There were generally enough supplies in here to clean an apartment complex, although at least half of them were unidentifiable.

Unfortunately, most under-sink cupboards still look about the same. So let's take one big step toward quicker and easier cleaning. Own and use what really works and get rid of the rest!

Truth #1: you don't need much.... When I wrote my million-seller *Is There Life After Housework?* back in '81 I included a list of the equipment and supplies we professionals use in it. This caused a trooping to janitorial-supply stores to get them, resulting in a lot of happy people. Soon people in remote areas like Milford, Utah, Havre, Montana, Chugwater, Wyoming, Lynx, Ohio, and Percy, New Hampshire who had no such stores nearby were writing to me for sources of pro supplies. So I created a mail-order operation called "The Cleaning Center" to provide people with a way to buy pro supplies at good prices by mail. Next I built a retail Cleaning Center store here in Pocatello. It has a nice big showroom that really frustrates me, because although we have almost everything you need to clean with in here, in all sizes, still the place looks half empty. I keep my eyes open every day for something else I could put in there to fill it up, but there is just little else we truly need to clean with.

The professional tools and supplies described in this chapter are available at janitorial-supply stores and from the Cleaning Center. Some of them are so popular now they can even be found at other outlets such as discount stores.

HOW TO DO IT
TABLE OF CONTENTS

A SHORT COURSE IN THE CHEMISTRY OF CLEANING

Don't wrinkle your brow, this isn't difficult and will help you choose and use cleaners more effectively.

There is one important difference in cleaners, and that is how acid or alkaline they are. This is measured by the "pH scale" which you may remember from high school chemistry or testing soils in the garden. The pH scale runs from 1 to 14: the higher its rating on the pH scale, the more alkaline something is; the lower its number on the pH scale, the more acid.

Many of the soils we clean up every day, including grease, oil, most foods, and body discharges, are at least mildly acid—have a pH below 7. Because acid soils are more easily removed by alkaline solutions (remember from high school chemistry, too, how acids and alkalis neutralize each other?), many detergents, soaps, and other cleaning products are alkaline. There are a few alkaline soils, however, and these are best dealt with by an acid cleaner. Hardwater deposits (or "lime scale") are alkaline, as are rust stains, and stains from coffee, tea, and liquor.

Tough cleaning jobs like the heavy coat of airborne soil that collects in a kitchen, or the burned-on grease that collects in conventional ovens, call for a high-pH cleaner to cut the grease, because grease is acidic. On the other hand, the hardwater deposits we find on showers and toilets, which are alkaline, need a strong acid cleaner. High and low pH cleaners, which we use for jobs like these, are good at what they do, but they are hard on household surfaces, and can be dangerous to work with, too. Most ordinary, everyday household cleaning can be done safely and effectively with a cleaner that is near the middle of the pH scale, about a pH of 7 to 9.

A cleaner like this is called an all-purpose or "neutral" cleaner, and it's great for all-around cleaning.

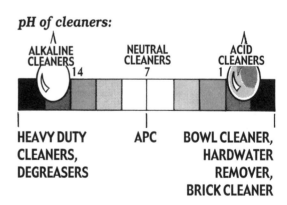

pH of cleaners:

ALKALINE CLEANERS 14	NEUTRAL CLEANERS 7	ACID CLEANERS 1
HEAVY DUTY CLEANERS, DEGREASERS	APC	BOWL CLEANER, HARDWATER REMOVER, BRICK CLEANER

APC (all-purpose cleaner)

While I was doing an unrehearsed TV news segment once in a surprised homeowner's kitchen, a neat box of products was brought forward from under the kitchen sink—eight different bottles and brands of cleaner. "Guess what," I said, as the camera moved in for a closeup of each one, "all of these different cleaners can be replaced by one single all-purpose cleaner." The audience gasped in relief.... "Really?"

All-purpose cleaners are the cleaners that are best for most ordinary household cleaning. With a neutral or only slightly alkaline pH, they are versatile, easy on your hands, and safe for most surfaces—you can use them for general cleaning and soil removal anywhere. A gallon of APC concentrate (so you can mix up your own solution) is inexpensive and will last for months. Liquid dishwashing detergent makes a good APC in a pinch.

There are specialty cleaners that work better in special situations, of course. If you are cleaning something super greasy, for example, you need a stronger cleaner such as a heavy-duty cleaner/degreaser. APC also won't clean glass well, clean off hardwater deposits, or soils that need a solvent to remove them. Some surfaces (like bathroom fixtures) will benefit from a disinfectant cleaner, but regular cleaning with APC kills most of the "germs" we commonly encounter in household cleaning.

The best way to use APC is to have several spray bottles of it mixed up and ready, so you can have a bottle in all the places you need it.

Use cleaner concentrate

You can buy "ready to use" cleaners, but why not buy cleaner concentrate and mix your own? It's much cheaper to just add your own water, and saves lugging all those heavy bottles home from the store and disposing of them after they're empty. Even the major home cleaner manufacturers have seen the wisdom of this, and are moving in this direction now. For example, a quart of spray glass cleaner mixed up yourself from concentrate from a janitorial-supply store costs about 18 cents, versus $3.93 for the same amount of a popular ready-to-use type from a supermarket.

Heavy-duty cleaner mixed yourself from concentrate is 43 cents a quart, versus $3.61 for a quart of same from the supermarket. Even all-purpose cleaner you mix up yourself from a bottle is 18 cents a quart from the supermarket, versus 4 cents a quart for the same from janitorial-supply concentrate.

To make your own cleaners just add water and the right amount of concentrate to a spray bottle or bucket, shake or stir, and you're ready to go. Concentrated cleaners are available in bulk by the quart or gallon, or premeasured into little plastic envelopes. These packets prevent waste and wrong dilution, they're easier to transport and store, and reduce container trash even more. Just snip and mix!

Another way to assure accurate dilution every time is to use a professional meter bottle. These measure cleaner concentrate for you quickly every time you need to use it. Squeezing the bottle forces just the right amount up into the measuring cup.

YOUR BASIC CLEANERS

Four basic cleaners will do most of the cleaning that needs to be done in the average home.

1. **All-purpose cleaner.** A gentle cleaner that can be used for almost any type of cleaning.

2. **Glass cleaner.** A fast-evaporating alcohol-based cleaner for small windows, appliances, some countertops, mirrors, glass knickknacks, bright work, etc.

3. **Disinfectant cleaner.** A cleaner that contains quaternary disinfectant and detergent, for bathrooms and other areas that need germ-killing action.

4. **Heavy-duty cleaner/degreaser** for tougher, harder to break down greasy grime and soil you may encounter in spot clean-

ing, appliance cleaning, kitchen cleaning, and the like. Soilmaster and SuperOrange diluted according to directions are excellent degreasers.

When you use a cleaner...

We now have some of the best cleaning chemicals imaginable. But good things still have to be used correctly. So when you use a cleaner:

Use the gentlest, mildest cleaner first

Before resorting to anything stronger. Don't just automatically reach for the heavy-duty cleaner or the bleach bottle.

Match the cleaner to the soil

An APC may be able to take care of things eighty percent of the time, but the other twenty percent (when we're up against heavy grease, hardwater buildup, or certain kinds of spots, for example), we need to match the cleaner to the culprit. Identify the soil first: what are you cleaning? Grabbing detergent to clean off an oil spot is a waste of time and product. A simple inexpensive solvent, on the other hand, (one that dissolves oil-based soils) will give you a perfect cleanup job in a few seconds. That same solvent used on vomit is of no avail. Be sure to use the right *type* of cleaner for the soil in question.

Dilute it properly

Cleaning products are tested and retested as to the amount needed in the bucket, the washtub, or the spray bottle of water. However we are always trying to "upgrade" this by increasing the amount of cleaner we put in.

Rather than enabling us to clean more quickly or efficiently, too much destroys the balance of the cleaner with the water. This causes the solution to clean poorly and leave a lot of residue behind (which is often worse than the original dirt).

Give it a chance to work

Let the cleaning chemical or solution do most of the work. The molecules in it are moving, just like your body does when you clean. Once a solution hits a surface it begins its job of softening, dissolving, and removing the soil, and the more it does, the less you have to do.

Put it away when you're done with it!

When you're done, return all your cleaning gear to its proper storage place, so you can find it easily when you need it next. In short, clean up from your cleaning! It cuts cleaning time, reduces clutter, and is safer for little ones and pets, too.

The four basic steps of cleaning

1. **Eliminate** Remove all the loose soil you can first—with a brush, broom, vacuum, scraper, whatever.
2. **Saturate** Wet the surface well with your cleaning solution.
3. **Dissolve** Leave the solution on there a minute or two to give it a chance to dissolve the dirt. This is easier and safer than rubbing and scrubbing.
4. **Remove** Now you can just wipe away the softened and loosened dirt. In some cases you may need to follow this with rinsing.

Your cleaning closet and its satellites

I once did a consulting study for a big company which revealed that providing convenient, adequate space to store custodial supplies in a building would save the owners more money than if they rented the space out. I can't promise you that a home cleaning closet will save you money, but it will save you time!

Don't just take any old odd corner to store cleaning stuff—make a place!

1. It takes very little room, especially if you use the right things to do your cleaning.
2. It will encourage the family to help.

The kitchen is a good place for a cleaning closet. We're always in the kitchen or end up there, and when cleaning we clean our way there. If whoever built your home didn't give you an adequate storage space for cleaning supplies in the kitchen, then make it yourself. Most kitchens have a pantry or broom closet to which you can add hooks, hangers, and shelves so that your cleaning tools and supplies will be organized, accessible, and safe from the little ones. Another good location for a cleaning center is a little-used coat or linen closet in a handy hallway.

YOUR CENTRAL CLEANING CLOSET

Safe, convenient, contained!
- mount as much as possible up off the floor
- wire baskets are great because they don't collect dust and they give sponges, brushes, and cloths a chance to dry
- mark the places on the shelves for things
- put anything harmful higher

No more under-sink messes!

You want some mobile mini-closets (cleaning caddies) too—see following.

Make sure everything in your cleaning closet and your satellite cleaning kits is ready to go! Keep spray bottles refilled and make sure that cleaning cloths and dustcloths are clean. If you put a vacuum somewhere, make sure you have the attachments and bags there, too.

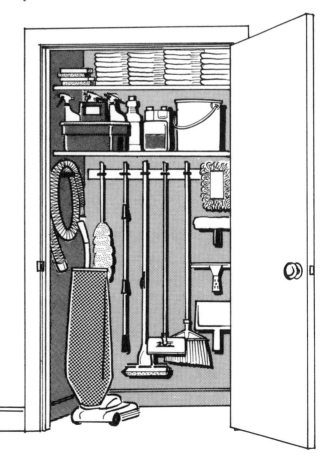

Cleaning caddies

When we only have only ten minutes to clean, we don't want to spend seven of them finding and assembling tools and supplies.

A cleaning caddy is the answer—a small, sturdy plastic basket that can carry your basic cleaning kit, or just what you need to clean a particular area. This keeps all your gear organized, together, and ready to go, and it can be stored easily and grabbed quickly.

Caddies are inexpensive enough that you can stock them up and keep them handy in many areas in your home. I have one under each bathroom sink with everything needed to clean the bathroom. This saves things like cultured marble countertops from ending up with acid-ring burns because wet bottles of bad stuff were set down on them.

If there are children in the house, caddies make it easy to put the cleaning chemicals up out of reach. Best of all, they make the wherewithal available to everyone, for cleaning up after themselves.

(All of the items in the following lists are explained later in this chapter.)

BASIC CLEANING KIT

professional spray bottles filled with:
    all-purpose cleaner
    glass cleaner
    heavy duty cleaner/degreaser
terry cleaning cloths
electrostatic or Masslinn dustcloth, and/or
    lambswool duster
white nylon scrub sponge, or antibacterial
    scrubber/sponge

BATHROOM CLEANING KIT

professional spray bottle filled with
    disinfectant cleaner
spray bottle of glass cleaner
white scrub sponge
quart of Showers-n-Stuff
foamer nozzle
grout brush
quart of bowl cleaner such as Safety Foam
toilet swab
pumice stone
rubber gloves, safety glasses
terry cleaning cloths

To clean more efficiently

Direction can make a big difference in your cleaning efficiency. Maintaining a clear-cut direction of work also helps us to remember where we are and not forget anything.

For speed and smooth work flow, clean:

1. Back to front. You always want to start at the back and bring the dirt to the front, so you are never moving from a dirty area into a clean one.

2. Top to bottom (when doing things like dusting).

3. And in a counterclockwise pattern. Most right-handed people work faster if they move in a counterclockwise direction (from right to left) within a work area. Cleaning the rooms in a house in this direction as well helps eliminate unnecessary steps.

4. It's usually a good idea, too, to work your way from the dirtiest area in room to the cleanest—get the big, bad stuff off and away first, to avoid contaminating cleaner areas.

CLEANING SAFETY

When we're cleaning, we climb and lean and stretch and reach. We use acids and solvents and other strong and poisonous chemicals, and often work on wet surfaces. We lift and carry heavy things (such as furniture and rugs), work around and with electricity and glass objects. And we're often doing all this when tired or distracted, which just about doubles the chance of an accident.

Being in a hurry is no reason to shortcut safety. A unexpected trip to the emergency room, or sudden injury will make a **real** dent in your to-do lists! So:

- Stay alert at all times when cleaning.

- Read the labels and instructions on cleaning products—**before** you use them.

- Don't mix different cleaners or chemicals together. Most won't work as well, and some mixtures will create fumes that can KILL you.

- Don't use flammable solvents for cleaning, or any solvent around open flame, or while smoking. Don't leave oily, or polish- or solvent-soaked rags around or put them in a dryer.

- Store any dangerous cleaning supplies in a safe place, out of the reach of children. Throw away any containers, bottles, or cans holding anything other than what it says on the label.

- Don't clean wearing loose, floppy jewelry, baggy clothes, or shoes that don't give you secure footing.

- Wear rubber gloves when working with harsh or dangerous chemicals.

- Always pick up broken glass and splintered substances with a broom or brush and dustpan, never your hands.

- Don't push down trash in a trash can with your hands. Use the bottom of another trash can, or some other hard object.

- Don't drink or take drugs and drive your cleaning equipment around the house, work on stairs and ladders, etc.

- Never stick your hand under the lip of a beater-bar vacuum while it's running.

ETY

- Wear safety glasses when changing fluorescent lights, using bowl cleaner or any strong chemical, or whenever there is a danger of getting particles or dust in your eyes. Remember we are limited to two eyes per lifetime.

- Use good ventilation, dust masks, or respirators as necessary to protect yourself from dangerous or damaging fumes and dust.

- Don't clean up bodily fluid spills without taking proper precautions.

- Don't leave acid cleaning solutions in the toilet bowl after cleaning. They could splash up on the next user, or be sampled by the cat.

- Keep people aware of wet floors, and off them until they're dry.

- Get more light when and if you need it. Often too little light in an area can triple the chance of a slip or fall.

- Get rid of broken and defective tools of any kind, and don't use faulty electrical equipment.

- Don't plug anything in with wet hands, or unplug something by yanking the cord from across the room. It can cause sparks to arc out.

- When cleaning any light fixture, keep moisture to a minimum. Don't spray cleaner into electrical outlets or switches. Unplug anything electrical before cleaning it.

- Bend at the knees and keep your back straight when lifting heavy things. When moving heavy furniture, get someone to help.

- Never carry a load that blocks your vision. If you can't see where you're putting your feet, don't go.

- Don't pull things off a high shelf. Something heavy, breakable, or easily unlidded could come crashing down on you.

- Climbing is one of the most dangerous parts of cleaning. Don't climb on furniture, boxes, or fixtures, to clean. Use only nonslip stepstools, sturdy ladders, or scaffolding, if you need it.

- Make sure a ladder is firmly anchored and set at a safe angle (one foot from the wall for every four feet of height).

- Never reach more than an arm's length while on a ladder.

- Stepladders should have all four feet on firm, even ground, and the spreaders should be locked before you climb on the ladder. Never stand on the top rung.

- Don't use metal ladders around electric lines.

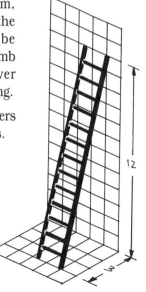

One foot from the wall for every four feet of height.

CLEANING TECHNIQUE: DUSTING

DUS

As one Southern gentleman told me...

❝*Ah love ma dust, it is protecting ma furniture from the elements, and also marks the spots so I can put things back where they belong when ah move 'em....*❞

Now there's a positive opinion of the stuff we've been fighting for centuries! Dust isn't the worst of our cleaning problems, but it somehow got to be THE gauge of clean, something that could swing the "clean house?" verdict for or against us. Dust matters, but it doesn't matter that much, and it's not a hard problem. There are some good reasons to get rid of it, though:

▶ Dust in the air means dust we breathe. Some of us living in heavily populated areas breathe in about 400 thousand million particles of dust a day.

▶ Dust in indoor air, especially, provides food and a breeding medium for bacteria, fungi, and other harmful microorganisms.

OUR DUST REMOVAL ARSENAL

What do you need to combat dust the way the professionals do? Tools that will capture dust, rather than just stir it back up into the air.

A good vacuum cleaner with a dust-trapping bag

A vacuum is the best tool of all for dusting, because it's the one most likely to gather the dust up and remove it, not just scatter it around. But a vacuum can do some dust scattering too, if it doesn't have a good bag. Best of all are the "micro" or "hepa" type filter bags, which remove ninety-nine percent of the particles from the air that flows through them.

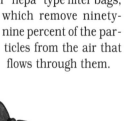

Central or built-in vacuums are the ultimate vacuum for dust removal, as everything the vacuum picks up is sent to a central vacuum unit with a good filter and all exhaust air goes outside. For more on central vacuums see p. 64 and 135.

Dustcloths

The disposable chemically treated Masslinn dustcloths (available at janitorial-supply stores) and the washable electrostatic dustcloths such as the Wonder Dustcloth by Dupont are both designed to pick and up and **hold** dust. You should keep these not just in your cleaning kit, but near the TV, computer, and in the car.

Damp cloth

A clean, lightly dampened cotton cloth will do a good job of dust removal on things that will tolerate moisture, IF you keep turning it to new fresh sides as you work.

Lambswool duster

Lambswool attracts dust like a magnet and will grab and hold not just

TING

- A buildup of .042 inches of dust on heating or cooling coils can decrease their efficiency more than twenty percent, according to the EPA.

- Dust depreciates the surfaces it falls and rests on, as it wears on them like ultra-fine sandpaper.

- In areas like the kitchen, airborne grease and oil combine with dust and attract more—look on top of your fridge!

- Dust and lint that settle in our computers and other electronic components can trap damaging heat and cause heat failures if not removed periodically.

cobwebs but fly wings and hornet snouts and the like. The synthetic fleece ones don't hold dust as well as a genuine wool duster. Lambswool dusters are available with long handles that make high and low dusting easy, and some can be used with an extension handle for the really high places. Lambswool dusters are soft enough to be used safely on delicate surfaces, and can reach into uneven surfaces (just don't use them on anything rough that will snag). When a lambswool duster gets full of dust, shake it outside.

Feather duster

Genuine ostrich feather dusters such as those made by Texas Feathers don't just flick dust off, they hold it. Cheap ones just scatter the dust. Feather dusters are great for detail dusting, and for dusting things such as knickknacks without touching or moving them. When a feather duster gets loaded up with dust, gently vacuum it or shake it outside.

Heavy-duty dust brush

A husky, longhandled duster for heavy dust and cobweb buildup, such as on exposed beams or rafters, under the house eaves, or in the storage shed or garage. The bristles are stiff enough to dislodge even embedded dirt. You'll find many uses for this.

Dustmop

Much better than a broom for de-dusting floors. Use a small mop with a twelve-inch head at home. For best results always treat first with dustmop treatment (available from janitorial-supply stores) according to directions. See p. 140 for dustmopping technique.

DUSTING TECHNIQUE

No matter what you use:

1. Dust before you vacuum.

2. Dust top to bottom, so you won't have to go back and redust anything.

3. Work your way around the room in one steady direction, so you don't forget anything. Right-handed people can work most efficiently in a counterclockwise direction, and left-handers, clockwise.

Direction to dust.

4. Dust with a smooth wiping motion, don't whip and flick your tool (and the dust!) around.

5. Turn your cloth or duster over to a clean side as soon as it gets loaded up, and shake it out or replace it before you start spreading dust rather than collecting it.

6. Don't use furniture polish every time you dust—it just builds up into a sticky, streaky coating that shows fingerprints and attracts dust.

HOW OFTEN?

▶ A once-a-week once-over-lightly is enough for the average home.

▶ Monthly, hit door frames, window blinds, valances, and light fixtures.

▶ Dust rafters and the like at least twice a year, using an extension handle.

SOME OFTEN OVERLOOKED DUST COLLECTORS

Here are some very efficient dust collectors that many of us miss when cleaning.

1. The bottom of furniture, such as the legs of wooden furniture, actually accumulates more dust than the top parts. Since we often don't see it, it's rarely removed.

2. The lower parts of walls. We pros always dust the bottom three feet of all the walls with our lambswool dusters because plenty of dust collects here from foot traffic and static cling. Few home cleaners ever think of this.

3. Upholstered furniture. Slap a chair cushion in a shaft of sunlight and watch billions of particles become airborne.

4. Bedspreads! We often keep a bedspread on for six months or longer between cleanings. We vacuum the carpet around the bed every week or so, yet the spread is catching about as much dust as the floor!

5. In the carpet. Once dust works its way from the surface to the backing it stays and starts to damage the fibers and nourish dust mites.

6. Along the jambs and casings of doors. As heating and cooling air flows through doorways, dust accumulates here.

7. Inside of drawers.

8. Inside of air conditioning and heating ducts. The dust in here gets recirculated every time the fan comes on. Regular filter changing and periodic duct cleaning will help here.

COBWEBS

Have a bad reputation in cleaning circles, but they're really harmless. Cobwebs aren't an index of your cleaning ability or a serious liability to your dwelling—they're just dusty spider webs.

Cobwebs are best removed:

1. Often

2. Dry

For cobweb removal you want a genuine lambswool duster because it will catch cobwebs and hold on to them. A light, quick pass of the duster will easily detach those webs from the fan, light fixture, wall, room corner, or ceiling, and transfer them to the duster. The duster can be vacuumed or washed when you're all done. To wash, just swish the duster head around gently in a sink or tub of soapy water, rinse well, and spin the handle in your hands to remove the worst of the water before you set the duster somewhere to air dry.

Cobwebs can appear overnight, so a regularly scheduled de-webbing is not necessarily the answer. It's more of a "see and swoop" process, fun and easy.

TO CUT DOWN DUSTING:

You can dramatically reduce dust, and your dusting chores, by the following:

▶ Put professional-quality doormats inside and outside every entrance to your home. Up to eighty percent of the dust and dirt that gets into a house comes in through the doors, and by using the right kinds of mats you can stop it in its tracks. Good "walkoff" mats will reduce dusting and many other kinds of housework. See pp. 41-42 for all the details on mats.

▶ Seal cracks: Cracks, holes, and crevices anywhere, inside or out, can let in, collect, and harbor dust. Cracks around doors and windows are a prime source of outdoor dust brought in by wind. Caulk, weatherstrip, or do whatever you have to close any air leaks. If there is any access at all, dust can and will get in.

▶ Seal concrete: Concrete is wonderful and enduring. However concrete floors will bleed dust with each sweeping and cleaning, plus they have a thousand pores per inch to collect dust. Seal concrete floors with a clear concrete sealer to stop dust bleeding and provide a surface that can be cleaned quickly and easily.

▶ Seal other floors: Keeping a good floor finish or "wax" on many types of hard floors gives them a slick surface that makes dust much easier to remove. See p. 158-160.

▶ Have a pest control program and keep it up—insects create dirt and dust.

▶ Keep all floors, carpeted and hard floors, vacuumed, dustmopped, or swept regularly.

▶ Put dust-collectors behind glass! Don't set yourself up for constant dusting and handling of delicate collectibles and decorations. Put them into built-in or other glass cabinets or cases, that can be cleaned with a quick spray and wipe.

▶ Keep your furnace and air conditioner filters cleaned and changed. This will do a lot to cut down airborne dust and dirt. The electronic or electrostatic filters are the most effective at removing fine particles.

▶ Make sure your vacuum isn't leaking dust back into the air. To check it out, put it in a darkened room, turn it on, and shine a powerful flashlight beam on it. Escaping dust will show up in the light beam. Check to see that the bags and bag gaskets of uprights are sealed tight, too, and use disposable, fine-particle trapping bags on both uprights and canisters. Even better, consider a central vacuum system.

▶ Keep your parking area and driveway (the approaches to your living space) clean—hose those babies periodically. Dust from the neighborhood, the atmosphere, and miles away will gradually settle here and be tracked into the house. Grass or pave any bare earth in your yard, and replace gravel driveways with concrete or blacktop.

CLEANING TECHNIQUE: VACUUMING

How to DO IT!

VAC

Vacuuming is how we keep carpet looking good and prolong its life, and it's also the best way to remove dry dirt and dust from many other household surfaces, including hard floors.

VACUUMING TOOLS

The vacuum is our most important piece of home cleaning machinery, the one we use most often and that can do the most to improve the looks of our home in a hurry.

The vacuum you choose can make a difference in how much time it takes to clean. There are lots of good machines out there today, so base your choice on the following factors:

▷ **size and weight** (how easy will it be for you to handle it and maneuver it around?)

▷ **effectiveness** (how well does it work?) How much suction does it have, and how well does it pick up things?—Dirt, not steel balls! To remove embedded dirt, a vacuum needs a beater bar or motorized brush roll.

▷ **durability** (how long will it last?) Does it appear to be well constructed, of durable materials?

▷ **suitability** (how well suited is it to the particular type or types of vacuuming you most often have to do?)

▷ **capacity** (how much does it hold and how large an area can it be used on?)

▷ **repairability** (how often is it likely to need repairs?) What is the repair history of this brand or model? A vac repairperson can tell you.

▷ **bag change** (how easy is it to change or empty the bag?)

▷ **noise level**

▷ **storage** (how easy is it to store, and where will you keep it?)

▷ **cost**

MY OWN ANSWER TO "WHICH VACUUM IS BEST?"

Is again to use what that the pros use. Professionals clean the same kind of carpet and surfaces you do every day, only faster and on a big scale, and they need to have vacuums that perform well and last.

The ideal combination for home vacuuming, in my opinion, is a professional-quality upright and a small canister vacuum. I don't like the detachable suction hoses and hang-on attachments for the multipurpose uprights—they're bulky and heavy, always clanking, or you lose them when the machine tips over. So I recommend a simple, uncluttered, easy-to-maneuver upright for vacuuming carpet, and a separate lightweight canister vac for all the rest.

A pro upright

In a week of traveling recently I was in seven major hotels and visited four janitorial companies that clean carpet every day. **Every one of them** used the same vacuum I use myself at home and work: a sleek commercial upright model called the Eureka Sanitaire.

You can buy these through vacuum shops or janitorial-supply stores, and the price range is $250-$400, depending on the model and options. A vacuum like this is powerful, rugged, extra durable, easy to use, and easy to repair—superior in all respects to the overpriced deluxe home models.

UUMING

A small canister vacuum

For corners, edges, stairs, baseboards, and above-floor cleaning such as drapes, furniture, blinds, and door frames—I use a compact canister. By this I mean an easily carryable canister of at least five horsepower with the attachments you need for above-the-floor vacuuming. A good quality model of these can have suction equal to any large canister. Compact canisters are easy to store, too, and relatively inexpensive ($100-$150 with all attachments).

I like machines that are easy to use, service, care for, and store—both of these are. And I can't think of a vacuum job in a house they couldn't do, except wet vacuuming. You can get both of these—a pro quality upright and small canister vac—for under $500 and they should last for many years if you take care of them.

Built-in or central vacuums

Are the third type of vacuum I recommend and an excellent addition to either a new house or an old one. Central vacuums save the hassle of lugging the vacuum from room to room and up and down stairs, and all those dents on walls and furniture from banging the vacuum into them. The motor that creates the suction in a central vac is located in the basement, garage, or other utility area, and then plastic tubing is run to outlets all over the house. All you have to do is insert a light hose into the outlet and you're ready to roll!

Central vacs are easy to install and without question the cleanest of all vacuums on the market. This helps everyone breathe better, especially

The collection tank of a central vacuum.

anyone with allergies. I like the quietness of a central vac—no whine, roar, or rattle. And when you find a bit of litter or debris on the floor, or in your pocket, there is a little wall inlet you can flip back, drop the litter in, and away it goes! You don't have to hunt down a wastebasket.

There are a number of major central vacuum companies, and any building contractor, vacuum shop, or dealer can direct you to them.

When you're installing a built-in:

1. Put in a few extra outlets. When outlets are closer together, you can use shorter hoses. A fifteen- or twenty-foot hose is nicer to work with than a twenty-five- or thirty-foot one, and it's easier on wall corners and door casings.

2. Be sure to include outlets in the garage and workbench area, in the kitchen for crumbs, and in all guest quarters.

3. Buy the bigger model—you get lots more pull and power for just a little more money. It will also mean you can run the carpet beater brush attachment without electricity, off of the air power. There are only about $150 price increments between the small, medium, and large (two-motor) units. I have giant, two-motor commercial units in my home and corporate office, and I love them!

4. Buy the attachments that work the best, not just the ones that are most popular. Your dealer can help you here.

The top vacuum choices:

Central vacuums or built-ins are the cleanest, quietest, most convenient vacs on the market.

Or a combination of:

Sanitaire upright: The fastest, most efficient way to clean carpet.

And a small canister vac: Easy to carry and handle, yet has enough suction and capacity to do all the above-the-floor vacuuming.

FOR SPECIAL VACUUM NEEDS

Wet/dry vacuums

These are canisters that can pick up either dry material or liquids. Home models of wet/dry are available all over at reasonable prices. These are great machines to have on hand for flooding basements or toilets, etc. Be sure to get a floor squeegee tool with the attachments.

Backpack vacs

In some situations you might want to consider one of the torpedo-like backpack vacuums. Although they lack the advantage of a beater head or bar to help loosen the dirt, for routine cleaning of hard and soft floors, and high places, they are wonderful. We pros use them in tight quarters, such as offices and manufacturing facilities where you can't be dragging, pushing, or pulling a vacuum around. These do have to be plugged in, but they strap to your back and give you much greater freedom of movement in your cleaning operations.

Backpack vacs come with all the usual attachments, and can be purchased at janitorial-supply stores for $400+.

Wide-track vacuums

If you have a huge house with acres of carpet, you might consider a wide-track vac such as the Sanitaire. These clean a swath fourteen to sixteen inches wide that will help speed your vacuuming chores.

BETTER BAGS MEAN CLEANER AIR!

Old style cloth and paper bags do catch visible dust, much pollen, and some fungus spores. But the finer particles often escape (to be blown back into the air), or quickly clog the pores of bags like these, restricting air flow and reducing suction.

Our increased concern with indoor air quality in recent years led to the development of "micro" and "hepa" filter type bags, much improved, which remove ninety-nine percent of the particles from the air that flows through them. This means almost zero dust recirculated back into our living spaces. These better filter bags are a bit more expensive but now widely available at vacuum shops and elsewhere. If and when you switch to bags like these, your indoor air quality will improve and allergy sufferers will appreciate it.

VACUUMING TECHNIQUE

▷ Police first. Before you start, be sure to pick up all the "big stuff" that is only going to clog and injure your vacuum—all those toy trucks, pieces of gravel, nuts and bolts, broken crayons, dropped quarters, etc.

▷ You also want to dust before you vacuum. This way the dead bugs, orange pits, fingernail clippings, plant leaves, and pet hairs that the duster knocks on the floor can be picked up by the vacuum.

▷ Vacuum into a room, not backing out of it. This is much safer, easier on you and the furniture, and faster, too! The cord will be behind you and you won't run into things.

▷ The traffic patterns are where most of the dirt is, so concentrate on those areas. Here is where soil and grit are going to be ground in under foot to ugly up and damage your carpet. Pay special attention to places like entrances and hallways. You don't need to vacuum lightly used areas or under and behind furniture as often as you vacuum the "trail."

▷ Likewise, don't sweat the edges! The edges won't be worn out by ground-in dirt because we don't walk along the walls. Twice a month or so, before vacuuming, sweep along the baseboards and in the corners to flick the accumulated dust out where an upright vacuum can reach it. Or run over the corners and edges with your canister vac and a crevice tool. You can let the edges go even longer than that as long as they don't LOOK bad.

▷ Vacuum slowly, and overlap your strokes. One leisurely stroke will beat three quick swipes any day. Take your time and let the vacuum work for you. It needs time for the beater bar to loosen the dirt and for the air flow to suck it up.

▷ Stairs can either be done with a canister vac, a handheld vac with beater bar, or an upright. The center of the stair is where most of the dirt ends up, so concentrate your efforts there. If you use an upright, wipe the corners and inner edges of the stair first with a damp cloth to move any dust or debris out where the vacuum can get it.

▷ Never use a beater bar on hard-surface floors, especially wood. Use a floor brush attachment.

▷ Use your canister vac and upholstery tools to clean cushions and all the nooks and crannies of furniture.

▷ Use the air bleeder on your canister vacuum's hose when vacuuming things like drapes. It'll reduce the suction just enough that your vacuum can pick up the dust without swallowing the curtain.

HOW OFTEN?

It depends on the kind of use an area gets. Vacuum traffic areas often. Little-used areas can go two to three weeks!

VACUUM TLC

To keep your faithful servant running long and strong:

• Don't ignore that little knob called "pile adjustment." If it's set too high the beater bar won't be able to reach the carpet to vibrate the dirt out; too low a setting will interfere with both beater bar action and air flow (suction).

• A vacuum isn't a battering ram—don't use it like one. You'll nick, scrape, or gouge the vacuum as well as baseboards, doors, and doorways. Make sure the rubber bumper guard is in place, if your vacuum has one.

• Never run over the cord or let it be pinched in doorways. And remove the plug from the outlet with your hand, not a yank from across the room.

• Don't let string, thread, and hair accumulate on the beater brush. It will reduce your vacuum's pickup power, and it's hard on the bearings, too. Work the point of a scissors under all this and snip away until the brush spins freely again.

• Don't pull vacuums up or down stairs, or drop them. Things like this take their toll over time, if not immediately!

• The bag has to be replaced or emptied **often.** Some people go months without emptying the bag, and then wonder why their vacuum seems to be losing suction. If the bag is anything over one-quarter full, it will reduce your vacuum's cleaning power.

CLEANING TECHNIQUE: SWEEPING

Sweeping usually means removing all the dust and dry debris from hard flooring. You want to get all the loose dirt off your floors before it has a chance to be ground into the finish. Sweeping it up with a broom isn't necessarily the best way. Brooms are fine for quick cleanups of small areas, but a hard, smooth floor of any size can be "swept" quicker and better with a dustmop. Sweeping is a short, easy job and does wonders for preventing mopping, stripping, and premature floor replacement.

SWEEPING TOOLS

Dustmop

A dustmop is by far the fastest tool for sweeping large areas of hard flooring such as vinyl, wood, or tile. It's also easier to use than a broom, picks up more of the fine dirt and dust, and doesn't kick anything up into the air. Pros dustmop far more than they sweep.

Get a professional dustmop with a swivel handle at a janitorial-supply store—an 18-inch head is a good size for home use. You can also use the dustmop head on a Scrubbee Doo (see p. 157).

Dustmop treat

Dustmop treatments are usually oily or waxy compounds applied to dustmops to make sure they pick up and hold fine dust. Dust treats are available as aerosols such as Endust, or as liquids you can buy at janitorial-supply stores and put in your own spray bottle.

Vacuum

Vacuuming is slow, but it's the best way to be sure you get every bit of dirt, dust, and debris, especially in the corners and crevices. Use a canister vacuum with a floor brush, and use the crevice tool or dust brush as necessary. But don't try to vacuum big things like pebbles, paper clips, and toy cars—remove them by hand first, or you'll clog and hurt your vacuum.

Angle broom

For sweeping household floors (not the garage or sidewalk), a nylon "angle broom" with flagged tips will shed less than a corn broom and get more of the fine dirt and dust. The angle cut on the bristles helps you reach into corners and is better suited to our natural sweeping stroke—the whole head of the broom, not just part of it, is in contact with the floor. Always hang plastic-bristle brooms up when they're not in use, to keep the bristles from getting bent.

E P I N G

Magna broom

Made of fine castor oil fibers that grab hold of the dust as you sweep—you can even sweep up sugar without leaving a speck behind! The unique head design of this broom lets you push it or pull it to get in corners, around table legs, etc. Also great for wall and ceiling dusting.

Counter broom

For whisking off counters, window-sills, tabletops, or any flat surface, and sweeping in close quarters and tight spots. Get one with ny-lon, flagged-end bristles—you'll be able to get the finest dirt easily.

Push broom

For patios, sidewalks, driveways, and large areas of rough or textured floor-ing, a push broom is a must. Push brooms can also be used to scrub a wet surface, and they work better than a shovel on "skiffs" (light snowfalls). Choose bristles to match the job: stiff bristles for things like gravel and coarse sand, and soft bristles for things like sawdust and sheetrock dust. Most of us can get by with one "all-purpose" push broom that has stiff outer bristles and softer ones in the middle.

For home use an 18 or 24-inch push broom is fine, and be sure to get one with angle braces to keep the head from unscrewing as you work.

Dustpan

The job of sweeping isn't done until the all the dirt is captured and in the garbage can. This is the job of a good dustpan. Get one that will hold a decent amount of dirt and has a lip that really hugs the floor. A molded plastic pro-fessional dustpan does both, and won't rust, break, or damage any-thing.

Longhandled dustpan

You've seen these in beauty shops and theater lobbies, and now you can have one at home. It takes more room to store, but also takes all the bending out of sweeping.

Wall organizer

Brooms and mops should be hung, not set on the floor or leaned against something, and a wall-mounted tool organizer makes this easy to do. My Cleaning Center has one that will accommodate five longhandled tools plus six accessories such as counter brushes and dustpans.

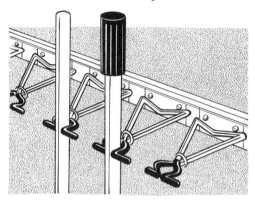

SWEEPING TECHNIQUE

Sweeping with a broom:

1. Hold the broom handle at a slight angle and drag the tips of the bristles across the floor. Don't hold the broom up straight and flick the dirt along—it stirs up too much dust.

2. Sweep corners and edges first and work toward the middle, moving the dirt with you as you go.

3. Finish by sweeping your dirt pile into a dustpan.

4. When using a push broom, push the dirt ahead of you in a straight path, and drop your sweepings at the end of each swath. This leaves you with a row of dirt at each end of the area, which can be swept into two piles and

Push broom technique.

picked up with a dustpan.

Sweeping with a dustmop:

1. First treat the mop head with dustmop treat according to directions—don't use too much or too little—and then wrap the head up in a plastic bag, preferably overnight, to fully absorb the treat. As you use the mop, you'll have to apply a little more treat from time to time, to keep it at full pickup power.

2. Before you start mopping, use a counter brush or angle broom to clean the edges and corners and other tight spots.

3. Mop with a smooth, steady motion, always keeping the same edge of the mop forward, and never lifting the head off the floor. If you follow these two rules you'll never lose any of the dirt.

4. The pros like to mop with a side-to-side "S" movement, but you can also mop in a straight line. If you mop in straight lines, shake off the dust load at the end of each pass, and mop all of your little piles together at the end.

Dustmopping side to side.

5. You can hold the dustmop in your right hand (if you're right-handed) and use your left hand to move chairs and the like out of the way.

6. Shake or vacuum out the head when it gets loaded up, and wash it when it gets really dirty. Don't forget to retreat after laundering.

7. Hang your dustmop up to store it—if you lean it against a wall or leave it on the floor, it'll leave an oily spot.

FOR A FAST PICKUP!

One of the few things in life we can be sure of is spillage. Regularly there will be tipped over buckets and pop cans, toilets running over, rainwater flooding in windows, diaper disasters, pet potty "accidents," and vomit in the worst imaginable places. Never underestimate spills or the mess they can create.

The key thing is to get them up, before they ruin the surface or someone slips on them. When I was speaking at a pizza convention once, one of the vendors had an eight-foot folding table loaded with gallon jugs of condiments, salad dressings, mayonnaise—all with the lids off. Suddenly the table legs gave out under the weight and the table collapsed. When all those open containers hit the carpet they shot out like slow-motion cannons, spattering people thirty feet away. Catsup and mustard exploded onto the carpet in swirling globs of color, five gallons of liberated salad dressing mixing artistically with everything else. In an instant that nice university carpet was literally covered with deep, gooey sludge. Someone came running into the lecture auditorium, "Mr. Aslett, they need your help!" The cleanup that followed was simple, a system you can use yourself.

First you need to get the bulk of the spill up and not let it bleed or soak into anything else. We put plastic bags in cardboard boxes and then used squeegees to sweep the sludge into plastic dustpans and then deposit it in the boxes. (You can also scrape or sweep a spill up, anything that gets the majority of the mess up and off the surface quickly.) It took just minutes to do this, and then we brought in a carpet extractor and quickly cleaned the carpet. The accident occurred at 8:30, and by 9:30 there wasn't a trace of stain left—the carpet looked perfect again.

Getting rid of the bulk of anything first is smart. Too many people try mopping up a big spill and soon they are spreading the spill all over with stained cloths and dripping mops.

Trying to pick up wet or yucky messes with a piece of cardboard is 19th-century stuff—keep a small window squeegee and a plastic dustpan handy for the purpose. For large areas of liquid pickup a floor squeegee (see p. 157) and dustpan is what you want.

You can also use a wet/dry vac to get up the worst of any spill. Wet/drys are great for toilet, dishwasher, or water heater floods.

No matter what the spill, I always spray a little APC solution on the area afterward, wipe it up, and then do a rinse-wipe. You can use a home extractor (see p. 164) to clean carpeting after removing the bulk of a spill from it. Make sure spillage areas such as carpet or upholstery dry quickly or you may get mildew and moisture damage—open a window or put a fan on the area.

CLEANING TECHNIQUE: MOPPING

MOP

Mopping is a light washing and rinsing of a floor to get the stuck-on soils a broom or vacuum can't get. When we mop we go over the floor twice—once to soften and dissolve the soil, and once to remove it.

MOPPING TOOLS
Get the right mop for the job:

String mop

If you have lots of hard surface flooring, a good string mop is what you want. String mops cover more ground faster, and pick up and hold the dirt until rinsed out. A 16-ounce cotton/rayon mop is a good choice for home use, and a screw-on handle makes mop head replacement easy.

Quick mop or smaller string mop

For a moderate amount of hard surface flooring, a smaller (12-ounce) string mop or a Quick Mop (the mop head on a Scrubbee Doo—see p. 157) will do the job quickly and easily. A Quick Mop does have to be wrung out by hand.

Sponge mop

For small areas and largely carpeted homes. Remember that a sponge mop only has a few square inches of contact with the floor, so it gets dirt-saturated quickly. Get a professional-quality sponge mop with a sturdy built-in wringer and replaceable head.

Mop bucket (for string mops)

For a string mop you need a mop bucket with a built-in roller wringer. For home use four or five gallons is a good size, or go all the way to a professional size mop bucket if you have acres of hard floor.

2 regular buckets (for Quick Mop or sponge mop)

One for your mopping solution, and one to wring the mop into. See p. 147.

All-purpose or neutral cleaner

Plain water won't do it—you need a cleaner to remove soil. Use neutral cleaner such as Top Sheen (to minimize cleaner residue) or APC, but don't use too much—too much detergent will just dull the finish, cut any wax, and leave residue behind.

PING

MOPPING TECHNIQUE

1. ALWAYS sweep or vacuum before you mop. Otherwise you'll just be making dirt soup.

2. Prepare your solution. Mix up APC or neutral cleaner according to the directions, or use a short squirt of dish detergent in a bucket of water.

3. Dip the mop into the solution and wring it out well. Excess solution will only run out all over and cause problems.

4. Spread the solution over the floor, wetting the surface well but not flooding it. When using a string mop, mop all the way around the room or area first (don't go too close to the baseboard, if there is one), and then do the middle, in overlapping figure-8 strokes. Move backwards as you mop, working your way from the front of a room to the back.

5. When mopping with a string mop, "flop" your mop (keep turning it to clean sides) until it is thoroughly dirty, then rinse and wring and continue. For a top-quality job use your fingers to push the mop strands into corners and other tight spots the mop can't reach into.

6. Leave the solution on the surface a minute or two to dissolve the dirt.

7. If you come across stubborn soil, scrub a bit with your mop. If necessary, use a green nylon scrub pad or plastic scraper.

8. Now wring the mop as dry as possible, and go back over the floor again to remove the dirty solution. When using a Quick Mop or sponge mop, wring the dirty mop into a "slop bucket" to help keep your cleaning solution clean. If using a string mop, change the mop water when you can't see a quarter dropped into it.

9. If the floor was really dirty or you want to be sure and have a shiny, streak- and residue-free result, rinse-mop the floor now with clear water.

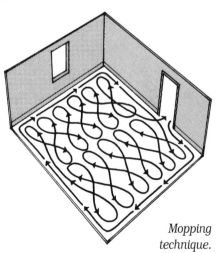

Mopping technique.

CLEANING TECHNIQUE: SPRAY AND WIPE CLEANING

With a spray bottle you can apply cleaning solution faster than you can with a cloth, and reach all the nooks and crannies easier. And your hands don't have to touch harsh cleaning chemicals.

Pulling the trigger on a spray bottle of cleaner you mix up yourself is just as easy as pressing the button of an aerosol, and much more economical. And there's no need for environment-damaging propellants.

When I say spray bottle I don't mean the cheap throwaways you get when you buy ready-to-use cleaner at the market. I mean the same high grade of spray heads and bottles we professionals use in commercial and industrial work. These are available at janitorial-supply stores, and by mail from the Cleaning Center.

These bottles are strong, longlasting, and inexpensive. A commercial spray bottle complete with spray head runs around two dollars.

For most cleaning situations or "keep up" cleaning, use the one-quart size. This works well for spot cleaning many different surfaces. Twenty-two ounce bottles are also available if you prefer a smaller and lighter bottle.

Buy good commercial spray bottles! They work, they last, and don't dribble and leak!

YOUR BASIC CLEANERS

I keep spray bottles of four basic cleaners in my home kits.

1. **All-purpose cleaner.** A gentle cleaner that can be used for almost any type of cleaning.
2. **Glass cleaner.** A fast-evaporating alcohol-based cleaner for small windows, appliances, some countertops, mirrors, glass knickknacks, bright work, etc.
3. **Disinfectant cleaner.** A cleaner that contains quaternary disinfectant and detergent, for bathrooms and other areas that need germ-killing action.
4. **Heavy duty cleaner/degreaser** for tougher, harder to break down greasy grime and soil you may encounter in spot cleaning, appliance cleaning, kitchen cleaning, and the like. Soilmaster and SuperOrange diluted according to directions are excellent degreasers.

Identify them now:

Sometimes the color of the cleaner can serve to identify it, but for safety I'd write an identification—Bathroom Cleaner, Glass Cleaner, All-Purpose Cleaner, whatever—right on the bottle with a permanent marker.

SPRAY AND WIPE TECHNIQUE

1. Always measure the amount of cleaner you're putting in a spray bottle, don't "glug and guess." More isn't better. It doesn't just waste cleaner, it dulls and streaks the sur-

face of what you're cleaning, and can even damage it. It will make the solution LESS able to do its job of dissolving and suspending dirt, and will call for extra rinsing, too.

2. Put the water in first, then add the concentrate. This prevents a four-inch head of foam and dangerous chemical splashes. Fill the spray bottle with the desired volume of water and then just add the cleaner concentrate, shake twice, and it's ready to use.

3. A spray bottle nozzle can be adjusted, from a fine mist to a thin stream, so adjust the nozzle for the job you're doing. The coarser settings put more solution on the surface faster, and the fine spray is great for covering large areas. When spraying things like disinfectant cleaner, especially in confined areas, you don't want to atomize the cleaner. If you do, it can be inhaled easily and it's not good for you. Better to set the sprayer to deliver droplets.

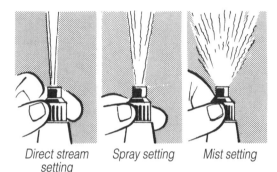

Direct stream setting   Spray setting   Mist setting

4. Make sure what you're cleaning can tolerate a spray. You don't want to spray anything electric or electronic or where water may seep in and harm or destroy things. For mirrors, TV fronts, computers, and other surfaces that overspray or excess moisture might harm, lightly spray the cleaner onto a clean cloth (not directly on the item), then carefully wipe the surface with the cloth.

5. Basic spray cleaning technique (for most surfaces such as counters, sinks, doors, windows, wall spots, and handprints):

- Spray the surface—wet it well, but not so much that the solution runs down or all over. If you get a run, wipe it up quick to avoid streaking below where you're cleaning.
- Leave the solution on the surface a minute to dissolve the dirt.
- Remove the cleaner, and polish the area dry, with a cleaning cloth (see following).

Terry cleaning cloths

Absorbing moisture, removing cleaner residue, and polishing or buffing are important parts of cleaning, and these are the jobs of a good cleaning cloth. The "rags" homemakers often hoard and use for these purposes aren't the answer, however. These are linty, full of seams, buttons, and zippers, and often made of materials that won't absorb water well or even repel it.

Get some thick cotton terrycloth (old towels are fine for the purpose) and cut it into squares about 18"x18" and hem all the edges. The result will be like magic on the end of your arm. Cotton terrycloth is ultra absorbent, and all of the little "nubs" on the cloth reach down into textured surfaces. Terry will give you quick, streak-free drying, and is strong enough to protect your hands while you're working with it, too. I was converted to cloths like these a half-century ago, and nothing is as good or as fast. Once you start using them, you'll never go back to rags. Cleaning cloths are cheaper and easier on the environment than paper towels, too.

You can also make cleaning cloths in the "tube" or "sleeve" style many pros prefer: after cutting the cloth into 18"x18" squares, hem all the edges of each square and fold it over once. Then sew the long side together firmly and you'll have a "tube" of terry. Fold it once, and then again, and it'll just fit your hand. As you use it, it can be folded and refolded and then turned inside out to give you sixteen fresh sides to clean with.

Make yourself up a couple dozen cleaning cloths and you can wash them as needed and tumble them dry, and then reuse them. Any color will do, but I like white because when I use them for stain removal I can see if the surface I'm cleaning is colorfast and if the stain is coming out. Cleaning cloths are also available pre-made and ready to use, from the Cleaning Center.

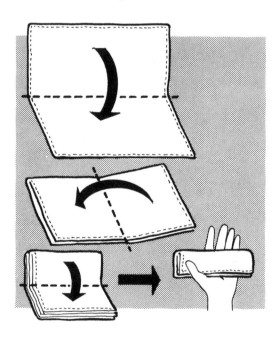

THE "TWO-BUCKET" CLEANING SYSTEM

A great way to avoid the old problem of finding yourself (halfway through the cleaning process) cleaning with cloudy, murky cleaning solution. The two-bucket method can be applied to any surface you wash with cleaning solution—walls, counters, tables, appliances, entryways, bathroom surfaces, floors—just about anything.

TWO-BUCKET TOOLS

Bucket half-filled with cleaning solution

An **empty bucket**

A **sponge** or spray bottle

A gentle white nylon **scrub sponge** (see p. 150)

Terry cleaning cloths

TWO-BUCKET TECHNIQUE

1. Dip the surface of the sponge about a half-inch into the cleaner.

2. Apply the cleaner: start at the top (or back) of the surface and spread the cleaner over an area the size of a comfortable arm's reach. You can also use a spray bottle to apply the cleaner.

3. Let it work: give the cleaner a minute or two to dissolve the soil.

4. Remove the dirty solution: go back over the wetted area with your sponge, or the white nylon side of a scrub sponge if needed, to dislodge and remove the dirt.

5. Dry the surface: wipe the sponged area with a folded cleaning cloth.

6. Get rid of the dirt: squeeze (don't wring) the dirty sponge into the empty bucket.

7. Repeat until you're done. Your cleaning solution will stay crystal clear the whole time you're working with it and the waste bucket will end up full of dirty water.

CLEANING TECHNIQUE: SPOT CLEANING

Is another kind of "keep up" cleaning—one of the ways professionals keep a house or an area looking good, without a big cleaning campaign. Spot cleaning simply means keeping the visible dirt, marks, and handprints cleaned off of things. Eighty-five percent of spot cleaning can be done by the spray and wipe method. The trick is just to find and remove all the spots.

How to Do It!

S P O

SPOT CLEANING TOOLS

spray bottle of APC
terry cleaning cloth
white nylon scrub sponge

SPOT CLEANING HOTSPOTS

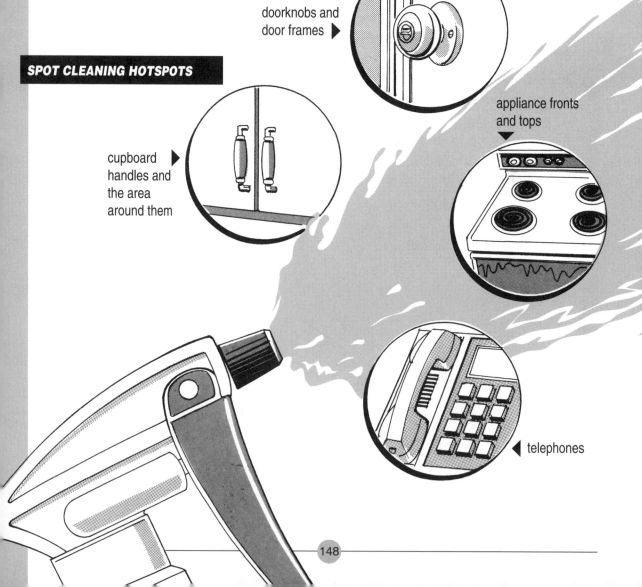

doorknobs and door frames ▶

appliance fronts and tops ▼

cupboard ▶ handles and the area around them

telephones ◀

T CLEANING

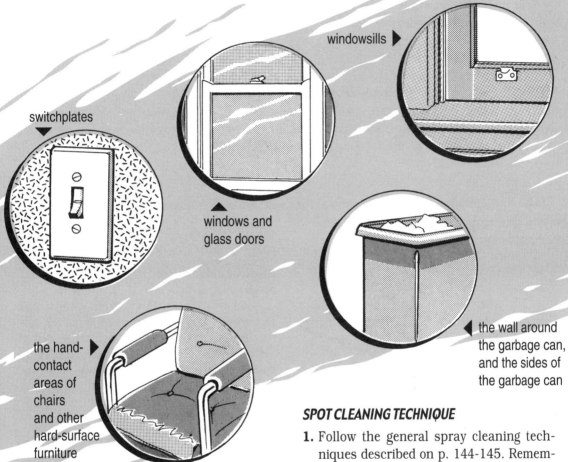

windowsills ▶

switchplates ▼

windows and glass doors

the hand-contact areas of chairs and other hard-surface furniture ▶

◀ the wall around the garbage can, and the sides of the garbage can

▲ sink and tub hardware

SPOT CLEANING TECHNIQUE

1. Follow the general spray cleaning techniques described on p. 144-145. Remember that for anything electrical, or otherwise sensitive to water, to spray the cloth sparingly and use it to wipe the object.

2. For stubborn marks or hard blobs, use a wetted white nylon scrub sponge. Leave it in contact with the spot for a few minutes if necessary. If that doesn't do it, saturate the corner of a cleaning cloth with an appropriate solvent, and apply it to the spot. Then pat the area dry with another cleaning cloth. Don't use abrasive pads or cleaners on spots—you may get the spot, but leave an ugly scratch or big dull patch behind.

CLEANING TECHNIQUE: SCRUBBING

Scrubbing, which we pros call "agitation," is sometimes needed to help loosen and remove soil from a surface.

But first, be sure there really is a need to scrub. Vigorous scrubbing, especially with the wrong tool, can scratch, mar, and prematurely wear out surfaces. Always try gentler measures first. Apply cleaning solution and give it a chance to work. If the surface will tolerate it, lay a damp cloth or sponge on stubborn spots such as hardened food for a minute or two, to soften them for easy removal. Clean drips and smears up promptly, and you won't need to scrub.

SCRUBBING TOOLS

White nylon scrub sponge

For many jobs nylon mesh pads are better than brushes. Sponge-backed white nylon scrub pads, such as those made by 3M, are one of the safest and most versatile of this type of tool. They're perfect for sink or bathroom cleaning, or anywhere a little scrubbing is needed to ease off the dirt, and they won't hurt a thing. You have to try one to appreciate how much a simple, inexpensive thing like this can do to speed up chores.

Hourglass scrubber

These are made of a 3M material that looks and feels as aggressive as sand-paper, but won't scratch. Just a little larger than a big bar of soap and flat as a pancake, hourglass scrubbers are thin enough to fit in tight spots and extra-easy to rinse out. Great for all the jobs you use a white nylon scrub sponge for, but with more scrubbing power for faster cleaning. Inexpensive, too.

Green or other colored scrub sponges/pads

You have to be cautious with any dark-colored scrub pad—they usually contain abrasives that may get the dirt and deposits but mar the surface in the process. Use colored nylon scrub pads only on tough surfaces that can take it, such as concrete, stone, and rugged metal.

Utility brush

When you do need a brush to scrub, get a professional "utility brush" from a janitorial-supply store. It has firm, springy, longlasting nylon bristles that really reach into corners, crevices, and uneven surfaces to remove the dirt. And they're easy to clean and sanitize afterward. They also keep your hands up away from the job, clean and protected. Brushes like these last a lifetime. They are also available now with long handles, and softer bristles for jobs like miniblinds and car washing.

UBBING

Grout brush

The better professional version of that staple of home cleaning, the "old toothbrush."

A grout brush is bigger and easier to grip, and it still gets in all the cracks and corners, from tile grout (where it got its name) to window tracks.

Scrubbee Doo with nylon scrub pads

A Scrubbee Doo is a simple, highly effective longhandled floor tool to which different types of heads can be quickly attached for mopping, dustmopping, applying wax, or scrubbing. Three different nylon scrub pads (light, medium, and heavy duty) are available, for scrubbing anything from delicate surfaces to glass to garage floors. A Scrubbee Doo eliminates scrubbing on hands and knees, and it can also be used to reach up and scrub walls and ceilings. See p. 157.

Plastic scraper or putty knife

The safest way to remove hardened blobs of catsup and the like from soft surfaces such as vinyl flooring.

SCRUBBING TECHNIQUE

1. No matter what tool you use to scrub, be sure to wet both it and the surface you're scrubbing before you start. Generally, the wetter, the better—this both enhances the cleaning solution's ability to lift the dirt, and lubricates the cleaning process, preventing damage.

2. When scrubbing with a brush, don't scrub in circles. Scrub first in one direction, then go back over the same area in the opposite direction—scrub east/west, then north/south. This way you get the dirt out of even an indented surface, clean much better and more efficiently!

3. When you're done scrubbing, remember that much of what we scrub off ends up in the pad or other "scrubber." If you leave it in there it will harden or ferment. So take a few seconds when you're done to rinse your scrubber out nice and clean, so it will stay sweet-smelling and sanitary for the next time you need it.

DRY CLEANING HARD SURFACES

How do we clean surfaces such as acoustic tile and other soft, porous ceilings, wallpaper, flat paint, and wall murals? When cleaning solutions are applied to surfaces like these, they will suck the dirt and moisture right in, or the moisture may cause staining problems. The answer is a professional tool called a "dry sponge." We professionals use dry sponges to clean up after fires, before painting, and anywhere we cannot wash. Dry sponges are also a good way to clean wood paneling, vinyl wall coverings, and oil paintings, and to remove the bulk of the dirt from washable surfaces before washing them.

A quick stroke with a dry sponge across a surface removes the soil almost like magic. Dry sponges will remove ordinary soiling or smoke deposits but not grease, flyspecks, smudges, or fingerprints—just the surface film of dirt.

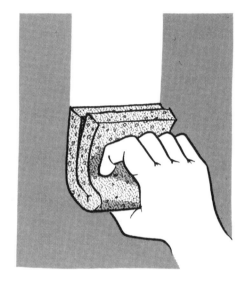

DRY SPONGING TOOLS

Dry sponge: a soft rubber pad available at janitorial-supply stores, some paint stores, and the Cleaning Center. Two types of dry sponges are available: a pad and a cube. Pads are far better—they cover more surface for the money. Pads can be folded and refolded in such a way that you have eight fresh surfaces to clean with.

DRY SPONGING TECHNIQUE

1. The pad is held in your hand, folded as shown; the cube is usually used on a pole holder.
2. Wipe the sponge lightly over the surface in overlapping three- or four-foot strokes. The sponge will absorb the dirt and begin to turn black.
3. When one area of the sponge becomes saturated with dirt, refold the sponge to a fresh area and keep going.
4. When the sponge is thoroughly dirtied on both sides, discard it, and switch to a new one if necessary.

SOME HOUSEWORK EASERS

We are all getting older, and as much as forty percent of we Americans, according to statistics, have some kind of minor or major handicap. Even those of us who think this will never happen to us can count on some degree of disability eventually. And there are all kinds of temporary disabilities, from pregnancy to sore backs and sprained wrists. No matter what the reason, if you find that some of the chores seem harder to accomplish than they used to be, here are some "housework easers" you can take advantage of:

Grasping and holding Innovate here if you need to, and put smaller or larger handles on your tools, or even extra handholds if you need them.

Lifting Buy lighter tools and machines if you find lifting a problem. You can always go back to junior size on spray bottles, buckets, shovels, and rakes, and use lighter ladders. Forget the giant economy size if lifting a two-quart container is easier and more convenient. If you find it hard to haul a big vacuum around, buy a little 7.5 pound Oreck, or consider a self-propelled vacuum. Make storage lower and easier to reach, so you don't have to lift things above your head.

Bending Go through your place and move low things and frequently used drawers to a waist-high location.

Longhandled tools (see following) save bending down and getting on your hands and knees. If you are going to kneel, buy a pair of good knee pads. I learned early in life, picking potatoes and thinning beets, that I could do an amazing amount on my knees and save a sore back.

Reaching You don't have to climb or stretch to reach things. There are now longhandled dustpans (see p. 139), longhandled utility scrub brushes, and extension handles to reach anything from high light bulbs that need changing to second-story windows. Extension handles are made for all kinds of tools—to wash things, dry them, dust, etc. Trust me, they are worth it. Anything that can save bending and climbing is faster and safer. Find and buy what you need here—it's a good investment.

Stairs Move, or get yourself help to do stairs if cleaning or using them bothers you. Stairs can go a long time between cleanings, but do keep them decluttered.

Seeing Get all the light you can on the subject, when you clean. We all need more light to see well as time goes by. Move a lamp over or shine a portable work lamp or flashlight on anything that is poorly lighted and will take a while to clean.

Walking If your cleaning involves too much walking: get smaller quarters, get help, clean less, or centralize your living area/s.

Balance If balance is a challenge: stay off ladders! Don't clean with a cold, or wearing ear plugs. Add handrails. Use nonslip mats or treads in any vulnerable spot.

Share your own ingenious ideas for easing housework with me and I'll share them with everyone in my next book.

QUICK GUIDE TO FLOOR CARE

Floors are one of the hardest-used parts of our homes and other buildings, as well as one of the things people notice most when they're passing judgment on "how clean" our place is.

Floors are the most used and abused surface in a home—they get more wear and tear than walls, counter tops, and windows all put together. Yet many of us spend more time worrying about how our second-story windows look, than about the floors.

Though there are more precise divisions and designations, for simplicity we can divide modern flooring into "soft" (carpeted) and "hard" floors. The latter include vinyl, wood, ceramic or clay tile, concrete, terrazzo, brick, stone (such as marble, granite, or slate), and the newer laminate floors.

The following are three things that will lengthen the life of any floor as well as keep it looking good.

SELECT IT

The type of floor and its design and color should be well suited to its future use. If you are lucky enough to get to decide on your own flooring, take the decision seriously. Whether you are creating an entirely new floor in a new house or home addition, or replacing the flooring somewhere in your existing home, don't make a quick decision based on how pretty something is, or the fact that it's on sale. Shop wisely. Ask around, among your friends, neighbors, and family, and talk to builders and contractors who have experience with a variety of different flooring types.

Pick a surface and color that is compatible with the use and occupancy you have in mind—a big family with pets and active games, for example, or quiet lounging for one or two. Consider how durable the surface is, how well it will hold up over time, how well it hides dirt and lint, how much care it needs, and even how well it matches the soil in your area! You cannot gain efficiency with a non-efficient floor. When considering a flooring type, ask yourself: Can it give the room or area I have in mind low-maintenance good looks?

The lowest-maintenance flooring has some variance, such as more than one color, or a pattern in it. Floors that are all one color, and very light or dark colors, will magnify any dirt, whether it's a crumb on a white floor or a string on dark carpet. Variation in texture is also important because flat, uniform surfaces also highlight dirt. Some patterns of laminate flooring, for example, have a highly uniform surface that will make any dirt on there more apparent. Patterns like these might be a better choice for a home office where dust is the main concern, than a kitchen that seems to need sweeping hourly.

Once you have a floor in mind, visit somewhere such a floor has been installed, and see how it looks after time and use, and ask the owner if he's still pleased with it. For more on making low-maintenance choices, see Chapter Six.

PROTECT IT

Floors don't have to wear out before their time. Many can serve elegantly your whole lifetime if cared for properly, and that same care will cut your cleaning time. The first step in protection is reducing the amount of damaging dirt that reaches a floor by using door mats (see Chapter Four). A regular routine of sweeping and vacuuming is critical, too, to remove dirt that does reach a floor before it can be ground into it. Preventing damage of other kinds is important, as well, because the stain from a spilled glass of red punch might never come out of carpeting, and a cut in vinyl flooring from juggling knives in the kitchen can't be repaired. So you want to exercise some

"crowd control" by making household rules such as no food on the carpet. Carpet can be also protected with soil retardant, regular vacuuming, and occasional deep cleaning (professional shampooing, preferably by the extraction method). Sealers and finishes are an option for many hard floors, too, to keep them shining, make them easier to clean, and help protect them from the daily damaging grind.

INSPECT IT

Floors can do **too** good a job of camouflaging soil. If you have a busy household and let dirt and grime remain on your floors for days or weeks, no one might notice but the floor does. As dirt and grit is stepped and stomped in, chairs are slid across it, etc., the surface of the floor will wear and deteriorate. Hard floors will eventually have a porous, scratched, and pitted finish that is much harder to clean when you do get around to it. And that same neglected dirt and grit will sink down into the roots of carpet and grind away at the fibers. Any floor needs to be cleaned—swept, vacuumed, or dusted—and have spots removed regularly. Even when you can't see the dirt! Foot traffic itself doesn't hurt hard or even soft flooring all that much. It's the grit and grime between the foot and the floor that eats them up! A floor today may be sold as "needing little or no maintenance," but most of us don't read the fine print to discover this means only if no one walks on it!

CARING FOR HARD FLOORS

One of the foremost floor care experts in this country, when asked how to take care of this floor and that floor, answered: "A floor is a floor is a floor!" Meaning that all hard floors are cared for similarly, if not the same, and I'm with him in this appraisal.

The basic process of caring for hard flooring is simple, and applies to all floors, with a bit of adjustment for the particular type and size, and a few exceptions, such as laminate floors.

First: Have door mats at every entrance, to keep out as much dirt as possible. Make sure you read p. 41 about this, because all mats are not created equal, and matting, done properly, can cut eighty percent of the flow of dirt into your home.

Second: Keep floors swept or vacuumed often to remove dirt, grit, gravel, and other debris before it is ground into them. Even dried food particles can cause damage to hard floors. Regular sweeping or vacuuming and good door matting will keep abrasive particles from wearing away the surface of hard floors and damaging the fiber of carpeting. How often you need to sweep or vacuum depends on the use

an area gets—a family of six with young children might need to sweep their kitchen twice a day, and a retired couple who eat out a lot only once a week.

You can use any sweeping tool or system you want—vacuum, broom, or dustmop. For small areas a commercial angle broom lasts longer and works better than the old corn broom standby.

Hang the broom in a handy place, with a counter broom and dustpan right beside it. If the broom always goes back there when you're done, you'll be amazed how it speeds things up. And how much less resistance you get from helpers, when you take the searching out of the job of sweeping.

For larger areas of hard floor use a dustmop—these work great on wood, vinyl, and tile floors alike. For sweeping, many efficient housecleaners also favor a compact canister vacuum or a built-in vacuum, so you can just vacuum the dirt up and there is nothing to deal with after you're done.

D FLOORS

Scrubbee Doo

A Scrubbee Doo or Doodlebug is a beautifully simple tool for basic floor care. This is a long wooden handle with a plastic swivel head that has Velcrolike teeth that hold on a variety of attachments: mop head, dustmop head, wax applicator, and different grades of nylon scrub pad, for gentle to more aggressive scrubbing. This handy tool was originally developed by the 3M Company and it is good! You can scrub or mop a floor with it in minutes without ever bending over or going on "hands and knees." I use a Scrubbee Doo all over the house even though I own a whole room full of big buffers. Scrubbee Doos are fast and convenient to use, inexpensive, easy to store, and last for years.

Floor squeegee

This is a tool few have, and all should. A pro floor squeegee is longhandled, heftier version of a professional window squeegee that can be used inside or out to quickly round up and remove water.

When you're washing, scrubbing, or stripping any floor, a floor squeegee can be used to swoosh the spent solution into a dustpan—the floor will be clear in seconds. Floor squeegees can also quickly and efficiently pick up spills, and remove light snow and loose ice.

The floor squeegees you've seen and admired in service stations aren't nearly as good as the nice "push/pull" models pros use, which can be used in any direction.

A floor squeegee with an eighteen or twenty-four inch head is just right for the home. Ettore brand is the best, and can be found in most janitorial-supply stores. A squeegee like this will last twenty years if the neighbors or in-laws don't make off with it.

Third: Remove spills immediately. The homes that get the most help from everyone have a "spill center" with APC and plenty of cleaning cloths ready for the next inevitable spill. Kids (and adults, too) would usually rather clean up than fess up.

Fourth: Remove stuck-on soil regularly by mopping. Depending on the size and type of floors you have there are different tools you can choose, but the process is the same.

Damp mopping is just that—taking a mop and wringing it out until it's almost dry and then quickly mopping the surface. This is done when a floor is not very dirty or on a wood floor with a poor finish.

Regular mopping means spreading mopping solution over the entire floor and leaving the solution on there a minute or two to make sure it has a chance to dissolve grease and grime. In most cases the scrubbing action of the mop is sufficient to help the cleaner do its job. Sometimes a quick scrub with a nylon pad (see p. 150) is necessary for neglected or heavy soil. Now wring the mop dry and pick up the dirty solution. This mopping process can be done with a sponge mop, Quick Mop, or a larger string mop. See pp. 142-143 for more on mopping tools and technique.

If you just follow a regular maintenance program with your hard floors, and never let them get really grungy, you will spend half the time and use half the chemicals on them. They will also look new longer.

Fifth: I personally like to keep an acrylic (clear waxlike) finish on most of my floors. I use a professional self-polishing finish such as Top Gloss.

Finish is a friend of many hard floors because:

1. It protects them. The wear and scratches will be on the finish, not the floor.
2. It makes them easier to clean. Soil, black marks, and the like are on the finish, not embedded in the floor. It's much easier to remove dirt from a finish than from the floor itself.
3. It makes them beautiful. Finish fills in the tiny pores and any little scratches in the surface, which means maximum light reflection and more shine.

There are scientific studies proving that a shiny floor will do more to make people buy in a supermarket than what is being offered on the shelves.

4. It makes them safer. People think of "waxed" floors as slippery, but modern floor finishes actually make hard floors less so.

Today's floor finishes or "waxes" are non-yellowing and often don't need to be stripped off for years. When you're applying floor finish, go easy on the corners and edges and under things, anywhere the floor is not really used, or finish will accumulate in places like these and eventually need to be stripped. I "wax" the whole floor once and then apply two or more coats (and future coats) only in the traffic areas, where it is sure to be worn off.

WHICH FLOORS SHOULD YOU "WAX"?

Not all hard floors can or should have a finish applied, however. If you tell your local janitorial-supply store what kind of floor you have, they will let you know if a finish is desirable, and if so be able to provide the best, the latest, and what we pros are using.

Here are my own recommendations for some of the most widely used hard-surface floors.

No-wax floors

These are wonderful floors, made of sturdy vinyl that lasts, and the no-wax claim is made because of the extra-glossy clear "wear layer" that is added atop the vinyl. If the floor gets little or no use (you have no kids or dogs, and walk around on it in stocking feet), it will stay beautiful forever. However normal household use will dull even no-wax floors eventually—roughen the surface a bit and reduce the shine. Once it does start to dull, apply a professional floor finish, such as a self-polishing, metal interlock finish from a janitorial-supply store. The right wax will make a floor shine like new again and will last months before it has to be reapplied.

Wood

Care of wood is a little more involved—you want to preserve and protect the original urethane finish on wood floors as directed earlier, with an emphasis on good door mats and keeping the floor dirt and spill free. And damp-mop only, when mopping is needed.

The factory finish on any newer wood floor is so tough it doesn't require any protection, but like almost any surface it wears over time, and at this point a maintenance coat of urethane should be applied. In most homes these maintenance coats are needed about once every four or five years. Waxing a wood floor is not recommended in an ideal world, but most homes aren't in that neighborhood. There are times when you aren't ready to refinish a wood floor or even apply a maintenance coat of urethane. The floor in this case can be instantly enhanced with a coat of acrylic floor finish (wax). Realize when you do this that it will require more work later to remove that wax before the wood can be recoated with urethane. But for a quick beautiful floor, waxing is an option.

Older wooden floors that have been treated with a penetrating sealer followed by paste wax should be rewaxed with paste wax. If there is a buildup of old, dirty wax, it should be removed with a steel wool pad or screen on a single-disc buffer, then paste wax should be reapplied.

For a complete guide to care of wood floors, send $9.95+ $3 shipping to *The Guide to Easy Wood Floor Care and Maintenance*, PO Box 700, Pocatello, ID 83204.

Laminate flooring

These floors have a built-in satin sheen and don't need any type of finish added to them. Don't wax these! Maintain these floors following the basic steps outlined earlier. To mop, use a mop only lightly dampened in plain warm water or, for heavier soil, a solution made with a half cup of ammonia to a gallon of water. Here is one case where you don't want to use soap or detergent of any kind, because it will leave a dulling residue behind.

Tile

Most tile is made to withstand wear and tear for years without showing any sign of it. I don't recommend ever waxing tile. It will change the appearance of the tile and cause more maintenance down the road. Most floor tile is designed to not have wax, and wax won't even stick to some tiles. Acrylic finish won't bond well to ceramic tile, for instance. Tile can be treated with a penetrating masonry sealer, however, to seal any pores in the tile and prevent the grout from staining and make it easier to clean.

Concrete

Raw concrete will shed dust all of its life, and that dust from the garage or basement will end up in other areas of your home. I recommend sealing concrete—giving it a clear, permanent coating so that the dust is sealed in and the stains from family and cars are sealed out. If you've ever been in a wholesale store with concrete flooring you have seen an example of this. I've seen some beautiful concrete floors in schools and retail stores that have been sealed with concrete seal and main-

tained with a floor wax polish. I like to wax my own sealed concrete with a professional self-polishing acrylic finish such as Top Gloss, but you may not wish to do so unless the floor is in a living area such as a basement.

Stone and Mexican tile

These surfaces are designed to be rough and rustic looking. People like the look until they have to take care of it—it can be a maintenance nightmare. If easy maintenance is a priority I would put a coat or two of concrete seal on tile of this type. This will seal some of the roughness and make the surface easier to clean. It will change the appearance of the floor, however. Be sure to test the sealer first on an extra tile to make sure you like the results, because this type of seal is almost impossible to remove.

At-a-glance Guide to Hard Floor Care		
FLOOR	**WET CLEANING**	**WAX OR FINISH**
No-wax vinyl	Mop with no-residue (neutral) cleaner	Wait until shows wear
Dull vinyl	Regular mopping	Can be a quick appearance boost
Laminate	Damp mop with plain water	NO!!
Matte-finish ceramic tile	Regular mopping	Not recommended
Shiny tile	Mop with no-residue (neutral) cleaner	Won't stick
New wood	Damp mopping only	Not recommended
Old wood	Damp mopping only	Can be a quick appearance boost

Baseboards

Here's your chance to make a million dollars, not cleaning these, for sure, but inventing a new one. For more than forty years I've cared for baseboards made of wood, metal, tile, and vinyl or rubber (the worst)! And between where they are located and the punishment they take, cleaning baseboards is a real pain. Lint and floor fallout is attracted to them, floor mopping often splashes dirty water up on them, and brooms, vacuums, furniture, and toys beat them to death. So even when clean, baseboards often look bad. And wood baseboards (both painted, and stained and varnished) not only have to be cleaned regularly, but touched up with paint or polyurethane often.

Baseboards should be dusted, swept, or vacuumed during regular cleaning. Soils collect against walls, and wiping baseboards down once a month with a cloth or sponge lightly dampened with APC solution will work wonders.

Be sure, prior to repainting or refinishing baseboards, that all old waxes and oils are removed from the surface (lightly sand it if necessary to accomplish this), or the new paint or whatever won't adhere properly.

To touch up stained and varnished baseboards:

Clean them first, then lightly sand the marks or gouges and fill them with wood putty. When the putty is dry, sand it to level with the surface, and rub on a matching stain, carefully blending it with the rest of the finish. When the stain is dry, recoat the entire baseboard with varnish or polyurethane.

My favorite baseboard is carpeting with a braided top—a truly new approach that solves most baseboard problems in carpeted rooms.

CLEANING TECHNIQUE: CARPETING

CAR

Carpet is better than ever: the quality, the colors, and its durability and soil resistance can hardly get any better than it is now.

And as for caring for it, there are only three simple steps, to keep carpet looking good and make it last: regular vacuuming, prompt spotting, and occasional shampooing.

Vacuuming is covered on pp. 136-137. Spotting is simply immediate removal of spills and stains. See the Spot Removal chart on the back cover. For a complete guide to spot and stain removal, see the book *Don Aslett's Stainbuster's Bible* (see p. 201).

Here's the pro lowdown on carpet shampooing now.

SHAMPOOING

Shampooing is the everyday term for the deep cleaning we have to do every so often to remove the dirt and soil that gradually accumulates in the carpet pile. If carpet is of good quality and frequently vacuumed, and not in a high-traffic area or a place where a lot of cooking and eating is going on, it can go a long time (two years or more) without shampooing.

The goal of shampooing is to get all the dirt out, leaving the carpet as dry and with as little detergent residue as possible.

The following are the most common methods used today and their pros and cons.

Hot water extraction or "steam" cleaning

Of the three main ways of modern carpet cleaning I believe extraction is by far the best, and most carpet experts agree. In extraction a jet of hot cleaning solution is shot into the carpet and then a strong wet vac on the same

applicator head pulls it right back out. Extraction will usually remove loose soil even from deep in the carpet, but it often doesn't do so well with hard, crusty, stuck-on soil. That's because the solution isn't on the carpet long enough to have a chance to break down stubborn dirt, and there's no "agitation" or scrubbing action to help get it out.

An extractor at work.

If you use this method be sure the carpet is presprayed and prespotted, to soften stubborn soil ahead of time, and give the cleaner a longer time to be in contact with the carpet. The solution also needs to be hot enough (150 degrees F. or more) for effective cleaning. This usually calls for professional truck-mounted equipment, or a high-ticket rental.

Rotary shampooing

A foaming carpet shampoo is scrubbed into the carpet with a rotary shampooer, and then the foam (or as much of it as possible) is removed with a wet vac. Some shampoos dry to a crystalline powder which encapsulates the soil and then can be vacuumed out.

Rotary cleaning does an excellent job of loosening difficult soil, but may not then actually remove it all. This method is also slow and usually leaves shampoo residue behind that can accelerate resoiling.

P E T   C A R E

Dry cleaning

Is done with a powder containing solvents and detergents, which is worked into the carpet with a brush or machine, then vacuumed up when it is thoroughly dry.

There's no water involved and no long waits for the carpet to dry. But this method is usually a little slower and more expensive than wet cleaning and it's not easy to get all the powder vacuumed back out.

Combination method, or "showcase cleaning"

The best method of all is a combination of rotary cleaning and hot water extraction, which gives you the best of both worlds. The whole carpet, or at least the badly soiled parts, is scrubbed with a rotary shampooer, and then rinsed with an extractor, using clear water. This kind of "showcase" cleaning can also be accomplished by an extractor that has an agitator head.

DO IT YOURSELF, OR HIRE IT DONE?

If you own your own home, or rent but have a green light from management to handle the rug cleaning, you have two basic choices: calling a professional or doing it yourself.

Should you do it yourself?

There are lots of reasons not to. This is one operation a pro can definitely do quicker and better. The average person doesn't have access to equipment capable of doing a really good job, and is all too likely to end up with an overwet carpet, too much shampoo resi-

due, stains that are still there, and a strained back and ripped car upholstery from hauling rental equipment around. The odds of a disappointing job of cleaning and damage to household furnishings are good. And if you counted the value of your time not just doing the job but picking up the equipment and returning it, and the aggravation of it all, doing it yourself is probably more expensive than having it professionally done. If you can afford it, leave your carpet cleaning to the pros.

If you're dead set on doing it yourself, get the most powerful extractor available and be sure to use hot water. Try to rent something stronger than the supermarket rental extractors, which only recover sixty or seventy percent of the moisture they put into a carpet. Sharing the work and rental cost with a neighbor will make the job easier, both physically and financially.

If you shampoo carpet yourself, there may be stains you can't remove, and the cleaning process you use may even "set" stains, making them permanent. Pro carpet cleaners have specialized training and chemicals to deal with problem stains such as lipstick, dyes, nail polish, candle wax, and red food and drink stains.

When hiring a pro

If you decide to let a professional do the carpet cleaning, get and check references on the company you have in mind, and then get them to quote you a firm price before they start. Make sure you know which cleaning method the quote includes. Some cleaners quote "bonnet cleaning" at very attractive rates, but bonneting does not deep clean a carpet.

The quoted price should include all necessary pre-spotting and stain removal, and should be guaranteed to get the job done to your satisfaction.

Often you will see seductive ads such as "Three rooms of carpet cleaned for $29.95." Yet when the carpet is finished the bill is $129.95, counting all the extras and add-ons after the cleaner arrives—another case of the old "bait and switch." Deal with contractors who give a written bid for a job and don't offer "deals," and you can avoid this. It also helps to ask all and any questions you may have about the service **before** the price is established or anyone comes to do the job.

The cost of carpet cleaning is usually estimated according to the amount of square footage that can be cleaned on one trip, so having a larger area or several rooms done should be cheaper. Some companies offer discounts for repeat customers. When the cleaner can clean an empty or nearly empty room it will also tilt the economics in your favor.

When a professional is looking over and bidding the job, point out any stains and odors to him, and ask what he can or will do for them. Pet stains, especially, need special treatment, so be sure to identify them in advance. Many old stains are just that, not spots but permanent stains, even damage, and nothing is going to remove them. A trained carpet person can and will, however, get a surprising number of stains out of the carpet.

If there is an additional charge for applying or reapplying soil retardant after the cleaning, make sure you understand how much this will add to the cost. This step may not be necessary in lightly trafficked rooms like back bedrooms.

Will shampooing get rid of fleas? Professional shampooing can help remove flea eggs from carpet, but only spraying with pesticide will eradicate the critters.

You can do a lot to aid the quality of a professional carpet cleaning by vacuuming the areas in question well, and moving all of the small stuff and clutter out of the way before the cleaner gets there.

What about those home extractors?

Small home extraction units are now available from a number of different vacuum manufacturers. You'll also find extraction units in the do-it-yourself rental departments of hardware stores and supermarkets. These somewhat larger machines can extract both carpet and upholstery.

As you might imagine, the big commercial units do a better job, because they're bigger and more powerful, and can recover up to ninety percent of the moisture they put into the carpet.

Most home extractors only recover sixty or seventy percent. However you can get okay results with a home unit if you follow the instructions below, and as long as you don't have exceptionally dirty carpet or problem stains.

One good thing about century 2000 carpet care, much in your favor and not mine as a professional carpet cleaner, is that competition has forced prices way down. Talented, knowledgeable carpet cleaners with $30,000 machines can and will do your carpets reasonably, extraction style. So before you race out to buy your own little extractor, or decide to go the rental route, call and have a seasoned pro give you a firm bid for your carpet deep cleaning.

If you find yourself renting an extractor often, and/or have a large extended family that could make good use of it, you might also consider buying an industrial grade extractor. These are portable and powerful (about the same size or a little bigger than the ones you will normally be renting) and cost between $1200 and $1800. You can call my Cleaning Center and we'll help you find a unit to fit you.

FOR BEST RESULTS WITH AN EXTRACTOR

Whether you are using your own extractor or a rental, here are some professional pointers that will make a great difference in the final result.

1. (An often overlooked step) READ THE INSTRUCTIONS that come with the machine, and on the carpet shampoo, before you embark on the project, and FOLLOW THEM when you're doing the job.
2. Vacuum the area thoroughly first. This is the real secret of good carpet shampooing. Remove as much soil as possible before you add water and make "mud" out of it. The pros who know use powerful vacuums to

do a thorough dry soil removal before uncoiling the water hose.

3. Block all furniture legs. If you can't move all the furniture out of the room before you extract or shampoo, block it up (set it up off the carpet on little pieces of cardboard, or waterproof material such as wax paper, foil, or Styrofoam). This prevents rust stains from wet carpet coming in contact with metal furniture glides, or bleeding of wood stain from the legs or base of furniture into the carpet.

4. The "prespraying" secret—prespray or lightly mist the carpet ahead. Detergents and cleaners work better when they have a few minutes to be in contact with soils. Too often, when using an extractor people zoom quickly over the surface of the carpet or upholstery, spraying the solution in and then instantly removing it. The wastewater they recover may look impressively dirty, but you can be sure they only got the surface soil.

That's because there wasn't enough "dwell time"—the solution wasn't on the surface long enough to break down all the difficult soils. To prevent this, put some carpet-cleaning prespray (such as Carpet Pretreat 61 from the Cleaning Center), or a traffic lane cleaner from a janitorial-supply store, in a spray bottle or weed sprayer.

Then lightly prespray the carpet five to ten minutes before you go over it with the extractor. The prespray solution will loosen the dirt, and then when you come zipping by with your extraction unit, you will clean twice as well. All the pros do this, but people at home seldom do—now you know! It's not necessary to prespray the carpet all the way to the edge—just the traffic areas.

5. Now extract.

6. Now stay off the carpet till it's dry! This should take about four to six hours if you ventilate the area well, or maybe overnight for carpet that has been thoroughly wetted.

7. If imprints from blocking materials remain afterward, rub them lightly with a cloth dampened in clean water. Then brush the areas up, and let them dry.

8. If it's a rental, nice people clean the machine before returning it.

CLEANING AREA RUGS

There are more breeds of area rugs than ever these days, from flimsy throwaways to priceless orientals. Our maintenance efforts here should be equated with value of the rug, of course, but whenever possible, do regular and careful vacuuming, and attend to any spots and spills immediately.

The less expensive types of rugs (if the label agrees) can be washed in a machine when they get dirty, but don't use bleach, hot water, or hot dryers—the rubber backings can't take it. Those that can be shampooed, you can do yourself with a home extractor. Be sure to move any rugs on wooden floors to a water-safe surface before proceeding.

Valuable and expensive rugs should be cleaned by a dry cleaner or other professional who is equipped to do fine rugs. For oriental rugs, I'd stick with the certified oriental carpet cleaner in the area—they are highly trained and know the special wools and dyes used in these rugs. Master carpet cleaners like these can even clean oriental rugs on site, right in your home.

As for those hooked rugs made with loving care, I'd send these, too, out to be cleaned if they are still nice.

Scrubbing isn't good for any area rug, as it can mash and distort the fibers.

SOME COMMON CARPET PROBLEMS

Odor in carpeting

Many odors in carpeting, such as pet piddle or smoke, are not just in the carpet, but have been absorbed by the rubber or felt padding beneath it. Rubber holds odors seemingly forever. If you have a very persistent odor problem, the carpet can be cleaned and deodorized rather inexpensively by a professional, and then all that is needed is to replace the padding. This too is inexpensive. Since the carpet is already there and sized, and the tack strips in place, an experienced carpet layer should do it for a reasonable price.

When shopping for a carpet cleaning of this type, make it clear that you want a product or process used that will remove the odor, not just mask it for a while with a perfume scent. See p. 181 for a discussion of "odor neutralizers."

Flooded carpeting

Must be taken care of immediately to prevent mildew and musty smells forever. If you get the water out and dry the carpet quickly, mold won't have a chance to start growing. Use an extractor to remove the water. Lifting up a corner of the carpet and putting a professional carpet blower under it will dry the carpet out in a hurry.

If you didn't take care of a flooded carpet right way, it may now need to be cleaned with disinfectant cleaner, then extracted to remove the solution. A good disinfectant cleaner for this purpose is Cide-All, available from janitorial-supply stores and the Cleaning Center.

In bad cases the carpet may need to be completely removed, cleaned and rinsed on both sides, and then dried well before replacing. Replace all of the carpet padding that got wet.

Extensive carpet flooding will usually be covered by homeowner's insurance, and a professional flood restoration cleaner is best called in.

That old carpet

Even after we take it up, we just hate to part with it. Though we are tired of it, it isn't quite worn out, so we keep it around forever in the basement or back room. Ninety-five percent of us will never use it again, and it takes up space, is stumbled over, and scrapes the walls. Why not get rid of it to someone who WILL use it? A friend of mine who had a half-dozen old carpets cluttering up his storage building got inquiries within an hour of the appearance of this ad: "200 yards of good used carpet suitable for summer cabin or other use. Call...."

Carpet groomer rake:

This resembles the good old garden rake, but instead of iron tines it has tough nylon teeth. We pros use carpet groomers to lift the pile of carpet prior to shampooing, and to work the mats and tangles out of long-pile carpeting. You can also use them to help work prespray solution into the carpet. A rake is most often used to "dress up" carpet, making the pile lay all one way so that it looks better, especially after cleaning. You can get one at a janitorial-supply store.

GLASS CLEANING

HOW OFTEN SHOULD WE CLEAN IT?

Since glass doesn't rust, rot, mildew, or absorb anything, it doesn't hurt it to get a little soiled. So don't get hung up on a "glass cleaning schedule." I've seen windows in some locations go years without cleaning and still look good and work fine. Sometimes only the bottom windows or part of a window needs cleaning. Look before you leap into it.

HOW TO DO IT

Here are three effective ways to clean glass.

In the sink

Anytime you can move or remove glass to clean it, washing it in a sink like a dish is the easiest way to go about it. This method is great for light fixture lenses, glass figurines and vases, and the like. Often things like this are not just dusty, but coated with airborne grease and flyspecks. Soaking them in dish detergent solution, scrubbing a little if necessary with a white nylon scrub sponge, and then rinsing leaves them perfect. You can air or cloth dry them afterward. If you have a rigid, cast iron sink, put a rubber mat in the bottom to avoid breakage.

Spray and wipe

For smaller windows and spot cleaning any glass surface, a spray bottle with a quick-evaporating alcohol-based glass cleaner like Windex is the way to go. For spray and wipe drying, a cotton cleaning cloth is better than paper towels—faster, more effective, lint-free, and easier on our forests.

If you have a lot of tiny panes up out of sight, I wouldn't bother spray-cleaning the outside. Just wash them down with a brush and detergent solution and then quickly flush them off with water. (If you live in a hardwater area, this will leave water spots.)

When spray cleaning, you need to be careful with things like TV and computer screens and the glass over framed pictures, where the cleaner can run to the bottom or sides and damage or warp things. On mirrors, too, you want to keep the cleaning solution off the edges to prevent black discolorations, caused by oxidation of the silver plating. In situations like this you want to spray the cloth, not the object itself, then wipe.

To keep dirt, dead bugs, cobwebs, and other window frame debris from getting on the window itself (especially when cleaning small-pane windows), simply wipe or wash the frame quickly **before** you clean the window, instead of after. Four quick wipes with a wet cloth will do it. Flushing frames with a garden hose works well for exterior windows.

For quicker cleaning:

If a small window is just dusty, wiping it with a clean, dry cloth is the quickest.

When spray cleaning, don't spray on more cleaner than is needed to do the job. The less you spray on there, the less you'll have to wipe away.

S S

Squeegeeing glass

For glass surfaces larger than 2'x2', it's much easier, faster, and cheaper to copy the pros and use a squeegee. Glass also stays clean longer when squeegeed. It takes a few minutes to catch on to how to do it, but you'll be glad you did.

Brain

So you won't attempt to squeegee in hot, direct sunlight. The solution will evaporate too quickly and leave streaks.

Squeegee

Be sure to get a professional quality twelve or fourteen-inch squeegee such as Ettore, with a replaceable rubber blade.

Window scrubber

A scrub head like this is much faster and easier than a sponge or brush for wetting glass and removing stubborn deposits.

Extension handle

A telescoping aluminum or fiberglass pole that attaches to your squeegee and window scrubber to extend your reach. This is a much easier and safer way to reach high glass than teetering on a ladder. A four-foot pole that extends to eight feet is a good size for most single-story work, and makes reaching over shrubs, stairs, etc., a snap. A longer pole is needed for second-floor windows.

A handle like this eliminates the need for a ladder in most cases. If you have a lot of high windows, you might also want a longer extension pole and a Super System squeegee.

Super System squeegee

This is a special squeegee head with swiveling action that makes problem windows, or any high windows, a cinch. With this you can do the "angling" you need to do odd-shaped or hard-to-reach windows. (See p. 171.)

Bucket

A bucket that can accommodate a window scrubber is best. You can get these at janitorial-supply stores.

Rubbermaid makes some great rectangular buckets now that are perfect for the purpose.

Cleaner

In glass cleaning, proper dilution of your cleaning solution is so important! You only need about five drops of dish detergent such as Joy in a bucket of water.

Razor scraper

I always carry a razor scraper with me when I'm window cleaning. (Never use a razor blade alone for scraping—it can damage both you and the window.) You can get a pro quality scraper such as Ettore or Wonder Blade at a janitorial-supply store or from the Cleaning Center.

SQUEEGEEING TECHNIQUE

1. Apply the solution to the window with the wand. Applying pressure to the wand, go over the glass twice—once to wet the surface, the second time to loosen the soil.

2. Wipe the squeegee blade on a clean, damp cloth before you start, and after each pass. This lubricates the blade and helps prevent skips.

3. To eliminate those frustrating drips from the top of the window, make a quick pass across the top of the window first with a tilted squeegee to clear a one-inch strip along the top edge of the glass.

4. Place the squeegee in the dry strip at the top and pull down.

5. Wipe any drips at the bottom of the window away with a clean dry cloth.

6. Don't worry about any little drops at the edges of the window—after they dry you'll never notice them. If there is a tiny streak or splash somewhere in the middle of the glass, just wipe it away with your bare (dry) hand or finger. Trust me, it works!

7. If you come across a sticker, drop of hardened paint or mortar, bird dropping, etc., first dampen the window, then scrape it with a razor scraper. Only push the scraper in a forward direction. If you push and pull back and forth, you can scratch the glass if something hard like a grain of sand gets caught under the blade.

   Any gummy residue left after sticker removal can be removed with a citrus cleaner such as De-Solve-It or Goo Gone.

Side to side

Some windows can be more easily squeegeed side to side. If you want to squeegee sideways, then clear a strip of glass at the side before you start.

After a little practice you'll be able to "fan" a window in a continuous figure-8 pattern like the pros do. You can clean the whole window without lifting the squeegee off the glass!

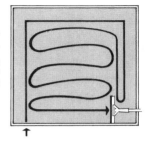

Fanning a window with a squeegee.

Preventing those first-time problems

1. **Squeegee jumping and skipping:** Hold the squeegee angled down in your hand, just gliding over the glass. If you hold it straight out, with the blade at a 45-degree angle to the glass, it will jump along.

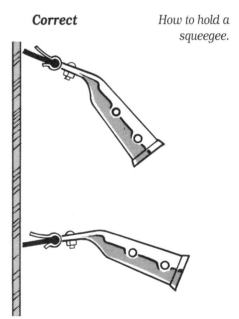

Correct

How to hold a squeegee.

   If you wipe the squeegee in between swipes with a clean, damp cloth as noted earlier, this lubricates the blade and allows it to sail over any dry "lapover" area.

2. **A white chalky residue left on a squeegeed window** means you are too generous with the detergent. Back off a little. It only takes five drops—half a capful—in a bucket of water.

Removable storm windows

Even if they can be removed, I've found in more than forty years of cleaning thousands of homes that it's best to clean them right there in place, don't haul or move them around. You can do it with either a squeegee or spray bottle of alcohol-based glass cleaner, whichever is most efficient given the size, location, and accessibility of the window.

You'll probably want to take down removable screens, though, and flush them with a garden hose or pressure washer. See p. 172.

Odd-shaped or hard-to-reach high windows

Cleaning high windows can get tricky sometimes because an ordinary squeegee on an extension pole may not be able to be "angled" correctly to reach odd-shaped windows, or windows in an awkward location. (When we're doing windows near the ground, our hand and arm make such adjustments easily.) For windows like these switch to a Super System squeegee, available from janitorial-supply stores or the Cleaning Center.

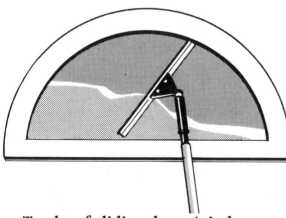

Tracks of sliding doors/windows

That sticky black or brown gunk that collects in the bottom was once dry dust, insect parts, and all sorts of other fallout, plus airborne grease and soil. Moisture from condensation and other sources mixes with all of the debris collected in there, and creates "gunk" that not only looks bad, but eventually affects the performance of the door or window.

The easiest way to clean a track is to spray APC solution into it—flood it—and leave the cleaner in there a while, five or ten minutes if necessary. Then wrap a terry cleaning cloth over the tip of a large screwdriver or a paint stirring stick, and run it over and through the now softened goop. Several passes like this will clean and polish the track, and then dry it. Don't forget to slide the window or door over when doing this, so you get both ends of the track!

Prevention pointer:

If you zip the vac nozzle over the windowsills and tracks when doing your regular above-the-floor vacuuming, you'll reduce or eliminate the problem of "icky track."

THE PROFESSIONAL WAY OUT

If you decide to have your windows done by a pro:

1. Always have them look at the job **before** you decide on price and when. Windows range from easy to extra-difficult, depending on height, type, and accessibility.
2. If your windows have hardwater deposits, be aware that removing them is an often time-consuming process that a window cleaner won't do on a regular call.
3. Make sure the person you have in mind to do your windows has professional insurance.
4. Keep yourself, your children, and pets out of the window cleaner's way—they go for speed!

SCREENS

Get a gradual buildup of dust, dirt, bug residue, bird doo, and the like. Screens get ugly, their pores get clogged, and they have to be cleaned. It's not a hard task.

SCREEN CLEANING TECHNIQUE:

1. Always take screens down to clean them. If you try to clean them in place, you'll make a mess, not get all the dirt off, and be likely to stretch and sag the screens.

2. Lay the screen out on an old quilt, blanket, or the like, on a flat surface outside or in the tub. Be sure you lay it screen side down (so the screen is perfectly flush with the surface), so it won't be damaged by stretching.

3. Scrub the screen **gently** with cleaning solution and a soft brush. The quilt or whatever underneath will get detergent-soaked and clean the other side by itself.

4. Rinse with a hose (or with the shower) and then give the frame a rap with your hand to shake most of the water loose. Let it sun or air-dry the rest of the way and it's done.

5. A pressure washer on a low setting can also clean screens safely and well. Be sure not to set the pressure too high, or you'll stretch the screen material.

BLINDS

Cleaning blinds isn't anyone's favorite job, but the way to make it more bearable, believe it or not, is to do it more often. The big secret of blind maintenance isn't any "magic fingers" you send away for. It is simply dusting them often. If you dust them regularly, instead of when it can't be put off any longer, the dust won't have a chance to combine with oils and moisture in the air into a stubborn, sticky coating.

DUSTING BLINDS

If you dust blinds regularly the dust will still be loose and easy to remove. Dust blinds twice a month or more with a Masslinn cloth or better yet, a lambswool duster. Close the blinds up flat, dust one side, then close them the other way and dust the other. If you're using a lambswool duster, be sure to make good contact with the surface, don't just wave it over the slats.

Verticals shed dust, so they can usually be done less often. Cloth-covered verticals, however, will absorb dust, so they should be done twice monthly too, and not with a treated dustcloth, because they will also absorb dust treatment. Use the dust brush on a vacuum.

DEEP CLEANING BLINDS

When hard-surface slatted blinds need to be washed, or deep cleaned (which is generally once every year and a half or so, depending the soiling conditions in your area and home), don't try to wash them in place. You will bend them, cut your hands, do a poor job, and it will take forever. Don't take them off and try to wash them in the tub, either.

Nor should you gun them with a pressure nozzle—I've bent blinds and punched holes in them doing this.

The following process is fast (takes only four or five minutes a blind) and it works. Your blinds will look like new.

BLIND WASHING TECHNIQUE

1. Spread the old quilt, blanket, piece of carpeting, or a couple of large mats, out on the slanted surface.

2. Take down a blind, let it out to full length, adjust the slats to flat, and lay the blind out on the quilt or blanket.

3. Mix up your cleaning solution, wet the blind with it, and scrub with a soft brush longways along the slats. Be sure to get up under the cords.

4. Then turn the blind over and do the other side. The quilt will be saturated with the solution by now and help to clean the blind.

5. Hang the blind on a clothesline or over a ladder (or have someone hold it up) and rinse it with a hose.

6. Then give it a good shake or run your fingers down the slats to shake off the excess water so the blind won't water spot. Dark-colored blinds need to be blotted or wiped dry to prevent water spots. The blower attachment on a vacuum cleaner is another way to speed drying. Blinds can be rehung while still damp, but not dripping wet.

Ultrasonic cleaning

This process, offered by professional cleaners you can find in the Yellow Pages under "Blinds," is the easiest and best way to deep clean blinds. The blind or shade is immersed in a tank of cleaning solution and gently "scrubbed" by sound waves. Ultrasonic cleaning isn't cheap, but it is the safest and most thorough method available, for either miniblinds or fabric shades.

VERTICALS

Vertical blinds with a smooth surface can be cleaned quickly by spray and wipe, using glass cleaner and a terry cleaning cloth. If you have a lot of verticals, photo-supply stores sell print squeegees that will squeegee the cleaning solution from both sides of a flat vertical slat in one pass—it makes the job go quickly. It won't work well on curved slats, though.

Cloth-covered vertical blinds can be wiped occasionally with a cloth dampened with carpet shampoo. Just spot clean them gently and let them dry. Do not immerse or soak. The shampoo dries to a powder which can be removed by vacuuming or dry brushing.

FABRIC BLINDS AND SHADES

Pleated fabric and cellular shades are cleanable to varying degrees, depending on the brand. It is extra important here to follow the manufacturer's recommendations for cleaning. Most fabric shades that are recommended for ultrasonic cleaning will also tolerate a gentle washing in your bathtub with lukewarm water and Woolite. If the shade has a metal header, be careful it doesn't scratch or mark the tub. If you have any doubts about the tolerance of a shade for wet cleaning, consulting with a pro blinds cleaner may be well worth the fee, to avoid costly damage.

DRAPES AND CURTAINS

Are pretty good characters when you think about it. They just hang there quietly, protecting us and our furnishings from the sun, the cold, and any potential window peekers. They're good-looking, they give a home spirit and dignity, and require almost no maintenance. They'll last quite a while if we thank them with a little looking after.

In more than forty years of professional cleaning, I've cleaned many a curtain and drape, from the curtains in tiny trailers to giant stage drapes. Here's how to make drapes a super simple part of your cleaning schedule.

1. Buy good quality drapes/curtains. That tiny bit more spent up front pays you back with years and years on the back end. Good quality window coverings always look better, hang nicer, resist soiling more, and even damage less when Cindy the Siamese decides to climb them.

2. In and near kitchen areas there is a lot of airborne grease and oil, and just as it collects on top of the fridge, it will on drapes, so install sturdy fabrics that are thoroughly washable or otherwise cleanable in such places.

3. Have curtains and drapes hung properly. I'm a good mechanic, patient, and can draw straight lines, but I've always struggled with drape hanging because few of us do it often enough to know all the tricks involved. If you don't know what you're doing, it's easy to damage the drapes, the woodwork, and your relationships in the process. In most cases it pays to ask an expert to hang them or have it included in the price if you're buying new ones. You'll be amazed at the difference in the final result.

DUST REMOVAL ON DRAPES

Drapes do accumulate dust and the way to get rid of it is by vacuuming. Vacuuming pulls the dust out of drapes, instead of just knocking it from the surface. Generally you can do drapes with vac attachments from a standing position and it will only take three or four minutes to do a whole drape well. A couple of times a year is generally enough.

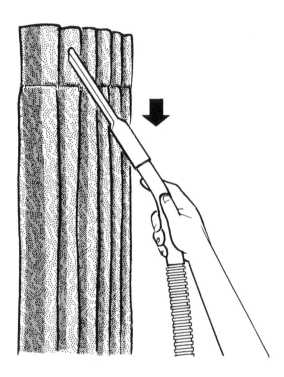

There is a secret to vacuuming drapes—being sure to "bleed" the vacuum suction. That little clip on the vacuum hose (in case you've wondered what it's for) opens a hole in the hose and lets air in, which reduces the suction of the vacuum so it won't suck in the whole drape or bend or crinkle the fibers of the fabric with too much suction.

Eighty percent of the dust will be on the top two inches and the bottom foot of the drape. Vacuum from the top down, always moving vertically, with the pleats or flow of the drape.

To remove dust from drapes not dirty enough for the cleaner, you can also tumble them in the dryer for a few minutes. Don't use this technique on fiberglass or anything resembling it. Tiny glass fibers will remain in the dryer and be picked by other clothes, causing irritations when worn.

Cleaning drapes

How often drapes and curtains have to be cleaned depends of course on where and how you live, and what they have to endure. For drapes in the average home, cleaning once every two or three years should be enough. If there's a smoker in the family, once a year cleaning is recommended.

Drapes or curtains in or near the kitchen will catch and absorb the airborne grease and oil from cooking, which will also make them collect dust faster. Curtains in locations like this will usually have to be cleaned twice as often as others.

For washability of either drapes or curtains, consult the label. When in doubt, be sure to use the gentle cycle, especially on curtains with ruffles or other frills. It was common in the past century to starch curtains after washing, to give them a crisp look and even a little dirt shedding factor. Most newer materials are designed to not need starching.

Drapes are relatively inexpensive to dry clean, in comparison to other home care costs. (And we usually only have drapes in a few places, like the living room and dining room, so the total cost shouldn't get out of sight.) For example, for 84" lined drapes the average price to have them dry cleaned, pressed, and pleated is around $1.20 a pleat. Unlined or shorter drapes will be less. Dry cleaners will be happy to give you a price quote or estimate. Don't be afraid to ask or call.

Most shops that handle drapes offer a (often surprisingly reasonable) take down and rehang service.

Choosing drapes for ease of care

Drapes, on the average, should last about ten years. Drapes seldom wear out just hanging there; sun rot is the biggest enemy. Kids and pets climbing on them is a close second. Think of these things when choosing and buying drapes. Some homes aren't meant for delicate, frilly, Victorian drapes, or Lincoln Center velvet curtains. Remember, too, that the more ruffles, valances, flounces, and tiebacks, the more layers of curtain on a window, the more time you will have to invest in care and maintenance.

Any fabric exposed to the sun will fade somewhat, and dark colored drapes or curtains absorb rather than reflect light, so they will fade more. Choosing good quality, longlasting drapes is another case of "it costs a dollar less to go first class." If you're really making an investment in a particular set of drapes, seeing or calling someone who already has that type might be a good idea.

Drapes can help save upholstery and carpets. Keep drapes drawn to keep sun out.

CLEANING TECHNIQUE: WOOD

Though wood is one of the best camouflagers of soil and damage (they blend right in with the grain to become almost invisible), wood does get dirty, especially where hands are often touching it. Soils such as handprints and grease have to be washed off—you can't just take a dustrag to them and polish them away. Washing means moisture, and the thought of using it around wood terrifies wood lovers. But most modern wood surfaces have several coats of seal on them (polyurethane, varnish, or lacquer). This gives them a tough, transparent coating that doesn't allow moisture to ever touch the wood itself—it's like a thin layer of glass over the wood. When you wash wood like this, you're washing the finish, not the wood. So applying a cleaning solution and then drying the surface quickly has zero effect on the wood. It just removes the soil from the surface of the finish.

Water can cause a problem if you flood a wood surface, or leave moisture in prolonged contact with it. When you do this that moisture will finally find tiny cracks, holes, or damaged areas in the finish and soak into the wood itself, causing swelling, cracking, splitting, or other damage. Pressboards and plywoods, especially, will swell up greatly when soaked with water, and not shrink back to normal as they dry like other woods might.

So the first and most important step in wood care is to determine just what kind of finish is on the wood, or if there is any finish at all.

WOOD WITH A WELL-SEALED FINISH

Most modern home furnishings made of wood that has a slick, shiny surface (such as kitchen cabinets, dining tables and other furniture, paneling, and glistening hardwood floors) have several coats of finish on them. When they need it, they can be damp-wiped or damp-mopped with a mild, neutral cleaner like Top Sheen or Wood Wash. Just remember to always wipe and buff wood floors dry immediately afterward with a cleaning cloth, to remove the moisture and any detergent residue that may remain. This allows the nice shiny surface to continue to shine. Cleaning wood this way will also leave the surface more resistant to resoiling, whereas applying and reapplying polishes and waxes will often cause the surface of wood to get gummy and sticky, which attracts and holds dirt. Paneling with a sealed surface can be cleaned by the two-bucket system, using Top Sheen, Wood Wash, or Murphy's Oil Soap.

If you encounter a hard-to-remove spot while cleaning sealed wood, scrub gently with a wetted white nylon scrub sponge.

When you need to polish

As noted earlier most wood with a well-sealed finish benefits more from cleaning (see above) than polish. Using furniture polish can help wood with a finish that is starting to look worn. Varnished and lacquered finishes can get dulled and worn from use, and a furniture polish will fill tiny scratches in the surface to help it look better for a while. If you use a polish, stick to the same type to avoid

O D

streaking. Professionals use a carnauba-based product called Wood to Wood when polish is needed, instead of oils that will only build up and encourage fingerprints. Carnauba is the original wood wax and polish. It adds beauty and luster to wood, and leaves behind a microscopic coating that resists dust.

OILED WOOD

The wood in some furniture and paneling and other home surfaces may appear dull and more "natural" looking. Chances are that finishes like these (including some floors) have been treated with tung oil or other penetrating oils, whose purpose is to soak into the wood and condition it, keep it from drying out and cracking and splitting. Most oil-treated finishes, even though they don't shine, will hold out moisture fairly well. So you can wash finishes like this, too, to clean them. Just do it more conservatively. This means, for instance, dipping your cleaning cloth into the solution and wringing it almost dry, and then going over the surface with it a couple of times to loosen and remove the soil. Then immediately follow this damp wiping with a dry towel to remove all moisture and detergent residue.

Oiled wood does need to be reoiled about once a year, to keep it stain and moisture resistant. Apply the oil, rub it in, leave it on a while, then blot up the excess. Don't use furniture polish on oiled wood.

UNFINISHED WOOD

Unvarnished or unfinished woods around the house (such as used in some kinds of "rustic" decor, for example) are handsome, and carefree in the sense that flyspecks, nicks, and overall aging often just enhance their rustic look. However grease and many other stains will sink into the porous surface and be hard if not impossible to remove. If unfinished wood gets stained or soiled, try first to clean it with a soft rubber "dry sponge" from a janitorial-supply store. If that doesn't work, try a cloth lightly dampened in APC (don't use too much water, or you'll just spread the soil or cause it to sink further into the surface). Individual not-too-deep stains can be sanded off carefully with fine sandpaper. If you find yourself trying to clean unfinished wood frequently, you should break down and clean it well and then seal the surface with a low-gloss urethane. Or limit the use of such finishes to places that get little human contact.

WOOD USED IN EATING OR FOOD PREPARATION UTENSILS

Whether it has an oiled finish or been coated with a more permanent sealer, it should only be damp-washed or immersed in dishwater quickly and then removed and dried immediately. **Never** soak wooden bowls and the like in water. Treat wooden utensils and surfaces of this type at least yearly with mineral oil (not just any oil). Oil the whole surface generously, let it soak in overnight, then wipe off the excess.

TO KEEP WOOD LOOKING GOOD

✔ Clean up spills and water leaks immediately, the minute they happen.

✔ Mat all approaches to wood flooring.

✔ Sweep, vacuum, or dust often, to keep damaging dirt and grit off wood surfaces, and damp-mop or wipe them when needed.

✔ Head off damaging footwear and toys, and people with sharp, heavy things that are bound to be set down on or dropped onto your nice wood table or floor.

✔ Always clean wood well before deciding it needs to be refinished. And refinish wood with a protective finish when the finish is badly worn.

REMOVING HARDWATER DEPOSITS

Hardwater deposits are the bane of the bathroom, especially, but we have better ways than ever to remove them without hurting either our household surfaces or ourselves.

WHERE THEY COME FROM

Water in many areas of the country has minerals such as calcium and magnesium dissolved in it. Drops of water are splashed and dribbled around as we bathe, shower, etc. When the water evaporates it leaves its minerals behind. Drops often form in the same spot, and as they dry, those minerals keep adding up.

This process continues for sixty showers or twenty lawn sprinkler sessions, and you end up with a rock-hard buildup that doesn't clean off like other soils. Hardwater deposits are most often found on faucets, shower heads, tubs, shower enclosures, and toilets (the infamous "toilet ring" is a hardwater deposit).

WHAT WE NEED TO REMOVE THEM

Bleach doesn't take off hardwater deposits, it only removes the color from them.

Hardwater deposits have to be dissolved to remove them. Because mineral buildup is usually alkaline, we use an acid to loosen and dissolve it.

Hardwater deposits in SHOWERS, TUBS, and on TILE:

Many of the popular bathroom cleaners don't work too well for this even though they do contain a mild acid. This is because the deposits in showers, especially, are often a combination of minerals plus soap scum and body oils, and acid doesn't work well on those last two. There is a shower cleaner that dis-

solves all three—yet won't hurt you or the surface. It's a professional cleaning product called Showers-n-Stuff, and the closest thing to it on the supermarket shelves is Comet Bathroom Cleaner. A degreaser followed by an acid cleaner can also be used for a two-pronged attack on bad cases of hardwater deposits plus soap scum.

Removal techniques depend on how much buildup there is. A week or so of hardwater traces can be removed rapidly with a light acid cleaner (Showers-n-Stuff diluted with water 1:5). However, if it's been months or years since you cleaned it and you almost can't recognize the tile, you need to apply a cleaner like Showers-n-Stuff full strength and let it sit on there a few minutes.

After the solution has been on the surface for a little while, help the cleaner out with some light scrubbing with a white nylon scrub sponge. The deposit will begin to come off and you will know when it's all off by the feel. The surface will be slick and shiny like when it was new. Rinse the surface down **well** now, and clean it more often from now on.

Some shower cleaners come with a "foamer nozzle" that enables you to shoot the solution on the surface in the form of a clinging foam. If the cleaner doesn't come with one, you can get one from the Cleaning Center or a janitorial-supply store. A foamer nozzle is a help even with a nonfoaming cleaner like Showers-n-Stuff, because it will not atomize the solution (turn it into tiny airborne particles that could be inhaled).

Hardwater deposits in TOILETS:

If you already have a hardwater buildup problem in the bowl, you will need bowl cleaner. This is usually phosphoric or hydrochloric acid—handle with care (wear rubber gloves and eye protection)!

Don't pour the bowl cleaner right into the bowl—all that water will dilute the acid and reduce its effectiveness. Instead, take a bowl swab and thrust it up and down quickly in the throat of the toilet several times. This will empty the bowl.

Then wring the water out of the swab and use it to apply bowl cleaner over the whole inside of the bowl. Be sure to include the "throat" of the toilet and up under the rim of the toilet where the little water inlet holes often become clogged with mineral scale that can interfere with the toilet's flushing action.

Leave the acid on a few minutes and flush to rinse. Reapply if necessary. Persistent rings can be removed this way, or with a WET pumice stone.

Hardwater deposits on WINDOWS:

Hardwater deposits can build up on the outside of windows, too. For light deposits, try a mild acid cleaner like Showers-n-Stuff, or the phosphoric acid tub and tile cleaners sold by janitorial-supply stores. Keep the surface wet with the cleaner for up to five minutes, and scrub with a white scrub sponge as needed to remove stubborn spots. In really bad cases a stronger acid cleaner (similar to a bathroom bowl cleaner) can be used to dissolve the deposit and then rinsed away. Be careful not to damage adjoining surfaces, such as mortar and aluminum. In severe cases, the mineral scale clings to the glass so tightly that it is virtually impossible to remove. Such windows can sometimes be salvaged by pro window cleaners using professional (very strong) acid cleaners.

PREVENTION

✔ Squeegee or wipe down the shower walls after you shower to remove the droplets before they dry. This goes a long way toward 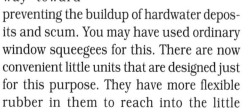 preventing the buildup of hardwater deposits and scum. You may have used ordinary window squeegees for this. There are now convenient little units that are designed just for this purpose. They have more flexible rubber in them to reach into the little curves in a tiled surface, and even come with a hook so you can hang them right there in the shower.

✔ Put the shower curtain inside the tub before you shower to reduce the amount of water splashed around.

✔ If you clean the faucets and shower head with disinfectant cleaner regularly, you will never have to face a heavy hardwater encrustation.

✔ Installing an automatic water softener will help, too.

✔ Outdoors, adjust or move sprinklers away from windows.

Grout
WILL MAKE YOU SHOUT!

"Tile would be a wonderful material if it weren't for that xo!#$%^ grout!" I agree and to make things worse, every 4" x 4" square of tile on the bathroom wall or wherever has sixteen inches of grout around it. Once grout gets impregnated with anything it stains and is ugly. Those stains are hard to remove and seem to return twice as fast the next time.

A professional grout brush (which you can get at a janitorial-supply store) is a great improvement over our usual cleaning tool, the old toothbrush, but it isn't a century 2000 answer.

Old grout

Remember a stain is often permanent soiling. If you regularly bleach your grout to get it white again, you are just getting temporary relief and oxidizing (damaging) the grout so it will stain even worse in the future.

The best thing you can do for old, badly soiled grout is to clean it really well using a grout brush and strong enough shower cleaner to release and remove soils. This one time you might even bleach the grout to get it whiter. Then go to a Color Tile store and get

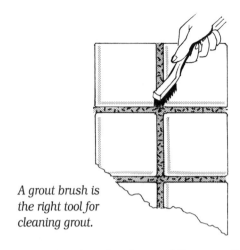

A grout brush is the right tool for cleaning grout.

some grout seal and one of those applicators that looks like a magic marker. Apply a couple of coats of the sealer to your grout with it, and let it dry. After this, soil should remain on the surface of the grout and be removable with regular cleaning.

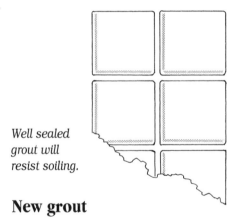

Well sealed grout will resist soiling.

New grout

Good news: most new grout has an acrylic hardener in it, which gives you "nonstainable" grout. If you have any doubt at all about its soil resistance, I'd seal my grout first thing, before it's ever used.

You can also get colored grout now. Remember both very light and very dark colors will show soils. A medium brownish or reddish color is the best camouflaging color. Whenever possible, lay new tile with narrower grout joints—1/8 or even 1/16th inch. It'll look better even when it's old and soiled.

HOME ODOR CONTROL

ELIMINATING BAD ODORS

We may be able to tolerate a little disorder when we're pressed for time, but bad odors have to go—now!

For more than forty years now, especially when cleaning old homes and apartments, and doing fire and flood cleanup jobs, I've fought the battle of bad odors. In the old days we professionals did more "masking" (covering up an unpleasant odor with a strong, more pleasant smell) than eliminating of odors. But in recent years there's been a real breakthrough, and now there are products on the market that actually eliminate or "clean up" odors. Among these are the odor neutralizers, which make chemical changes in odor molecules so that they are no longer perceived as bad odors by the tiny sensors in our nose.

One of my favorites is X-O, an odor neutralizer made of natural, organic ingredients. It will take care of unwanted odors instantly, safely, and economically. I recommend it for daily cleaning in odor-prone areas. Just dilute it according to the directions, and apply it to the surface (sponge, mop, or spray it on). In some situations you may want to apply it full strength, and it can also be added to washing-machine water and carpet shampoo solution, and used to fog the air in problem areas. The manufacturer says there's no odor it can't handle, and my Cleaning Center customers seem to agree. X-O is also available as an odor neutralizer combined with a disinfectant cleaner, to help combat the cause of odors.

An important thing to remember in all odor-removal efforts is that **odor has a source**, which is often bacteria or fungus growth of some kind. It may be dirty socks, a dead mouse, a rotting banana, or accumulated urine, but when this source is removed, the odor will usually be gone too. Too often we don't remove the source, but try to camouflage it instead with sprays and wicks and scented bags. Even when using an odor neutralizer, be sure to remove the substance causing the foul odor first—all traces of it—before applying the neutralizer.

When a bad-smelling organic liquid such as urine has been absorbed into a surface (such as carpet and the padding beneath it) that cannot be removed for cleaning, or ripped up and replaced, there is another weapon in the deodorizing arsenal that can be used here. That is a bacteria/enzyme digester, such as Eliminator. When mixed up and applied it will create a colony of friendly bacteria and their enzymes that actually consume the source of the odor. You have to follow the instructions on the label carefully, which includes not applying other cleaners first. Apply it and then keep the area moist for as long as the label tells you, to give the bacteria a chance to do their job. Bacteria/enzyme digesters can be found in many pet-supply and hardware stores. Eliminator is available from the Cleaning Center. See also p. 187.

"GERM-KILLER" CLEANING

Now that we know where diseases come from (bacteria, viruses, and fungi), there is a growing concern for eliminating and controlling these tiny troublemakers. We're almost a little paranoid about it—I'm amazed at the amount of disinfectant products people buy from my Cleaning Center stores, and one of the big sales promises on many new cleaning products in the supermarket is "germ killing action."

This is another place where we don't want to take a good thing too far—unnecessary use of disinfectant products (like overuse of antibiotics) can contribute to the development of "superbugs" that defy all germ control measures. So for the sake of our future safety we never want to use germkillers indiscriminately.

Our modern facilities for water treatment and waste disposal, and our more sanitary modern home surfaces do most of our sanitation for us. There is no need to panic if our home isn't up to hospital standards. In hospitals and the like, given the nature and risk of such places, very rigid procedures must be followed and special products used to achieve true disinfecting or "sterilization," which kills

WHAT TO USE

A disinfectant cleaner, used properly in the right places, kills bacteria and viruses on contact. As the name suggests, a disinfectant cleaner will clean surfaces and disinfect them at the same time. Ordinary cleaners do sanitize to a point—well enough, in fact, for most general purposes. But for bathrooms and other possible germ transfer areas, a disinfectant cleaner will do the job better.

There is a wide variety of disinfectant cleaners available today, in supermarkets and janitorial-supply stores. Disinfectants include pine cleaners, which have disinfecting properties if they contain at least twenty-seven percent real pine oil, and chlorine bleach, which is a disinfectant, but needs to be approached with caution.

The best all-around disinfectant cleaner for home use—the easiest to use, safest, and cheapest—is a quaternary ammonium compound. We pros refer to these as "quats" and they are inexpensive, generally odorless, and effective against a broad spectrum of microorganisms. You can buy them in concentrate form and mix them up in a spray bottle or your mop water, according to the directions. Then you're ready to go. You can get these at any janitorial-supply house, and they are what the hotels and motels use to keep their bathrooms so odor free. Regular use of a quaternary disinfectant cleaner will retard and prevent mildew growth, and is safe for most household surfaces.

The older phenolic disinfectants such as Lysol are actually more effective against certain types of organisms, but these have a disagreeable odor, can stain surfaces, cause skin irritation, and are more dangerous to some pets.

NFECTING

one hundred percent of microorganisms and their spores. At home this is usually neither practical nor necessary.

At home, within the family, or even moving in and out of other family homes, the risks are really minimal. So all we need to do is follow a few simple sanitizing procedures that will greatly reduce the "germs" in our home, our everyday living environment:

1. First: Keep our home surfaces clean and practice good general cleaning habits. How **well** and **regularly** we clean is more important than what we use, even when it comes to germ-killing.

2. Second: Remove any thing, or correct any situation that might house or encourage bacteria, viruses, or fungi. This means eliminate possible sources of bacteria growth, such as waste food, human or animal wastes, or dead animals.

3. Disinfect key areas regularly (see following).

4. If we do have a problem, deal with it immediately. Make sure anyone who has a serious disease gets medical attention and practice good sanitation measures to keep the infection from spreading to others.

When using a disinfectant

1. Whenever possible, clean before you attempt to disinfect. Remove any loose matter or heavy deposits from the surface, because such things reduce the effectiveness of disinfectants.

2. Never mix a disinfectant with other cleaners unless the label tells you to.

3. Dilute as directed—don't make the solution "stronger so it will kill germs better."

4. Really saturate the surface you wish to sanitize—be sure to get all the cracks and corners and crevices.

Always clean before you disinfect.

How to use it

You can spray, mop, or sponge disinfectant cleaner solution on, but be sure to leave it sit on the surface a while, ideally as long as ten minutes. This allows "kill time," to be sure it has a chance to come in contact with germs and kill them. Then wipe it off with a cleaning cloth, and the surface will be polished dry and won't need rinsing. In fact the bit of disinfectant residue left behind helps retard future germ growth.

Rubber gloves are recommended while using certain disinfectants—read the label. When applying disinfectant with a spray bottle and wiping afterward with a towel I don't use rubber gloves, but if a job involves dipping into a bucket or whatever of disinfectant cleaner, on go the gloves!

When spraying disinfectant cleaner from a spray bottle, set the nozzle so it delivers droplets, not a fine mist. Atomizing quats and breathing the vapor is irritating to the mucous membranes. Be sure to have good ventilation when you're using disinfectants—you don't want to be breathing disinfectant fumes for any length of time in a confined area.

Where to use it

1. Doorknobs, handles, faucets, switchplates, and anyplace in your home or car that gets a lot of hand contact.
2. The bathroom.
3. Waste containers and the area around them.
4. The floors in children's rooms.
5. In any mildew-prone area.
6. In and around pet areas.
7. In loads of laundry that need to be disinfected.
8. Floors, walls, bed hardware, and other furnishings in sickroom or home nursing areas.

Where not to use it

You never want to use quats or many other disinfectants around food areas, such as countertops, dishes, sinks, and refrigerators. (Check the label.) Regular thorough cleaning with dish detergent will keep areas like these sanitary enough. Using disinfectant on the kitchen floor is okay, just not anywhere that comes in direct contact with food or cooking utensils.

Mildew

Mildew isn't dirt, it's a fungus that thrives on moisture and temperatures between 75° and 85°F. Besides causing ugly stains and discolorations, it can and will eventually weaken and damage whatever it is growing on.

Mildew can grow inside the house (especially in bathrooms, basements, and closets), and outside, too, where its favorite hangout is the north or shady side of things.

TO HELP PREVENT MILDEW

1. Never put anything away wet (laundry, camping gear, etc.).
2. Reducing moisture will reduce mildew. Use a squeegee or towel to wipe the shower walls and any little "water traps" in the bathroom when you're done showering. Seal all cracks and holes anywhere in the house that may allow water leakage. Consider a dehumidifier in damp rooms. Packets or bags of chemicals like silica gel or calcium chloride will absorb moisture and discourage mildew growth in small, enclosed, mildew-prone places such as drawers and closets.

Heat cables or low wattage light bulbs can be installed in chronically damp closets.

3. Light retards mildew growth and can even kill it. If you have a mildew-prone area, increase the lighting there. Cutting overhanging tree branches will help mildew-susceptible rooms.

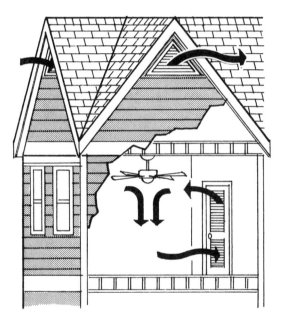

4. Ventilation—good air circulation—helps prevent mildew growth. Keep all areas of the house well ventilated. Fans, open closet designs, and louvered closet doors help out here.

5. Cleaning mildew-prone areas regularly with a disinfectant cleaner will slow down or stop mildew growth. In mildew-prone areas, after I've cleaned this way I spray a few last whisks of disinfectant cleaner on and don't wipe it off, just let it dry there.

6. To help prevent mildew on painted surfaces, additives (mildewicides) are available that can be mixed into paint.

REMOVING MILDEW
From clothing and other fabric items:

Vacuum or brush any mildew on the surface off immediately, and take dry cleanables to the dry cleaner. If mildew stains remain on washable fabrics, try bleaching with all-fabric bleach, or chlorine bleach if safe for the fabric. Soak fabric that cannot be bleached for thirty minutes in a quaternary disinfectant solution and then wash as usual. In some fabrics, mildew causes a stain that will not come out. If left untreated, mildew will eat and deteriorate fabric.

From leather:

Use denatured alcohol diluted 1:1 with water.

From hard surfaces:

Mild or surface mildew can usually be removed with a spray and wipe application of disinfectant cleaner. Use a white nylon scrub sponge if necessary.

Entrenched mildew (such as in bathroom grout or caulk) may be mixed with mineral buildup. Here you need to clean with an acid cleaner such as Showers-n-Stuff, or an acidic disinfectant such as Bac Down, to remove the buildup as well as kill the mildew. Use a grout brush or white nylon scrub sponge to scrub as necessary, and repeat the process if necessary.

When all else fails, a mixture of 1:5 chlorine bleach and water (and the help of a stiff brush) will also remove mildew from hard surfaces that can withstand bleach. Don't get this on carpeting, or any clothing you're proud of!

For mildew stains on siding, walks, walls, and other outdoor surfaces, see pressure washers, pp. 115-117.

PET MESS PREVENTION AND CLEANUP

THE BEST SOLUTIONS FOR PET HAIR ALL OVER

1. Groom pets regularly, especially pets with long hair or heavy coats, and any pet in shedding season. Get it before it gets all over.

2. A dampened cloth will remove hair from most hard surfaces well, and on soft surfaces like upholstery it will lift the hair so you can get it with a vacuum. A dry sponge is a good hair remover, too.

3. To remove hair effectively from upholstered furniture and other soft, smooth surfaces, you need a vacuum with a beater brush or power wand, or a handheld model with same, such as the Electrolux Little Lux.

4. A pet rake (available from the Cleaning Center) has stiff, crimped bristles that work well on carpet, soft furniture, bedding, drapes, car interiors, and the like.

5. A lint roller does a good, quick job on clothes.

6. A dustmop is best for hair on hard floors.

TO CUT DOWN CAT SCRATCHING DAMAGE

1. Provide a good scratching post, or more than one if necessary. Stiff, scratchy materials like tightly woven hemp are more attractive than soft materials like carpeting. The Felix company of Seattle, Washington, makes some of the best posts—sturdy, catnip-filled, and irresistible.

2. Trim your cat's nails regularly, using a cat nail nipper, and not going too close to the quick.

3. Avoid highly textured surfaces (including fabrics) in the pet's surroundings—they're much more likely to be clawed than smooth surfaces.

4. Avoid declawing unless the pet will be indoors all his life, and there is no other choice.

TO MAKE SURE CATS USE THE LITTER BOX, AND NOT OTHER PLACES

1. Plain nonfancy litters, and plain open boxes, are the best. Don't fill the box too full—a couple inches deep is enough.

2. Have more than one box if you need it.

3. Keep the box clean, or kitty will pass it up. Scoop out solids daily, and replace the litter and wash the box once a week. Remove the "urine clumps" carefully when removing solids, because they can cause more odor than anything.

THE TRUTH ABOUT FLEA CONTROL

1. To treat a flea problem, you have to treat the pet's whole surroundings, not just the pet. This means not just the pet bed but carpeting, upholstered furniture, drapes, cracks and crevices in hard floors, and even the yard areas your pet spends time around.

2. Use only fleakilling preparations designed for your particular kind of pet—i.e., only cat fleakillers for cats, etc.

3. Killing all adult fleas is not enough. Once you have a flea infestation, you have to treat the pet and his surroundings, and treat

MESS

again within two months to kill the newly hatched fleas.

4. Frequent vacuuming of carpet in flea problem areas helps keep down the flea population. Use a disposable bag and sprinkle some flea powder into it before you start. Hot water extraction cleaning of carpeting will also help kill adult fleas.

5. Flea traps are a safe, effective way to reduce fleas. You can make these yourself by setting out a large pan of water at night with a tiny bit of detergent in it, and a lamp arranged to shine on the surface of the water. Fleas jump for the light and drown.

TO KEEP THINGS SAFE AND SANITARY

1. Practice good basic sanitation around pets—wash your hands after handling them, etc.

2. Disinfect pet areas and articles every so often or when indicated. You can use an ordinary quat disinfectant as long as you keep pets away until the area or item has been rinsed and dried. Use bleach solution for special problems like parvovirus if so instructed by your vet.

3. When disinfecting, follow the instructions on p. 183.

4. Keep your pet at home, not wandering all over to cause problems and pick up infections elsewhere.

5. Keeping cats and dogs from killing small animals and birds will not only aid endangered species, but cut down on disease transmission.

POOCH POTTY PROBLEM PREVENTERS

1. Be sure to housebreak puppies as soon as possible, before they have a chance to ruin the furnishings and become problem dogs.

2. Install a stool digester in your backyard, to take care of the problem of "pet droppings all over." A stool digester is like a miniature (waterless) septic tank for pets—you install it in the ground, and then lift the lid to dispose of droppings.

THE BEST PET ODOR CONTROL PRODUCTS

1. Odor neutralizers like Nilium or X-O, when sprayed on or used in cleaning or rinsing solutions, will remove odors from hard surfaces.

2. When the odor of urine, vomit, and the like is entrenched, especially in soft, hard-to-clean things like carpet and padding, upholstery, and bedding, you need a bacteria/enzyme digester like Eliminator. This contains live beneficial bacteria that produce enzymes that literally consume the

organic compounds that cause bad odors. You do have to follow the instructions carefully when using them (such as don't use hot water, don't use any other cleaner or disinfectant first, keep the area wet while the solution is working, and leave the solution on long enough to do the job). Eliminator is a brand of bacteria/enzyme digester that works faster than some of the others.

3. Wick deodorizers such as those made by Nilodor can help with problem odor areas.

DEALING WITH PET INDISCRETIONS

Such as urine, droppings, or vomit:

1. Here, especially, prompt cleanup is important. Urine must be removed as soon as possible because after twenty-four to forty-eight hours it undergoes chemical changes that may cause permanent stains. Vomit contains strong stomach acid that will stain and bleach surfaces. And the odor of one pet potty mess on the carpet will encourage others to follow.

2. Pet mess on hard surfaces: Remove all you can first with paper towels or a small squeegee and dustpan, then wash the area with APC solution. Use an odor neutralizer/cleaner such as X-O Plus if the urine may have penetrated into cracks and crevices in the area.

3. Pet mess on carpet: Remove all you can first with paper towels or a small squeegee and dustpan. If the mess was vomit, now

rinse with water. Apply bacteria/enzyme digester according to directions, being sure the solution penetrates as far as the stain material did. If stain remains, use carpet spotter.

4. Old, widespread pet mess on carpeting may or may not be removable, depending on how bad it is. A professional odor removal technician may be able to take steps to salvage the situation, or you may have to simply replace not just the carpet but the pad beneath it.

MISCELLANEOUS PET MESS PREVENTION WISDOM

1. Make sure pets have clean, fresh water every day—don't just top off the water bowl every so often. Water bowls should be well out of the way, to avoid having them knocked over. Heavy ones are best.

2. Use strong, lidded cans to keep pets out of garbage.

3. A spray bottle full of plain water is a good way of discouraging cats from all kinds of problem behavior. They won't be hurt, won't know who did it, but they sure will hate it!

4. Take advantage of sealing and soil retardants (see p. 42) in pet areas.

5. If you permit your pets to lie on chairs or sofas, a washable cover over the pet's favorite spot(s) will make it easy to keep things clean.

6. Confining pets to certain areas of your home will reduce pet mess.

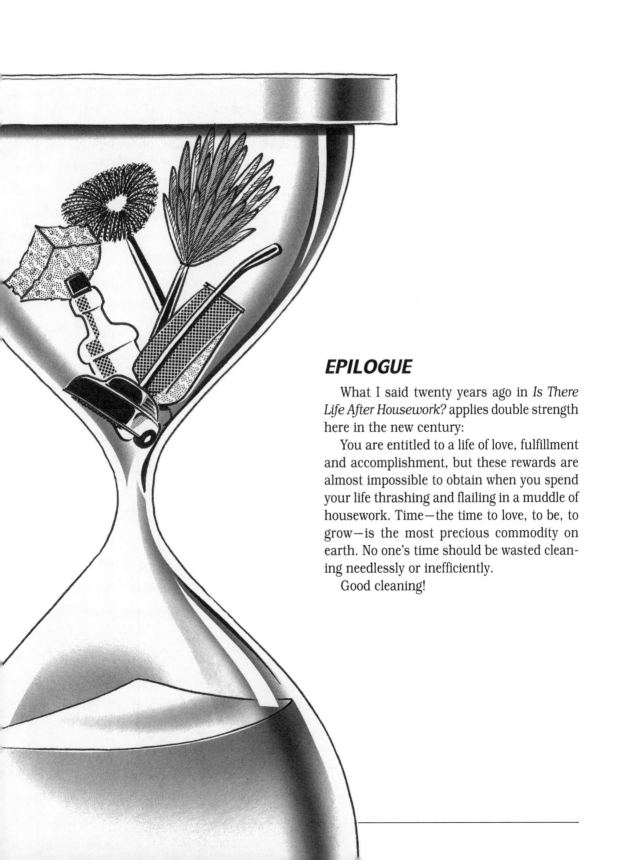

EPILOGUE

What I said twenty years ago in *Is There Life After Housework?* applies double strength here in the new century:

You are entitled to a life of love, fulfillment and accomplishment, but these rewards are almost impossible to obtain when you spend your life thrashing and flailing in a muddle of housework. Time—the time to love, to be, to grow—is the most precious commodity on earth. No one's time should be wasted cleaning needlessly or inefficiently.

Good cleaning!

About the Author

One of the questions most often asked of "the cleaning man," **Don Aslett**, is:

"Did you have any idea that the little college cleaning team you started in 1955 would end up being a worldwide cleaning corporation?"

His answer is:

"Yes, I foresaw and dreamed it, hoped for it, and then I lived the demanding schedule necessary to develop it. All because I just love to clean! And the rewards, more than three decades later now, are a large company with over thousands of employees, more than thirty books written and published (millions of copies sold), and over 5,000 media and speaking appearances about 'clean'."

Two decades ago, Don started revolutionizing the American home by sharing all the professional tools and techniques that can help us clean faster and better, and save us money, too. He gives home cleaners the "pro advantage" through his books, his appearances on national TV and radio across the country, his speeches, workshops, and seminars, his newsletter The Clean Report, his answering of cleaning questions on the internet, and his mail-order and retail source of professional supplies, The Cleaning Center. He has motivated millions to make "clean" not a chore but a personal choice for improved quality of life.

For a catalog of all of Don Aslett's books and videos

and

a copy of The Cleaning Center catalog/newsletter

THE CLEAN REPORT

please send your name and address on a postcard

to

The Clean Report

PO Box 700

Pocatello ID 83204

or fax 208-232-6286

or email AslettDon@aol.com

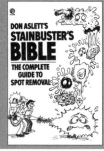
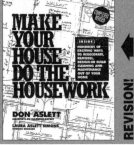

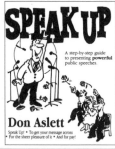
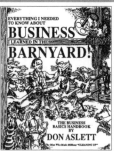

☐ Don, please put my name and the enclosed list of friends of mine on your mailing list for the **Clean Report** bulletin and catalog.

TITLE	Retail	Qty	Amt
Clean In A Minute	$5.00		
Video Clean In A Minute	$12.95		
Cleaning Up For a Living	$16.99		
Clutter Free! Finally & Forever	$12.99		
Clutter's Last Stand	$12.99		
✳Two for Twenty Special—above two books	$20.00		
Construction Cleanup	$19.95		
Don Aslett's Stainbuster's Bible	$11.95		
Everything I Needed to Know…Barnyard	$9.95		
How to Be #1 With Your Boss	$9.99		
How to Handle 1,000 Things at Once	$12.99		
How to Have a 48-Hour Day	$12.99		
✳Two for Twenty Special—above two books	$20.00		
How to Upgrade & Motivate Your Crew	$19.95		
Is There Life After Housework?	$11.99		
Video Is There Life After Housework?	$19.95		
Keeping Work Simple	$9.95		
LOSE 200 LBS. THIS WEEKEND	$12.99		Available this summer
Make Your House Do the Housework	$14.99		
NO TIME TO CLEAN!	$12.99		
Not For Packrats Only	$12.99		
Painting Without Fainting	$9.99		
Pet Clean-Up Made Easy	$12.99		
Professional Cleaner's Clip Art	$19.95		
Video Restroom Sanitation Includes Quiz Booklet	$69.95		
Speak Up	$12.99		
The Cleaning Encyclopedia	$16.95		
The Office Clutter Cure	$10.99		
The Pro. Cleaner's Handbook	$10.00		
Who Says It's A Woman's Job	$5.95		
Wood Floor Care	$9.95		
You Can, You Should Write Poetry	$10.00		
500 Terrific Ideas for Cleaning Everything	$5.99		

Shipping: $3 for first book or video plus 75¢ for each additional.		Subtotal	
		Idaho res. add 5% Sales Tax	
		Shipping	
		TOTAL	

☐ Check enclosed ☐ Visa ☐ MasterCard ☐ Discover ☐ American Express

Card No. _____ Exp Date _____

Signature X _____

Ship to:
Your Name _____ Phone _____

Street Address _____

City ST Zip _____

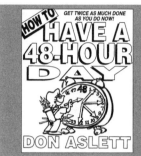

VIDEOS:

Mail your order to:
Don Aslett
PO Box 700
Pocatello ID 83204

Phone orders toll free:
888-748-3535

Keeping Work Simple

500 Tips, Rules, and Tools

Don Aslett & Carol Cartaino

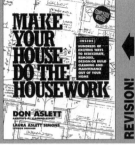

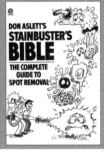

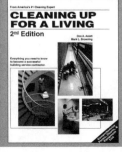